How To Get Sued

An Instructional Guide

J. Craig Williams

This publication is designed to provide accurate and authoritative information in regard to the subject matter covered. It is sold with the understanding that the publisher is not engaged in rendering legal, accounting, or other professional service. If legal advice or other expert assistance is required, the services of a competent professional should be sought.

© 2008, 2007 J. Craig Williams

Published by Kaplan Publishing, a division of Kaplan, Inc.
1 Liberty Plaza, 24th Floor
New York, NY 10006

Printed in the United States of America

June 2008
10 9 8 7 6 5 4 3 2 1

ISBN-13: 978-1-4277-9771-1

Kaplan Publishing books are available at special quantity discounts to use for sales promotions, employee premiums, or educational purposes. Please email our Special Sales Department to order or for more information at kaplanpublishing @kaplan.com, or write to Kaplan Publishing, 1 Liberty Plaza, 24th Floor, New York, NY 10006.

Contents

Foreword   vii

Preface   ix

Acknowledgments   xiii

Prologue   xv

Step 1 Pick Your Poison

Chapter 1: Fall in Love   3

Chapter 2: Own a Business   25

Chapter 3: Commit a Crime   45

Chapter 4: Go to Work   67

Chapter 5: Live on Earth   85

Chapter 6: Have Children   103

Chapter 7: Enjoy Yourself   119

Chapter 8: Indulge a Few Vices   133

Chapter 9: Own a Pet   155

Chapter 10: Own a Home   165

Step 2 Retain Competent Counsel

Chapter 11: Representation Is Priceless   177

Step 3 Go in Front of the Judge

Chapter 12: Tell It to the Judge   195

Step 4 Do Your Time in Style

Chapter 13: Lock It Up   217

Conclusion   229

Disclaimers   233

Appendix   243

Index   249

This book is dedicated to those who helped make it possible to write: the near-but-not-quite-yet Darwin Award winners.

Foreword

Ambrose Bierce, a favorite of lawyers because his distaste for them was no greater than his distaste for everyone else, described litigation as "a machine which you go into as a pig and come out of as a sausage." Although this rather neatly describes the prevailing view of the litigation process—and the lawyers who operate it—the fact remains that just as there are many people who love eating sausage (so long as they don't have to watch it being made) there are many people who find the litigation process hugely entertaining (so long as *all* they have to do is watch it being done).

This book is for those people. And you are probably one of them.

There's a certain schadenfreude aspect to reading the cases J. Craig Williams has collected. But it's not just the misfortune of others that is chronicled here, but also their very human weaknesses and foibles—and their hysterical efforts to overcome them once they get trapped inside the litigation machine. Just as it's difficult to avert your eyes from a train wreck, it's very difficult to put down a book that repeatedly illustrates not only how easily one can be swept into the sausage factory, but how hilariously difficult and Byzantine things can become once there.

Craig has compiled for us a "greatest hits" collection of such stories. Just consider the case of Hope Clarke. One lone marshmallow treat, a tiny bit of sugar at a campsite to make s'mores in

Yosemite, and suddenly, there's criminal charges to consider as she steps off a cruise liner in Florida. She allegedly had not paid the ticket issued by the Park Ranger for leaving the fixin's for the bears. You can almost hear pages from law books fluttering to the ground as eager lawyers search out confectionary precedents to cite to the bench.

Others, of course, aren't nearly as innocent as we must presume Ms. Clarke to be. Take Otis Cecil Wilkins from North Carolina who used a homemade bomb in an attempt to scare his former girlfriend from his property, but instead started himself on fire when an ash from his cigarette lit the fuse a bit too early. When questioned about making the threat, he passed off the presence of the bomb as a means of blowing up a beaver dam on his property, which apparently survived the attempt. The guffaws at the local constabulary echo from Craig's book.

Craig has toiled in the sausage factory for more than two decades. He knows it well. And he's gathered here some of its tastiest morsels as well as some of its most terrible offal. These are the kinds of cases that make judges wonder if they couldn't make a perfectly good living writing poetry or herding sheep.

Craig has provided you with an insider's guide to the American system of dispute resolution—a system admired and marveled at all over the world—and he's done it with some of the most outrageously funny tour guides you could imagine. Here you'll find the heights of human folly and the depths to which our noble intellect can sink. Here you'll find what happens to people who don't think carefully and what happens to people who think too much.

Whether you're contemplating entering the sausage factory or just thanking your lucky stars you've never had to, you'll enjoy this book. Beg, borrow or steal a copy. Come to think of it, though, if you don't want to be in the next edition, you'd better just go out and buy one. You'll send me a thank you note.

—Alex Kozinski, Chief Judge, U. S. Court of Appeals,
Ninth Circuit

Preface

Writing has been the journey of my life. It has taken many twists and turns, but has been one thing if nothing else: a constant. I've written practically every day of my life, for at least the last 30-plus years. It didn't start out all that well, however, or come that easily.

My church-secretary mother, who must have first started on a Royal, insisted I learn how to type, and in high school I got my first and only D—in business typing. Somewhere along the line, sarcasm snuck in, likely due to the overarching influence of my father and grandfather. Both were dry as a bone, and you had to be quick to catch the subtle joke they wouldn't repeat. My writing probably also had something to do with two years of grade-school Latin, because that grounding in the origins of English increased my vocabulary and made reading interesting.

My college communication arts professors gave me lots of writing assignments, and more than enough to get through, but nothing earthshaking ever made it out of my college electric Smith-Corona with the interchangeable, white-out-style eraser ribbon. I think I wore that thing out—the eraser part, that is. But the writing itself was not going well, especially as I entered the work-a-day world.

The antagonist of *The Devil Wears Prada* had nothing on my first boss, Kathleen O'Keefe Petty, at the telephone company in Virginia where I worked in the public relations department. She was a proud Irish woman. Despite her full head of shock-white hair, she never really lost the temperament of what-was-surely-originally very bright red hair. I can fully attest to and vouch for her heritage, though I didn't trace it genealogically. Nothing I wrote on my Selectric ever satisfied Mrs. O'Keefe Petty, who earned the second part of that last name not by marriage, believe me. At least I thought so at the time. Everything I gave her came back dripping red ink. Indeed, there was a steady trail of red between our desks from the blood that dripped off the paper she regularly rejected. Galleys were more like gallows for me.

She's the entire reason I now correct in blue ink. To this day, I can't stand red ink on something I've written. I have a deep-seated, knee-jerk, cringing reaction whenever I see red.

Later, law school and its very different writing style spun my head around. I started typing on a different keyboard. This one wasn't attached to a set of keys that flipped upright to whack fabric ribbon soaked in ink against paper. Nor was it attached to a small, round ball that banged a strip of black plastic against the paper and the platen. The words magically appeared as white letters on a blue computer screen in front of me. Now it was time to write persuasively. The structure was entirely different. Gone was the lead, hook, dénouement, and resolution. Something called IRAC (issue, rule, analysis, and conclusion) replaced my earlier "style." I wrote a square peg for that round hole called "introduction, argument, and conclusion," the only three categories in a brief. Oh right—once in awhile you threw in "facts." Creativity was out the window.

Or so I thought at first.

Our law school writing class, taught by professors at the Writer's Workshop at the University of Iowa showed us how to write fiction. What lawyers sometimes write in their briefs isn't far off from that fictional writing, actually. For me, it was a breath of fresh air and made the cram-down, highly structured format of legal brief writing tolerable. As I read court opinions, I learned some lawyers (well, judges and justices) could write amazingly well. Among many, there's the Justice Benjamin Cardozo, along with many other Supreme Court Justices, and our own Ninth Circuit Court of Appeals Chief Judge Alex Kozinski and California

Appellate Justice William Bedsworth, the latter two featured in this book.

The glove had been dropped.

Once out into the real world of writing and turning to computers with yellow letters on a green background, several more senior lawyers taught me their particular styles, and I learned to mold mine to theirs. But something had changed. Collegiality had snuck in. No longer were my papers dripping red ink. Sure some of the lawyers ripped my stuff apart and rewrote it, but as I watched, I learned, and finally graduated to a fountain pen. Recife, to be exact, now used to sign just about everything I write since I can finally take pride in my words.

As a budding writer, a legal writing class rocked my foundation. Bryan Garner taught "Madman, Architect, Carpenter, Judge," his four-step writing scheme for organizing a winning, persuasive brief. It worked, and I've been doing it ever since.

Time in my law practice ticked away, and the writing world changed as the Internet sprung into existence. Suddenly, everyone could become a pamphleteer, and I had three monitors to display my typewritten words along with a split and angled ergonomic keyboard not attached to anything. I started to write my blog, May It Please The Court. Somewhere, voice crept into my writing. It came as my confidence developed, and perhaps as the freedom to write as I listened to my client and in turn pictured my audience.

Lisa Stone, a full-fledged, legitimate journalist long before blogging came of age, built Law.com's Blog Network. She and Jennifer Collins picked May It Please The Court as one of the first two blogs in the network, which has now expanded to well over fifteen.

The Los Angeles Press Club decided to pass over the Los Angeles Times sports blog to give a nod to May It Please The Court as the Best Individual Weblog. My blog has since received several other very kind tips-of-the-hat, and I'm still trying to figure out why.

Hot on what I thought was worldwide acclaim for my writing, I promptly wrote a sample chapter for this book, created a book proposal and sent it off to book agents for immediate acceptance, a big advance and large royalties. As I truly expected, I got a stack of pink slips.

Somewhat daunted, I gingerly sent off a more thoughtfully revised chapter and book proposal directly to publishers, because the agents obviously had never read anything of quality in their lives and couldn't tell a good book from a barn door. Or something like that.

Not surprising, more pink slips arrived in the mail. Completely daunted, I put the project aside, intending some day to tick off the "publish-a-book" box on my lifetime list of things to do, perhaps by self-publishing it.

Instead, it sat on a shelf, gathering dust in the hard drive inside my computer.

Kelli Christiansen had been hired by Kaplan Publishing to expand the New York company's repertoire of test-prep books into more mainstream publishing. She sent an e-mail to me in the fall of 2007, and this book is the result of her interest in May It Please The Court, perhaps figuring that it might generate some content for a mildly interesting book.

In response to Kelli's request, a now very humble book proposal and sample chapter got dusted off, timidly sent by e-mail, but ultimately approved by Kaplan Publishing. Somehow the words were written, ink magically got applied to paper, pages bound in a cover, wrapped in boxes, sent to a bookstore, then off the shelf and into your hot little hands.

Now, it's up to you.

The true judge, dear reader, is whether you think Kathleen O'Keefe Petty was right, and whether I still need red-ink-editing or I can thank those who wove the fabric of my life and helped create the tapestry of my writing. Read on, and let me know.

Acknowledgments

The existence of this book is largely due to two people: Lisa Stone and Kelli Christiansen. Without them, it would have never been discovered. I also owe a debt of thanks to the entire New York Kaplan Publishing team, including Maureen McMahon and Susan Barry, who took the manuscript and made it into the book you're now holding.

Back on the West Coast, thanks too go to Leigh Dierck, the SAK of our Newport Beach, California law firm. She not only invented her own, apt title, "Swiss Army Knife," but she's also a woman who can do anything she sets her mind to. She has done that many times, making it possible for me to write this book.

The genesis of this book started with my blog, *May It Please The Court*. The website was ably created by Nigel and Ursula Nelmes of EPI International, Bryan Ventura of Bryan Ventura Design & Marketing Group, and Costin Tuculescu of CosNet. Rushabh Jhaveri of Neurosity Jennifer Kurrle of and Pixel 8 doggedly maintain it. Design kudos for the blog's recent makeover go to Bill Boyington and Dave Gottwald of Optimal Design Group.

The infamous and anonymous Ed Post also deserves some credit for his watchful guidance, suggestions, and fine corrections, many of which contributed to the text you're about to read.

I would be remiss not to also thank my law firm partner, and longtime dear friend, Craig Lindberg, who has weathered many battles with me and has always provided that "second set of eyes" to look over and correct my writing, and especially argue with me over grammar and spelling. He has been an invaluable help, and I am forever grateful for his friendship.

Other members of our law firm have assisted in ways they may never understand, but I nonetheless appreciate. Our paralegals, Jean Harries and Gayle Delcoure, our file clerk, Lupe Velazquez, and our receptionist, Jeff Boyd, have all been a big help. Our attorneys, Charles Bennett, Joe McFaul, Greg Granger, and Wayne Kistner provided many of the ideas that led to the content of this book, and frequently made suggestions to improve my writing. I sincerely appreciate their help.

Thanks, too, to Toni Moomaw, who encouraged me to step off the carousel long enough to sit and write, and regularly checked up on me. Without her, the book would not have gotten off the ground. In addition, three other book authors themselves separately challenged and inspired me to write: Paul Levine of the Solomon vs. Lord series, Tim O'Brien, author of *Leading Like a Champion*, and Wes Sierk, author of *Taken Captive*, a business book.

Speaking of book authors, special thanks and an abiding appreciation go to Alexandra Sheldon, who gave me the inspiration to negotiate this book contract, and to her husband Sidney, God rest his soul, who told me to tell my story. A tip of the hat, as well, goes to the master negotiator, Art Rose of Knobbe Martens, my publishing attorney.

My loving daughter, Julie Jo Ayer Williams, deserves a big hug from Dad for her unconditional acceptance and being the grounding force of my life. She has my unconditional love and grounding in return. Love you, Baby Girl. I'm grateful, too, to my sons Michel and Dean, who give their father, and mother, Connie, much pride.

Certainly not last, my deepest appreciation goes to my partner in life and crime, Lisa Chester, who willingly put up with me while I was lost in my computer, reading and typing for hours on end. She listened to me read, critiqued my work, and encouraged me to write. Along with Griffin and Strider, she gave me the space I needed to create. She has my undying love and eternal gratitude.

Finally, I'd like to thank that first blog post some five years ago, titled "How to Get Sued." It got the whole idea started.

Prologue

So you want to get sued. Now hold on a minute, here. You've certainly heard advice about how to avoid lawsuits and what not to do, but you think you might want a little taste of litigation? Really? You're sure?

There we go, then. That's the ticket. Ready to stick your toe in the water to see how it feels? Wonderful.

Now, just to be certain before we get started, let's make sure you're looking for a first-hand tour of America's legal system, to experience the inside view from the party-to-the-lawsuit's side of the courtroom. Really? Great! Then we're all set.

Oh, yes, and congratulations! You're about to embark on a grand—and for those actually involved in these cases—rather misguided adventure.

Of course, you can't just walk into a courtroom and demand that someone sue you. You'd be tossed out on your ear, and you'd be wiser to invest a lot of time and psychiatric consultations before you seek that kind of torture. Believe me, I've seen it. But if you're insistent on becoming a "party," then it's much quicker and easier to find yourself in court if you give someone a reason to sue you.

Think about it. Why would someone want to go through the effort and expense of hauling you into court? After all, litigation and lawsuits aren't cheap—thank goodness for us lawyers, because law school was expensive and we've got to pay for it *somehow*—so you've really got to provide someone with a good reason to sue you.

Luckily, this process isn't difficult, and there are plenty of willing participants out there if you'd prefer the sideline seat offered in this book, or if you're looking for a demonstration first. Indeed, there are dozens of ways to find yourself embroiled in litigation, from the mundane to the majestic. Some techniques are more popular than others, including the tried-and-true favorites among the "defendant set." I've outlined many of them here, but don't feel restrained by these options. If you can come up with a creative, unique way to cause a lawsuit, then please feel free. We lawyers always like a challenge.

The Top Ten Ways to Get Sued

It's time to pick your poison. What do you want to do to ensure you, too, have your day in court? Here are the top ten options (aka the first ten chapters in this book!):

1. Fall in Love
Meet Mister or Miss Right (and sometimes the Missus, if you're looking for a third or fourth participant). You could go out on a few dates, fall in love, get married, live happily ever after. That's how the story goes, right? Wrong. Time and time again, true love can lead directly to big problems. People change, feelings change—sometimes even gender changes.

2. Own a Business
Owning your own business is part of the American dream, but if you're not careful, then it can become the American nightmare. From office leases to purchases gone wrong, having a business can be like walking a legal minefield, where one misstep can cost you a ton of money—if not your company, or at least a large part of it.

3. Commit a Crime
Now, committing a crime is certainly not a daily activity for most of us, but who among us hasn't had the pleasure (and I use that word loosely, of course) of receiving a speeding ticket or possibly

of being guilty of another relatively minor criminal infraction? Perhaps you crossed the street against the light or had a campfire where it wasn't strictly allowed. These minor legal missteps can balloon into monumental hassles, with hardly any effort on your part at all. We'll even take a look at some of the more serious ways people get involved with the criminal justice system.

4. Go to Work

Work is its own punishment, or so the popular T-shirt reads. Yet the T-shirt is a bit shortsighted—there's more to it than just a level of pain. The workplace is rife with personal interactions that promise all parties involved all kinds of lawsuits, especially if the judge isn't really on your side during your day in court.

5. Live on Earth

You don't really have a lot of choice with this one—there are only a limited number of openings and working spacesuits aboard the International Space Station, and I'm guessing you're not an astronaut. Knowing that it's Earth or nowhere, a significant number of people turn to the courts to help protect our fair planet. The results? You could say they're not exactly out of this world.

6. Have Children

Our families are our pride and joy. We love our kids more than anything else in the world. At least, that is, until it's time to pay for the little darlings, make child-care arrangements, or take care of the million of other small details involved in raising a child. Then it becomes a story of either too much work or too much money. Luckily, there's an easy answer: Take it to court.

7. Enjoy Yourself

We all want to kick back now and then. Certainly, there's nothing wrong with having a little fun. The problem lies, however, in the sometimes conflicting definitions of *little* and *fun*, which are frequently inversely proportional and occasionally include a dash of insanity. What's entertainment for one man frequently is annoying for another, and your good time may go too far and end up injuring another person. Here's what happens when good living goes wrong. Way wrong.

8. Indulge a Few Vices

Saints are few and far between, and many of the ones identified in this book can't even lay a claim to possible canonization. Most people have a drink now and then, or sneak the occasional cigar. Vices, however, have prices. Here's what you can expect to pay.

9. Own a Pet

Fluffy and Fido might bring you joy, but feline and canine companionship is not equally appreciated by everyone. Take good care of your animals or you might wind up in court. Of course, turnaround is fair play—sometimes man's best friend can be your secret ally with the jury.

10. Own a Home

Our homes are our castles. And like the castles of old, our homes are constantly under siege. From predatory insurance companies to structural problems you never saw coming, here's how where you hang your hat can cause you big problems.

Epilogue to the Prologue

As you can see, most of the ways to get sued aren't unusual activities. In fact, most are everyday activities, even approaching the mundane. But somehow, our heroes and heroines manage to rise above the blasé and add a whole new dimension to living.

You even may have engaged in one or two of these everyday activities yourself. I'm guilty of some of them, too. But it's *how* you engage in these common, everyday activities that may get you in hot water—and just as important, what you do to get out of trouble once you're in it. As I told my middle son once, "I'm not punishing you because what you did was wrong. I'm punishing you because you got caught."

In each of the chapters that follow, I share real-life examples of how regular life can become real litigation with hardly any effort on the part of those involved.

Read on to discover which reason works best for you. Choose carefully, and if you're lucky enough, then you, too, might just wind up with a case on the docket sometime soon. When you do, give me a call—especially if you're in court in California!

Step 1

Pick Your Poison

Chapter 1

Fall in Love

Love is a many-splendored thing. It can uplift us, inspire us, drive us to become better people—or worse. Love makes the world go 'round. It's the emotion behind sunny skies, rainbows, and true happiness. If you don't have love, we're told, then you don't have anything.

That's the best-case scenario: the image of love that drives the greeting card and wedding industry. It's an ideal, propped up by endless media portrayals of perfect relationships and everlasting marital bliss. But in the real world, things don't always go as smoothly, as you likely already know.

Sometimes the person you fall in love with isn't really the person you thought he or she was. Other times, you might be in love but the object of your affection doesn't feel quite the same way. Or maybe that person is in love with your wallet, not with you. Perhaps you can see where that might be a problem.

On the other hand, in some cases the problem isn't a lack of love. In fact, occasionally, it's just the opposite. Believe it or not, there can be too much love, as evidenced by the polyamorous couples who want to expand their union to include a third, fourth, or fifth partner. Yet the local constable doesn't want to sanction these relationships. The solution? Take it to court.

Love is an emotion that doesn't occur in isolation. Where there's love, there's jealousy. There's anger. There's bad decision-making galore. And where there's bad decision-making, there usually will be a few attorneys and at least one judge more than willing to help you sort it all out.

Falling in love isn't a surefire way to wind up in the courtroom, but your chances are pretty good. Especially if you don't follow these five steps:

Step 1: Know Who You're Marrying
Step 2: Keep One Eye on Your Wallet
Step 3: Don't Lose Your Temper
Step 4: Respect Others' Feelings
Step 5: Conduct Regular Head Counts

You want examples? Well, here we go—let's have a run down the aisle first.

Step One: Know Who You're Marrying

People change. It's a fact of life. The sweet, pliable guy you met in college may become an inflexible curmudgeon by the time he's 50. Nah. I'm not talking about me (even though I just hit that magical number!)—I'm talking about all the other curmudgeons. How about that girl who loved dancing until dawn and living life on the edge? Soon she'll settle down and start scheduling her weekends six months in advance.

Perhaps some change is inevitable. Maybe it's a fact of life, and couples either accept it and adapt or they don't. It's sad, but not wholly unexpected.

At least most of the time, that is. Changing technology and social mores have led to a rather wide variety of possibilities that were nothing but the most speculative science fiction twenty years ago. This next case hinges on just such a change, one that almost no one could have seen coming.

There is so little difference between husbands you might as well keep the first. —Adela Rogers St. Johns

They Were He and She—Now He's a She!

Paul Spina and his wife, Sharon, have been married for 22 years. They have two children.

Paul recently went to Thailand and had a sex-change operation and came back as Paula Spina. Now, his wife wants an annulment.

There's a surprise.

In her lawsuit, Sharon argued that Paul (now Paula) was always psychologically a woman, and when (s)he married Sharon, it violated the state's anti-same-sex-marriage statute. But at the time, Paula was Paul, clearly a man. After all, he did father two children.

It is admittedly confusing. So they turned to the courts to work it out.

Apparently, Sharon lost the first round to Paul/Paula and the court refused to grant the annulment. Sharon appealed to the Kentucky Supreme Court, which likewise denied her request to annul the marriage. The couple has accumulated a large amount of assets during their time together because Sharon's family owned a car dealership, so chances are this case won't be settled any time soon.

We haven't heard the last of this one. The next likely step would be to file for divorce, which will have a very different result than the annulment. The parties likely will split the family monies rather than not share them at all. Had the annulment gone through, they would have gone their separate ways, money and all. Now, Paul/Paula may share in the wealth.

⌒∞⌒

Before you marry someone, it's a good idea to know a little bit about him or her. You might want to know a favorite color, for example, whether that person can swim, and, perhaps, if there are any allergies you should know about. There are other, some would say more basic, questions to ask as well, such as exactly what your beloved does for a living.

Here's a case that illustrates why that question might be important.

Getting divorced just because you don't love a man is almost as silly as getting married just because you do. —Zsa Zsa Gabor

When Stepmom Practices the Oldest Profession

Divorce is not a subject I usually tackle. Even if I did, I wouldn't want to represent either the husband or the wife in this case, but the opinion is definitely worth a look.

It involves a deceased construction worker and two women. One, his second wife (and alleged soon-to-be-ex), and the other, his daughter. After he died, the second wife and daughter together brought a wrongful death suit and hit the construction company where Dad had worked for $1.1 million. Then the problems came.

They couldn't decide how to divide it up. That's right: the fur started to fly.

The daughter alleged that Dad was going to divorce his second wife (who was in that capacity for just eight months before he died)—because dear old Stepmom was a prostitute. And, when Dad found out, he was about to send her packing.

At trial, Orange County Superior Court Judge Randall Wilkinson ruled for a 90/10 split, with the winner's share going to the daughter. Needless to say, stepmom appealed, and the Court of Appeals upheld the decision.

But then there was the matter of a blistering, 37-page dissent by Presiding Justice David Sills, who said the majority committed "a serious miscarriage of justice" and had "pretty much ignored about 150 years of California case law dealing with wrongful death damages." Indeed, Sills's dissent was longer than the main opinion.

Justice Sills thought that it didn't matter whether Dad was going to leave his second wife—he was still married at the time of his death, and argued that the "lion's share" belonged instead to the second wife because to hold otherwise would restore "fault" to a no-fault divorce state. In California, we don't lay blame for the divorce at either party's feet (no fault) rather than deal with all those nasty allegations back and forth about who caused the break-up (fault) of the marriage, leading to the divorce.

The California Supremes voted unanimously to hear the case, and Justice Sills's dissent made up the majority of their ruling. In fact, almost a year after this ruling, the California Supreme Court reversed the trial and appellate courts, and ruled as the dissenting judge advocated.

Step Two: Keep an Eye on Your Wallet

When everything's going well in a relationship, no one worries about money. But at the first sign of trouble, finances suddenly can take center stage. In fact, money is cited time and time again as the most frequent reason that couples fight.

Whether you fight before or after the relationship ends, one thing is for certain: if you can't come to an amicable resolution, then you'll likely wind up in court. These next three cases discuss the status of engagement rings and what should happen to them when the relationship ends—a contentious issue argued by many couples over hundreds of years. It points out why honesty is always the best (and cheapest) policy, and how much your time in the bedroom may really be worth.

Before marriage a man yearns for a woman. Afterward the "y" is silent. —W. A. Clarke

You Can't Put a Price on Love— Or Can You?

According to a Pennsylvania man, you can. In his blog, *www. onpointnews.com*, Matthew Heller writes about Janet Grace, a woman in Pennsylvania who got sued. She first accepted a $35,000, 2.35 carat diamond engagement ring from Mario Mele. After her suitor jilted her just two months after he proposed, she sold it for $11,000 and donated the proceeds to charity.

In her response to Mario's trespass lawsuit seeking the return of the furtive engagement ring or $50,000 in damages, Janet claims that before he proposed, her suitor asked her to "consider" what to do with her six other diamond rings from previous entanglements (was she married that many times before this proposal?). She contends she agreed to her suitor's request to give up the other rings, valued at more than $20,000. She fulfilled her end of the bargain by giving them to charity, with one family ring given to a niece.

Because she fulfilled her end of the contract, she's now claiming that it is instead her suitor who breached his contract with her.

Who wins? Heller opines that the suitor looks like the likely winner under Pennsylvania law, and says, "In 1999, the state Supreme Court said the giving of an engagement ring is conditional on performance of a marriage ceremony, not acceptance of a marriage proposal." In that case, *Lindh v. Surmand* 742 A.2d

643 (1999), the court ruled that the gift of this engagement ring, a 5.06 carat whopper, requires the parties to actually go through the marriage ceremony. Accepting a marriage proposal isn't the promise that turns the gift into a possession. The justices ruled the donor may recover the ring no matter who is at fault for the breakup. That decision, however, was a close one, with the justices splitting four to three, with one of the dissenting justices arguing "fairness dictates" that the innocent party in an "ill-fated romantic connection" should retain the ring.

Back in our case of *Mele v. Grace*, Janet, however, cites a more feminist-leaning Montana law, which ruled that a gift is a gift, and not a bilateral contract that can only be fulfilled through performance. Unfortunately, we'll never know the outcome. In our $35,000 case, Mele and Grace settled confidentially before the judge could make a ruling.

⤜⊗⊗⤛

Matrimony is serious business. It's certainly nothing to joke about, as one would-be bride discovered.

You know what we can be like: See a guy and think he's cute one minute, the next minute our brains have us married with kids, the following minute we see him having an extramarital affair. By the time someone says, "I'd like you to meet Cecil," we shout, "You're late again with the child support!" —Cynthia Heimel

Intended as Humor, "I Don't" Wedding Vow Cancels Wedding—and Other Marital Maladies—Real and Imagined

You've likely heard of the shotgun wedding, frequently used in old movies and in some far reaches of our country that may not yet have seen the sun. But hold on a minute here—perhaps we came by it honestly from one of the "old countries." Apparently in Austria, it's quite the thing. It's the only reason I can come up with to justify the Austrian law that cancels the entire wedding and prevents its reoccurrence for a ten-week period if either participant responds with "I don't" instead of "I do."

Just ask Tina Albrecht, 27, who tried to marry fiancé Dietmar Koch, 29, at a castle in Steyr, in Upper Austria. Trying to interject a little humor, she used the forbidden words, and invoked the law.

Wedding authorities promptly called off the wedding and blacklisted the couple for the ensuing ten-week period. All the guests were sent home.

But consider this result from a May/December wedding that did go through. On their wedding night, a 54-year-old husband forcibly tattooed his initials on his 22-year-old wife's backside. She called a women's rights organization for assistance, and police sought the husband for questioning, but allegedly she failed to press charges.

Even so, she probably wishes she had said "I don't," too.

Then there's "That Girl Emily," who wrote a blog by the same name, but turned out to be a viral-style promotion for a Court TV show about a private eye. The campaign was awarded "Best Integrated Promotional Campaign" at the 2007 Cannes Advertising Festival.

In any event, it's worth a read and worth a look because it's so outlandish it seems almost real.

Reading from the beginning of her blog, Emily is a normal, everyday housewife writing about her life with her husband, Steven. On July 24, 2006, she's covering exciting subjects like baking cookies.

Then one of her friends loses her job, and Emily goes over to her apartment to spend the night and console her.

But it's not what you might think.

On July 25, 2006, we read her next blog entry, and she's just discovered Steven and her best friend, Laura, in bed together—in Steven and Emily's bed.

She hires a private investigator, who catches Steven and Laura in the act, and Emily posts it on her blog.

Jilted, Emily then decides to go on a rampage. She chucks Steven's computer, golf clubs, and clothes on the street, and someone conveniently posted the episode on YouTube (see *www.youtube. com/watch?v=UVNzjx8fFys* or *http://tinyurl.com/eh77w*).

Hell hath no fury...except a billboard. Supposedly erected right next to his office (it actually appeared simultaneously in

Manhattan, Brooklyn, Chicago, and LA), it says, "Hi Steven. Do I have your attention now? I know all about her, you dirty, sneaky, immoral, unfaithful, poorly endowed slimeball. Everything's caught on tape. Your (soon-to-be-ex) Wife, Emily. P.S. I paid for this billboard from OUR joint bank account."

Ouch.

If it were real, then she really would have been wishing she had said "I don't."

The Court TV viral campaign was outed by netizens who discovered the true facts in record time, according to the *New York Times*, but who failed to tune in to the new TV show when it debuted. In states where fault is an issue, even assuming Emily was real, she would have done herself more harm than good, but as many women commented, she probably would have felt better about it.

Just like some marriages. The moral of this story? If you're getting ready to utter those two words, "I do," then you might want to think twice.

⚬⚬⚬

Like it or not, there are no secrets in this world. Entering into a marriage intending to keep something from your spouse is almost certainly a surefire recipe for being found out. And as illustrated in this next case, sometimes it can be a very expensive lesson.

There was a time when a fool and his money were soon parted, but now it happens to everybody. —Adlai E. Stevenson

Take My Ring, but Don't Take My Money

Lee wanted to marry Yang. He worked in the United States, she worked in Hong Kong. To entice her to marry him, he gave her an engagement ring, and also added her name to his bank accounts.

She moved to the United States and began living with him. She soon discovered letters from "men around the world" written to him professing their love. Apparently, he had several previous homosexual relationships that he had not disclosed to her.

Jilted, she called off the wedding. She also cleaned more than $350,000 out of their now-joint bank accounts, which included some of her money. Here in California where I practice law, and in most other states, a joint account holder can withdraw all of the money in the account, regardless of whether that joint-account holder deposited all of the money in the first place (check the laws in your state or county). In this case, our heroine left a $500,000-a-year job to move to the United States, and was only able to find employment at $70,000 per year.

After she withdrew "his" money, he sued, of course.

The court ruled that because he made the accounts joint and there was no written agreement, she was entitled to the money.

As a consolation prize, the court gave him back the diamond that came out of his grandmother's engagement ring.

Next time, I'm sure, he'll get any banking arrangements in writing.

⌘

Infidelity broke up that relationship, but it presented far more dire consequences for the straying fellow in the next case.

If a man take no thought about what is distant, he will find sorrow near at hand. —Confucius

When Your Hand Gets Numb and the Mouse Stops Moving, It's Time to Stop

This woman would give Lorena Bobbitt a run for her money.

He Ling and Jiang Ming of Chengdu City, China, had a newborn son, but Jiang was addicted to the Internet—addicted in a bad way. He loved engaging in video chats with other women on the Internet.

Needless to say, his wife, He Ling, was none too happy, especially considering his absences required her full-time attention to their son.

After she confronted him, he promised to be a more faithful dad. Jiang committed to stay off the Internet and devote more attention to mom and son.

It didn't last. Jiang just couldn't stay away. He snuck off to Internet cafés and resumed his addiction. In fact, his addiction was so bad he didn't pay attention to what was happening around him.

I'll let Jiang tell the rest of the story from here.

"I suddenly felt a numbness in my right hand. The arrow on the screen stopped moving. Then I found my right hand was on the mouse pad and blood was shooting out," he related to the *Chongquing Evening News*.

His wife had cut his hand off, in what has now become known as the Chengdu Chop, based on the name of the city where the incident happened. Despite his missing hand, Jiang pled with the court to release his wife from jail because it was his fault. "I'm the one who broke my promise," he told the judge.

Now there's an understanding husband—how would you react if this happened to you?

⚮

Disability payments are usually pretty straightforward. Lose a limb or suffer an injury that renders you unable to work, and you'll be compensated. What happens, however, when your disability keeps you from performing in the bedroom?

This next case answers that question.

She was "honeychile" in New Orleans, the hottest of the bunch,
but on the old expense account, she was gas, cigars and lunch.
—Anonymous

Deprived or Depraved? Damages for Spousal Dysfunction

OK, I'll bite. While I was reading slip opinions (appellate court rulings written on "slips" of paper before they get published in the permanent law books), I ran across this teaser: "Coverage under 'bodily injury' clause of defendant's insurance policy does not include nonphysical, or mental, harm."

Huh? Now we're splitting hairs (pardon the pun) between body, mind, and soul. Is there coverage if your soul is harmed?

Essentially, the case turns on a different issue—the per-accident limit of uninsured motorist coverage. Sounds boring, but hang on.

The more interesting aspect of the case is a loss-of-consortium claim, and whether that claim amounts to a physical injury. In other words, does the spouse who suffered the loss of consortium (i.e., the one not receiving the "spousal functions" according to the court) have a claim against the insurance policy under its "bodily injury" coverage?

Some courts generally say yes, but a California appellate court put a different spin on the claim and said no. This lower court rejected the belief that a lack of spousal functions causes a separate physical injury, and thus, no payment from an insurance policy when your spouse can't "perform" due to an otherwise insured accident. The insurance company pays only the injured victim for his actual physical injuries, not his spouse for her "emotional injury."

I feel their pain.

Step Three: Don't Lose Your Temper

Relationships can get stormy. When you're dealing with strong emotions, it's easy for an argument to escalate. Before you know it, you've moved right past the "lover's spat" and directly into full-fledged trouble. That last step is rarely a good idea. Just ask the following folks.

Anyone can be passionate, but it takes real lovers to be silly.
—Rose Franken

Blowing Up the Beaver Dam

I couldn't make this stuff up if I tried.

CNN Law posted a story about a 45-year-old North Carolina man who had two problems: an ex-girlfriend and a beaver dam. Sure, some jokesters out there have already picked up on the pun, and certainly some are busily chuckling under their breath. But believe me when I tell you it gets better.

Much better.

Our hero, Otis Cecil Wilkins, wanted to get rid of a beaver dam on his property, which he planned to do by blowing it up. At least that was his implausible excuse, according to his public defender in court. Yep, you guessed it; he's now a defendant in a criminal matter. Get ready for the facts: Otis Cecil had threatened his ex-girlfriend to stay away from him, but she wouldn't listen. As she drove her car into his yard, Otis Cecil was distracted from his original task trying to deal with the beaver dam. Instead, when he saw his ex-girlfriend, he tossed the homemade bomb at her car.

Did I also mention that Otis Cecil smokes?

Unfortunately for our hero, some hot ash from his cigarette fell onto the fuse before he tossed it, which promptly started to burn. I'm guessing here that the early, short fuse wasn't part of Otis Cecil's original plan. When he tossed the homemade bomb, it immediately exploded into a fireball.

This part is where it gets better.

Otis Cecil must have been so surprised by all the commotion that after he threw the homemade bomb, he forgot to jump out of the way. The homemade-bomb-turned-fireball rolled back toward him, which next caught his shorts on fire.

Otis Cecil, quoted by CNN, said "[I] ain't no terrorist. It was just a little bit of black powder. It was just a little boom thing." This startling denial came from Otis Cecil, as recorded in a law enforcement report filed last year at the time of the incident. He spent three weeks in the burn unit recovering.

Perhaps fortunately for the district attorney, the ex-girlfriend became uncooperative. I say fortunately because in the trial, I don't think the prosecutor could have kept a straight face while trying to present these facts to the jury. In a plea bargain because of this uncooperative witness, Otis Cecil pled guilty to three counts of assault, and agreed to a ten-month sentence.

Reportedly, the beaver dam is still intact.[1]

∽◈∾

One hopes that Cecil eventually calmed down, but other lovers and former lovers out there share his, shall we say, fiery temper. That's too bad, because sometimes love just goes up in smoke.

---

[1] Although Otis Cecil Wilkins managed to miss the beaver dam, he did manage to garner international attention—including coverage on renowned columnist Dave Barry's Blog: *http://blogs.herald.com/dave_barrys_blog/2006/05/creeping _fascis.html.*

Zane had said now that we have a chimney, Santa can come in the real way. —Marcieau Matthews

What, No Cookies and Milk?

At 3:30 A.M., you're likely not going to hear screams of pain coming from your chimney, if you're lucky enough to have a real, working fireplace. Think about that statement for a minute, and reflect on the comfortable position you now occupy.

You're not stuck in a chimney, it's probably not 3:30 A.M., and there's no fire underneath you.

Alejandro Valencio, however, was in exactly that position. Plus, as you can imagine, he was drunk. He wanted to see Connie Deweese, of Evansville, Indiana, whom he had known for seven or eight months, according to the Associated Press (AP).

She apparently did not want to see him. She had locked him out of the house, but Alejandro managed to get himself up on the roof and partway down the chimney.

When the firefighters arrived to rescue him, they brought their axes into the house, ready to break through the wall. Connie would have none of it. "I told them to leave him in the chimney and let him die," she told the AP. She was cited for blocking the chimney and received her own set of misdemeanor charges for disorderly conduct and interfering with a firefighter.

One mantle piece and numerous bricks later, Alejandro was free and on his way to the hospital, only slightly bruised and battered.

The worse was yet to come, however. He showed up at Connie's with his figurative hat in hand, offering to pay for the damages. Nonplussed, Connie picked up and threw some glass bottles and a trash can at him, landing hits each time.

"I've dated a lot of psychos in my life, but nobody like that," Deweese told the AP reporter.

"Everyone do [*sic*] stupid things when they're drunk," Alejandro said.

Connie wasn't buying it. She told him to get off the porch and never come back.

No winners in this fight. No cookies or milk, either.

༄

Some passions never die. Or perhaps I should say death is no obstacle. At least not when one of two lovers are determined to be together.

Ay, go to the grave of buried love and meditate! There settle the account with thy conscience for every past benefit unrequited— every past endearment unregarded, of that departed being, who can never, never, never return to be soothed by thy contrition.
—Washington Irving

There's Aggravated Assault, and Then There's "Aggravated Stupid"

When someone dies, life goes on for others around them. Still, there are those who never seem to get over it. Living, I mean. Not dying.

Let me explain.

48-year-old Martha lived with Roger for five years until he died. When his teenage daughter Sierra buried Roger, she apparently didn't invite Martha. In most places in the United States, I'm guessing that girlfriends don't have the same rights as family members.

Especially when there's been a divorce, like in Roger's situation. The Associated Press story doesn't say, but it's my guess that Sierra and her mother (Roger's former wife) intentionally forgot to invite Martha to the funeral.

Like the old adage says, "Hell hath no fury like a woman scorned." The corollary to that adage is "Hell hath no fury like a woman scorned by another man's wife and daughter."

Don't believe me?

As Exhibit A, I offer into evidence Roger's ashes. "Nice try," you say, but if you said that, then you're missing my point. Remember I said Sierra buried Roger? Oh yes. Six feet under.

That's right. Scorned Martha got her Roger back, ashes, urn, and all.

She dug him up.

She is being prosecuted for felony vandalism, probably because Ohio never got around to enacting a grave-robber statute. But Athens County prosecutor David Warren sees it differently, according to the AP: "I have a category of crimes that I like to refer to as 'aggravated stupid,'" Warren said. "I have been doing this for almost 30 years now and I have never had anyone steal someone's ashes."

Step Four: Consider Others' Feelings

Remember the Golden Rule? That's the one that dictates we should treat others the way we ourselves would like to be treated. Ignore it at your peril, lest other people start treating you the way you treat them.

In these cases, one woman failed to respect another's privacy, with dire consequences. Understanding how someone else feels can be a valuable skill, especially when your finances depend on making the most of those feelings. Just ask the lady in the second case below.

Of course, you might have to wait until she gets out of jail.

You don't know a woman until you've met her in court.
—Norman Mailer

The Merry Wives of E-mail Theft

According to CNN, a woman named Angel Lee fraudulently obtained her husband's ex-wife's e-mail user name and password. No, you don't need a consanguinity chart to figure out that relationship. I probably just should have said "the former wife," or just her name, Duongladde Ramsay, which would have been a lot easier to understand.

Angel and her husband, Jeffrey, were engaged in vicious divorce proceedings, according to reports, and she was none too happy he was seeing someone else—his ex-wife. After Angel got Duongladde's e-mail password, she went into the ex-wife's account and read 215 e-mails. It had to be tremendously interesting stuff to have read that many. In a criminal proceeding separate from the divorce, and after admitting she invaded the ex-wife's e-mails, she was prosecuted for intercepting wire communications and sentenced.

Stating that "privacy is still a cherished value," U.S. District Judge Richard P. Matsch sentenced 28-year old Lee, of El Mirage, Arizona, to 60 days of home imprisonment.

The judge thought Angel should stay home with the kids rather than go to jail. Too bad he didn't take away her computer, too.

∞◊∞

Perhaps Angel Lee was just a victim of too much curiosity. Filled with a burning desire to know what the ex-wife was writing to family and friends (presumably *not* the ex-husband, right?), she broke the law. But in this next case, there was no burning desire—except the burning desire to take some money.

Now I ain't saying she's a gold digger... —Kanye West

You Thought Elizabeth Taylor Was Bad: 15 Husbands!

If 1 husband is good, then 15 is probably better—especially if you're "sharing" their money. Maybe the better way to characterize "sharing" is as "scamming" them.

An apparently lonely man on the Internet engaged in a series of electronic chats with a woman named Kyle McDonald. A few months and e-mails later, Kyle and Donald Rice were married. He was no longer lonely, and she was into his pocket.

Donald noticed his wallet was perpetually empty and his wife seemed to have relationships other than with him. He ran some Internet searches and discovered some of these prior relationships and the other husbands' complaints about her. The next call went to the local constabulary. According to police, her hand was into a string of pockets, also belonging to Kyle's husbands, some present and some previous. She is believed to have married 15 men and taken money from them all.

The Detroit police arrested Kyle, and she ultimately was sentenced to up to ten years in prison for defrauding just one of her husbands. Now, a few more lonely guys on the Internet are probably a bit richer for it.

Step Five: Conduct Regular Head Counts

If a little love is a wonderful thing, then doesn't it stand to reason that a whole lot of love must be better? The answer is obviously yes, at least according to the people in these cases. You see, they argue that polyamory—a relationship that includes more than two partners—is the way to go. Yet, strangely enough, the local court systems don't agree.

If you want all the benefits that marriage conveys, then you need to stick to the legal limit: two people per union. Otherwise, you'll learn firsthand where these folks are coming from—and going to.

Over the past few years, there's been a lot of changes in the world of marriage, at least as the concept pertains to same-sex couples. At least one state has legalized same-sex marriage, while a handful of others have created civil unions, granting couples some but not all of the protections of marriage.

These changes have created a lot of controversy and turmoil— and an interesting "me too" effect, as would-be polygamists try to hitch a ride on the same-sex marriage bandwagon.

Polygamy: An effort to get more out of life than there is in it.
—Elbert Hubbard

One of These Things Is Not Like the Other

Normally, I don't pander to prurient interests. Plus, who needs one more article about polygamy? But I can't resist this one, especially given how many people have been asking my opinion as a lawyer on the recent spate of decisions on same-sex marriages.

I can pick hot topics, can't I?

Well, here's a new twist on an old saw. An AP report reveals an avowed polygamist who believes his case is no different than the cases the courts have recently made in favor of same-sex marriages. With varying lasting success, several courts have ruled that same-sex marriages are legal because both are consenting adults, because of privacy claims, equal protection, and a host of other constitutional arguments. This polygamist sees it the same way. What's good for male/male or female/female marriages ought to be just as good for male/female/female and other such marriages.

As a lawyer, I can see his reasoning. If the social policy against same-sex marriages is based on lack of procreation, then this guy's more than made his point. After all, he's got 30 children.

But of course, that's not the "rest of the story." Apparently, according to the AP article, this polygamist allegedly "married" a 13-year-old girl, and he's up on charges of failure to pay child support. I make a good living, but I wouldn't want to see that bill at the end of the month. As with most, if not all, polygamy cases, his arguments didn't work. He was ordered to pay child support of $300 per month for each child and serve 40 hours of community service at a local soup kitchen. The child was removed from the home and placed in foster care. One of his other, older wives was ordered into counseling.

For anyone who's wondering, I don't endorse polygamy, though I have to admit…well, never mind. And to be totally clear, I'll quote the AP report, "Polygamy was renounced by the Church of Jesus Christ of Latter-day Saints in 1890 as part of a deal to grant Utah statehood, and the church now excommunicates those members who practice or advocate it."

There you have it. Notice how I completely avoided giving my opinion on these two issues? Well, if you have to know, I'm a libertarian, so I don't really care whether same-sex marriages or polygamy are approved.

But I do want to know if that polygamy guy succeeds. Maybe he's got something going there.

As of this writing, polygamy has yet to be recognized by any court in the country. That doesn't mean that advocates of multiple marriage have given up the fight, though. See *www.cbn.com /cbnnews/news/050721a.aspx* or click on *http://tinyurl.com/2gmmrq*.

❧

In a similar vein, but on a smaller scale, one couple wants official "permission" to grow into a triad. Here's their reasoning

One man's mediocrity is another man's good program.
  —Dr. Frank Stanton

Big Love: Eternal Triangles in Utah

I really don't like when people say "I told you so," but I did: I predicted we'd see a case like this.

Perhaps I wasn't as early as Justice Scalia, but then again, he's on the Supreme Court, and I'm not. I'm just a lowly and occasional pro tem judge in Orange County's Harbor Newport Beach Superior Court. But I saw it coming, too.

In *Lawrence v. Texas*, where the U.S. Supreme Court banned consenting gay sodomy, Justice Scalia predicted in his dissent that other public decency laws that ban "bigamy, same-sex marriage, adult incest, prostitution, masturbation, adultery, fornication, bestiality, and obscenity" would see similar challenges. In other words, he predicted the case here, where Utah residents G. Lee Cook and his wife, known in court papers only as D. Cook, sought a marriage license for both of them to "marry" a woman similarly known only as J. Bronson.

The case involves two consenting adults, male and female, who want to add another to the eternal triangle—legitimately. But there's a problem. Utah won't grant them a marriage license for a third person. The clerks refused to issue the license, so they sued. They argue polygamy is a matter not only of choice, but also religious belief. They invoked their constitutional right to free exercise of religion.

It didn't work. Back in 1879, the Supreme Court upheld the ban on polygamy in *Reynolds v. United States*, and the Utah courts upheld the clerk's refusal to issue the second marriage license to the third person.

Their argument is that their polygamous desires are no different than same-sex marriages, which the Big Court glanced at with the sodomy ruling, but wasn't biting. The rules are still pretty much the same as in the time of Adam and Eve way back in 1879. It takes two to be a married couple, not three. Nonetheless, it's an innovative argument, especially in Utah.

I just don't understand why it didn't happen in California first.

⌘

Not everyone is a romantic. Some people take a long, hard look at the state of marriage and see nothing but opportunity. That gives us situations like the following.

When people get married because they think it's a longtime love affair, they'll be divorced very soon, because all love affairs end in disappointment. —Joseph Campbell

They've Got Married Folks Coming and Going

You knew it was just a matter of time before someone figured out how to make money on both ends of marriage. If you think about it for a moment, too, the light bulb will immediately go off.

In Austria, just like everywhere else, the divorce rate is skyrocketing. Local wedding organizer Anton Barz saw divorce rates in Vienna hit 66 percent, and noticed at the same time that his marriage event bookings were slipping. At least it wasn't a lawyer who came up with this next idea!

Because he wasn't making as much money on the front end, Mr. Barz organized a weekend divorce fair. To maintain decorum and anonymity, he arranged for husbands to come in Saturday and wives on Sunday, avoiding what could be a rather awkward meeting. According to the BBC, they will "consult with lawyers, mediators, real estate agents, life-crisis experts, private detective firms, and DNA laboratories offering paternity tests."

Shudder.

Not only can you get counseling, but one fair exhibitor also offers a therapeutic weekend get-away package for the newly divorced.

It's certainly not a honeymoon. Maybe we could call that trip an "affair to forget."

Seriously Now: Lessons Learned

In a culture where divorces have become almost a norm, there are some steps you may want to think about before you utter those two famous words: "I do."

First, make sure you know who you're marrying. If it's a whirlwind romance, then pause for a moment. Ask about your lover's credit history, debts, past bankruptcies, spending habits, money in the bank, and generally make sure you understand your lover's financial condition. Some states follow community property laws, which means you not only get rights to half of your lover's money, you also get the "right" to pay half your lover's debts. Money is one of the most frequently cited reasons people get divorced. Why not check it out first before you make that big commitment? If appropriate, consider a pre- or postnuptial agreement. Consult with your favorite local attorney for the proper language.

Consider, too, that you may not be marrying Mr. or Mrs. Right. Meet family, friends, and business associates as you date. Employers conduct background checks—perhaps you may want to consider at least an informal check.

Second, give some thought to the financial arrangements. Adding your lover to your joint accounts generally (check local laws here) means that your lover can withdraw all the funds in the joint account without your permission. There's usually no such thing as "my money" in a jointly held account.

Third, if you're going through a breakup or divorce, then get some counseling. Rather than lose your temper or your mind and do something you'll regret later, just walk away and then talk to someone—anyone. It's perhaps an odd element of human nature that we tend to hurt the ones we're closest to—you'd think it would be the other way around. If you're the victim of harassment, then by all means take steps to protect yourself. Getting a court order preventing harassment may be the first step, but any divorce lawyer will say that a piece of paper will not stop a bullet or an angry spouse. There are halfway houses that protect abused spouses and children. Check your local phone book for their locations.

Fourth, the breakup of a marriage or relationship can be a knockdown, drag-out affair, and feelings of mistrust, resentment, and hurt tend to take away rational thought. People's emotions often control their otherwise well-behaved selves, and they do some of the things I've written about above. Before going down that path, however, it's best to talk to your spouse or lover to get their side of the story. Just remember what the word *assume* is made of.

Finally, it takes two to tango. Not three or four—unless they're part of your nuclear family. Crosby, Stills, Nash, & Young may have started it all with *Love the One You're With,* but that doesn't mean you have to follow their advice. If you're not happy with where you are, then find out why or leave. Life's too short. (Not that that's legal advice, of course.)

In this book's conclusion, I discuss full-fledged lawsuits and how they typically work in different types of cases. Before we get to that explanation, however, let's take a look at a few other ways you can be sued.

Chapter 2

Own a Business

Business ownership is part and parcel of the American dream. We're a nation founded on individual entrepreneurship. The largest retailer in the world started with just one man and a plan—and countless individuals try to follow in Sam Walton's and other successful business owners' footsteps.

Starting a business is hard work, and keeping it running is even more difficult. It's not surprising, then, that people run into trouble along the way—trouble that lands them in the courtroom. Some of the folks you'll read about here have taken over existing businesses, while others are creating an entirely new industry.

American Express may tell you that "Ownership Has Its Rewards," but these court cases will tell you that ownership has its drawbacks, as well. In this chapter, we're going to take a look at litigation that began in the workplace, with a special focus on the challenges faced by business owners.

Whether you're a lowly oboe player or a hardworking furniture dealer with a poor grasp of math, you're sure to find something here that resonates with you.

༻✦༺

Art, music, literature—creative professionals will tell you that their fields chose them. Their work is a passion, a calling, if not a vocation. They've no choice but to answer art's clarion call.

Of course, that doesn't mean they're not going to sue when they feel like they're getting the short end of the stick. Just check out this example from a European music hall.

Do re me fa so la ti do. —Julie Andrews

The Envious Oboe: I Play More Notes Than You

So, you're a violinist in a German orchestra, and you play more notes than everyone else. They're just like all the other violinists who play in the symphonies across the United States, and particularly out here on the Left Coast with the Hollywood Bowl Orchestra, my personal favorite.

Of course, the rest of us understand this allegation because we listen attentively to the music, or in my case, perhaps not. I go to the Bowl to watch the stars, have dinner, and an occasional glass of wine with some cheese and crackers. They play music?

As an overworked violinist, what do you do?

You sue for more money. According to the Associated Press, "sixteen violinists at the Beethoven Orchestra in Bonn argue that they work more than their fellow musicians who play instruments like the flute, oboe, and trombone." Disgruntled, they filed a lawsuit. Of course. Why didn't I think of that? I mean, I type more characters than the average lawyer. I publish every day.

Presumably, you do something more than everyone else, right?

I'll leave that one alone.

Ultimately, the 16 first and second violinists from the 106-member strong orchestra agreed to drop their lawsuit, originally scheduled to have been heard by a labor court in Bonn, and have instead negotiated a compromise with the city authorities, Bonn's mayor Barbel Dieckmann reported.

❧

Moving on to another art form—one that might justifiably lay claim to more fans than German chamber music—let's take a look at exotic dancing. There we ask the question, when is a performance protected intellectual property?

For a woman there is nothing more erotic than being understood. —Molly Haskell

The Stripper's Copyright

Stretching the bounds of copyright law, a pole dancer now has copyrighted her routine, according to a front-page article in the *Los Angeles Daily Journal* from February 2006. No, she's not performing her moves, known as the "Flirt," "Peek-a-Boo," and "Cat Pounce," in a dimly lit corner establishment. She's teaching them to other women as part of her exercise class.

With exercise boutiques (what should they be called?) in Los Angeles, New York, San Francisco, and Encino, the copyrighted routine has been featured on a number of national television shows, including *Oprah, 48 Hours, The View, Primetime Live, The Tonight Show,* and *The O'Reilly Factor.* You'd have to ask Sheila Kelley, the copyright holder, how Encino got included in that list of illustrious cities, but I'm sure it has nothing to do with the nightlife there.

The erotic moves merge striptease, pole dancing, and lap dancing into a cardiovascular exercise program touted as the latest fitness craze to develop in Los Angeles. And no wonder.

A two-hour class will set you back $50, but you can buy the DVD and/or book if you're not nearby. According to the website, you don't need a pole installed at home to use the book or video. You can learn the beginning moves on a floor mat.

Depending on the quality of your routine, however, I'm guessing that there may be certain establishments that would be willing to rent out their poles. For example, if this "exercise routine" takes off, then cities and counties might be able to add a new revenue stream by renting out fire station poles for classes. They'd probably be fairly well attended, too, but charging admission could raise some significant legal questions that I wouldn't want to answer.

On the other hand, you could help our copyright holder, Shelia Kelly, enforce her copyright by watching other, shall we say, "pole dancers," to see if they're performing the copyrighted moves. Of course, you'd have to own the DVD first.

⁓⊛⁓

Exotic dancers have to maintain a certain appearance in order to draw crowds. There's a dress—or undress—code, if you can imagine.

That requirement certainly is not unique to the profession; other employers require their employees to look a certain way. Is that fair? You decide.

Kiss and make up—but too much makeup has ruined many a kiss. —Mae West

The Question Is to Be with Makeup or to Be without Makeup

I have little experience with wearing makeup, except perhaps in high-school plays or during Halloween, so I'm ill-qualified to address 44-year-old Darlene Jesperson's termination from her long-time job with Harrah's Casino over the company's requirement that she wear makeup on the job. But, as you've seen, lack of experience rarely stops me from commenting.

Most American women, however, are quite the opposite, and some in the extreme. Wearing makeup, that is, not commenting (almost had you there, didn't I?).

Makeup is a question of degree, both in terms of appearance and in terms of attitude toward it. Let's first look at how some women view makeup. From Colette's *The Vagabond*, she ponders:

> Me. As that word came into my head, I involuntarily looked in the mirror. There's no getting away from it, it really is me there behind that mask of purplish rouge, my eyes ringed with a halo of blue grease-paint beginning to melt. Can the rest of my face be going to melt also? What if nothing were to remain from my whole reflection but a streak of dyed colour stuck to the glass like a long, muddy tear?

On the other hand, men are largely insensitive about makeup. Many don't notice it unless it's really bad. As a prime example, my dad used to say of some overdone women: "She's wearing enough makeup to paint a battleship and enough powder to sink it." Too much of a good thing can be, well, too much.

In quite the contrast, Darlene is an attractive woman, with or without makeup. She worked for more than twenty years at Harrah's, having started as a dishwasher and finally working as a bartender at its sports bar in Reno, Nevada. After a long respite of nonenforcement, Harrah's started to enforce certain appearance standards, and Darlene was terminated from her job as a result of her refusal to comply with the company's requirement to wear makeup.

She thought the unequal treatment was unfair. Generally, she had not previously worn makeup either on or off the job.

She filed a lawsuit against Harrah's, alleging sexual discrimination based on differing requirements for women and men. As the Ninth Circuit Court of Appeals instructs us at the beginning of *Jespersen v. Harrah's Casino*:

> "[Harrah's] standards required all bartenders, men and women, to wear the same uniform of black pants and white shirts, a bow tie, and comfortable black shoes. The standards also included grooming requirements that differed to some extent for men and women, requiring women to wear some facial makeup and not permitting men to wear any."

With that type of a gloss-over, the result was predictable.

The lower court held for Harrah's, ruling there was no discrimination, and the Court of Appeals agreed. But it's not the majority opinion that bears reading. Though the majority opinion is written by then-Chief Judge Mary Schroeder, many say it's apparent that most of the voting judges on the appellate court were largely men, perhaps many with the same disposition as my father.

There was one shining light, however, at the end of the opinion, little consolation that it was to Darlene after losing. It's quite an eloquent dissent by now cheif Judge Alex Kozinski, which is notable given the regular, high-quality writing we get in his opinions. As evidence of the creativity in his writing, consider this: in case you're looking for the record number of actual movie titles listed in a court opinion, its 215, and belongs to Judge Kozinski. You can read it in *U.S. v. Syufy Enterprises*, 903 F.2d 659 (9th Cir. 1990).

Judge Kozinksi took the majority to task for their ruling that Harrah's grooming standards didn't discriminate between men and women and the supposed lack of evidence of the cost of makeup. The beauty is in the simplicity of his observations:

> Nor is there any rational doubt that application of makeup is an intricate and painstaking process that requires considerable time and care. Even those of us who don't wear makeup know how long it can take from the hundreds of hours we've spent over the years frantically tapping our toes and pointing to our wrists. It's hard to imagine that a woman could "put on her face," as they say, in the time it would take a man to shave.

It's likewise hard to refute his commonsense logic:

> It is true that Jespersen failed to present evidence about what it costs to buy makeup and how long it takes to apply it. But is there any doubt that putting on makeup costs money and takes time? Harrah's policy requires women to apply face powder, blush, mascara, and lipstick. You don't need an expert witness to figure out that such items don't grow on trees.

Then there's the practical effect. Judge Kozinski gave the nod to Harrah's technical court victory, but invited the company to stand by their (wo)man:

> Finally, I note with dismay the employer's decision to let go a valued, experienced employee who had gained accolades from her customers, over what, in the end, is a trivial matter. Quality employees are difficult to find in any industry and I would think an employer would long hesitate before forcing a loyal, longtime employee to quit over an honest and heartfelt difference of opinion about a matter of personal significance to her. Having won the legal battle, I hope that Harrah's will now do the generous and decent thing by offering Jespersen her job back, and letting her give it her personal best—without the makeup.

Darlene Jespersen did not go back to work for Harrah's.

Moving right along, this next case illustrates the principle that size really doesn't matter. (No, we're not going back to exotic dancing!) In this next case, we're discussing furniture sales, and how the court discovered the planet-shaking revelation that a square foot in one location has the same dimensions as a square foot in another location.

Sometimes you make the right decision; sometimes you make the decision right. —Phillip C. McGraw

Let Me See That Ruler

Small retail furniture businesses in Hanford, California were upset that the city banned their businesses in certain parts of town, but exempted big department stores and allowed them to sell furniture as long as they limited the retail sales of furniture to something less than 2,500 square feet in their stores. This zoning exemption applied only to stores with more than 50,000 square feet of total space.

The smaller businesses cried foul under the equal protection provisions of the California Constitution, and sued.

The trial court agreed with the city and the big department stores, ruling that the city had a rational basis for the discrimination because the two kinds of stores were not "similarly situated." The smaller stores had approximately 4,000 square feet of retail space.

It took the appellate court only seven pages of opinion to reverse this ruling and determine that if the big and the small stores each limited retail furniture sales to 2,500 square feet, then they were similarly situated, and the city had violated the small businesses' right of equal protection.

The most surprising part of this lawsuit is that it took a city council, some big department stores, one small business, two or three sets of lawyers, and two courts to reach the momentous decision that no matter how you measure it, 2,500 square feet in a small store is the same as 2,500 square feet in a big store.

Let's suppose, just for a moment, that you don't have a storefront at all. You conduct your business alongside the road, free from any worries about zoning or square footage or whatnot—just you, your products, and pure profit. No problem, right?

Not necessarily. A lot depends on the type of inventory you carry.

I think it's about time we voted for senators with breasts. After all, we've been voting for boobs long enough. —Unknown

Give Me Your Tired, Your Poor…Just Don't Sell Your Pillows in Kern County

When you're tired, you put your head down on a pillow. According to the Kern County, California, Municipal Code, however, sales of certain pillows have been outlawed.

You may think that position is a bit outrageous, but in Kern County, they take these things very seriously. That's right, under Kern County Municipal Code section 9.12.010, the public sales of pillows is outlawed.

It's not just any type of offending pillow, however. It's "articles depicting female breasts," according to the code section. "Boobies pillows," to be exact.

Here's how the Kern County Board of Supervisors wrote it up:

> The hawking of those articles named by its vendor and sold as "boobies pillows" along the public highways is a species of indecency and vulgarity which cannot be ignored or controlled by passersby, which assails the eyes and minds of all who are required to use county highways, and which should be barred and controlled for the peace, safety, and welfare of the unincorporated areas of the county.

So you've been forewarned. Sell boobies pillows in Kern County (about an hour North of Los Angeles), and you'll get fined $500 and spend 90 days in the hoosegow.

You can probably find a safer place to rest your head. Safer, softer, and far more enjoyable, I'm guessing.

In the end, the sellers of the offending pillows closed down rather than challenge the constitutionality of the ordinance based on the freedom of expression clause in the First Amendment. As a justice of the Supreme Court once said, however, "I know obscenity when I see it," and boobies pillows might just fall into that category.

∽◦∾

Every business owner dreams about generating positive word-of-mouth about his or her operation. After all, word-of-mouth opinion is considered by many as better than advertising. If you can get people talking about your business, then they're more likely to patronize it.

That is, if the things they're saying are good. What happens if someone starts a campaign to badmouth your business? One California restaurant owner found out that there is some protection under the law—and that's not just idle chatter.

Free speech means the right to shout "theatre" in a crowded fire.
—Abbie Hoffman

Watch Your Words: Business and Free Speech

You have a First Amendment right to say whatever you want, even if it's critical, right?

Wrong.

There are limits. The typical example prohibits you from yelling "FIRE" in a crowded theater. That limit exists because to do so is dangerous. But what happens if you just want to be critical?

And critical and critical and critical. Almost like a protest.

Anne Lemen, a self-described Christian evangelist, found out the hard way. She apparently was upset with a neighboring restaurant, the Balboa Island Village Inn, a small bar and grill in Newport Beach. Lemen lives next to the restaurant, which she rather regularly defamed as part of her campaign to shut the bar down, telling anyone who would listen that the bar made sex videos, dabbled in child pornography, distributed illegal drugs, encouraged lesbian activities, had mafia links, was a whorehouse, and sold tainted food, among other things. The trial court ruled that all were false statements, and banned her from making them.

That's not all Lemen said, though. According to the California Supreme Court, she called customers "drunks" and "whores." She told customers entering the Inn, "I don't know why you would be going in there. The food is shitty." She approached potential customers outside the inn more than 100 times, causing many to turn away.

Lemen also had several encounters with employees of the Village Inn. She told bartender Ewa Cook that Cook "worked for Satan," was "Satan's wife," and was "going to have Satan's children." She asked musician Arturo Perez if he had a "green card" and asked whether he knew there were illegal aliens working at the Inn. Lemen referred to Theresa Toll, the owner's wife, as "Madam Whore" and said, in the presence of her tenant, Larry Wilson, "Everyone on the island knows you're a whore."

Aric Toll, who had bought the business in 2000, saw his sales drop, perhaps not too surprisingly, by 20 percent.

Despite these defamatory remarks, the Court of Appeals reversed the trial court's injunction, leaving only minor restrictions in place, such as preventing Lemen from videotaping patrons on their way in or out of the bar.

The California Supreme Court, however, reversed the reasoning in the Court of Appeals' decision, and ruled that a court can stop Lemen's defamatory statements and activities. In the court's words (despite two separate dissents and one concurring opinion), "a properly limited injunction prohibiting [Lemen] from repeating statements about [the Village Inn] that were determined at trial to be defamatory would not violate [Lemen]'s right to free speech."

There is a line, and Lemen crossed it. Now the case goes back to the lower court to redo the injunction and hold a trial on the damages Lemen caused the bar. Her trial in the Orange County, California, Superior Court was pending at the time of publication. I predict that trial will be an expensive lesson in "free speech."

꧁꧂

We business owners live, drink, and breathe our businesses. We're either always at work, thinking about work, or talking about work. There's no avoiding it: We need to be constantly connected.

That trait has spilled over to most of the rest of us: we want to be constantly connected, all of the time. Cell phones were perhaps the first step in this process, and now most phones can connect directly to the Internet. But for some people, that's just not enough.

The Internet is the most important single development in the history of human communication since the invention of call waiting. —Dave Barry

From one questionable idea to another: here's a look at a business idea that has "Huh?" written all over it.

She looks like she combs her hair with an egg beater.
—Hedda Hopper

You Can Patent Just about Anything, but Should You?

In the annals of bad ideas, the comb-over has to rank somewhere in the top ten. Probably even David Letterman would agree, if you asked him. Then again, like me, he's got a mostly full head of hair, so we likely fall into the category of those-who-shouldn't-judge.

But this is my book, so I'm going to judge away: the comb-over is a bad idea.

Just get over it and cut your hair. If you have any doubt, then ask a woman. She'll tell you. Cut it.

Perhaps the only thing worse than a comb-over is a patent on a comb-over.

No, I am not kidding. It's Patent No. 4,022,227, granted to Donald J. Smith and Frank J. Smith of Orlando, Florida, on May 10, 1977.

Here's the claim under their patent: "A method of styling hair to cover partial baldness using only the hair on a person's head.

The hair styling requires dividing a person's hair into three sections and carefully folding one section over another." The patent comes complete with drawings, if you dare imagine.

Can you believe it? Not just one person, but two, had the brilliant idea to patent what is likely the worst hairstyle in the world next to the mullet.

What were they thinking? Actually, it's probably not a bad idea, if you think about the practical application.

Imagine their enforcement program: "Hey you. Yeah, you with the comb-over. We've got a patent on that abysmal hairstyle. Pay us ten bucks or cut it off."

Now that I think about it, there are a few other things that deserve to be patented. Just be sure to regularly check the U.S. Patent Office listings to make sure you stay out of court. You wouldn't want to be a defendant in this patent lawsuit.

One of the most valuable assets any business has is its name. A name is an integral part of a business's identity, used to brand and market the operation. Most business owners are justifiably protective of their name—if you don't believe me, then just go start a fast-service hamburger joint and try to call it McDonald's.

It isn't just the mega-corporations who want to keep control of their names. Nope. Two small bars in Key West duked it out over a particularly profitable moniker.

Always do sober what you said you'd do drunk. That will teach you to keep your mouth shut. —Ernest Hemingway

What's in a Name?

When I was a kid, *sloppy joe* meant a very sloppy type of meat and sauce-dripping sandwich. It means an awful lot more to two bars in Key West.

To Sloppy Joe's bar, it means that Hemingway used to drink there.

To Captain Tony's bar, it also means that Hemingway drank there.

Hemmingway apparently did a lot of drinking.

Presumably, the tourists are attracted by where Hemingway drank. When I go to Key West, it's Margaritaville. Of course that also works for me in New Orleans and several other towns, but that's another story.

Apparently, there was a bar brawl between Sloppy Joe's and Captain Tony's over the use of the Sloppy Joe's name. You see, Sloppy Joe was a friend of Hemingway's, and he ran the bar where Hemingway drank. Now, there's a federal case over who gets to use the name.

Sloppy Joe's first dropped the gauntlet in the lawsuit, claiming that "Captain Tony's products are not of Sloppy Joe's quality, and the condition of its premises does not meet Sloppy Joe's standards. As a result, Captain Tony's has sullied Sloppy Joe's distinctive style and decor," the suit said.

Captain Tony was out of town and had no immediate comment.

The rest of the story? Florida's Monroe County historian, Tom Hambright, said, when asked which bar Hemingway drank at: "Both, as far as I can determine."

Now there's a surprise.

The suit was resolved by a settlement agreement. Captain Tony's still asserts its claim to be Sloppy Joe's, but the bar by the actual name Sloppy Joe's is the name of another bar, and remains in business today. Next time you're in Key West, just follow Hemmingway's advice: Have a drink at both places.

<hr>

You'd be amazed what falls on a simple baker's shoulders. The head of Krispy Kreme recently discovered that he's not only responsible for turning out a delicious product and turning a profit. Oh, no.

He has to tell the future too.

A doughnut without a hole…is a Danish. —Chevy Chase

Doughnut Maker Gets Creamed

Krispy Kreme's shareholders are upset at the doughnut business because they weren't warned that the craze for Atkins-like diets would eat into company profits.

Now there's a news flash. Shareholders expected the company to warn them about that? I don't know about you, but even if you don't watch the news, read newspapers, or (God forbid) scour blogs on the Internet, certainly one or more of your friends is on an Atkins diet, or, for that matter, some other type of diet. You don't have to be a rocket scientist to figure out any diet craze is going to hurt sales. In fact, even if you are a Krispy Kreme shareholder, then you've probably cut back on your own intake.

Disgruntled shareholders filed a lawsuit in North Carolina, which the company later settled for $75 million, including token payments from its former chief operating officer, chief financial officer, and a $4 million payment from its accounting firm.

Surely, a lot of carbohydrate-laden food companies blame Atkins for what may be their own mismanagement, and it's becoming a bit of a pastime to do so. But, maybe Krispy Kreme will turn the corner with a low-carb doughnut, as other companies have done.

Other people, however, consider the company's doughnuts part of a religion. I don't know about that, but they're holey to me, and they also taste great.

⌘

If you're like me, then your memory might not be what it used to be. You might be in the habit of jotting down notes from time to time, just to help you remember. You might even use them later, to prepare more formal documents.

You might want to make sure you keep track of all those notes. Otherwise, they could cost you a pretty penny.

Everything you have wants to own you. —Regina Eilert

Careful What You Doodle

Though this case isn't over yet, it certainly took a turn for the worse for Lawrence Taylor, a general partner of the Santa Monica Collection (SMC).

Well, apparently, Taylor asked Donald Sterling about purchasing real estate properties. Sterling agreed to purchase the properties. Sterling then prepared a handwritten document that listed three street addresses in Santa Monica and a sales price of $16.75 million.

Got that? A *handwritten* document.

Taylor never bought the properties. As expected, Sterling sued Taylor to enforce the agreement. A trial court decided that the handwritten document contained terms that were too uncertain to be enforceable under the statute of frauds.

In short, the statute of frauds requires that some contracts, including those for the sale of real property, be in writing and signed by the party that agrees to perform (here, Taylor).

To qualify, the handwritten note must at least include a description of the property and the price to be paid.

The California Court of Appeals, Second District, held that the handwritten document met those qualifications, and sent the case back to the trial court for the judge to decide if the agreement was actually enforceable under the remaining requirements of the statute of frauds.

Taylor may have to buy the three properties yet. With his luck, though, the value will have dropped, too.

Next time he wants to buy property, I bet he uses a lawyer to draft the purchase agreement.

⌘

There seems to be an endless supply of business ideas, but not every new idea is a good idea. The jury's still out on this one, not to mention the related litigation, but I have to say it may have some appeal for women.

American women expect to find in their husbands a perfection that English women only hope to find in their butlers.
—W. Somerset Maugham

Want to Rent-a-Husband?

I read. A lot. For my legal practice, that means I read slip opinions, like the one I discovered below. This case deals with civil procedure. Though a little on the boring side for most people, such issues are near and dear to the hearts of litigators. But what makes this case really interesting is the company: Rent-a-Husband (why didn't I think of that?!).

No, it's not what you're thinking. Rent-a-Husband has nothing to do with escort services or anything like lady sitters, the latter a Comedy Central skit.

It's a handyman business. You know, that honey-do list that never gets completed. Well, this guy does it. Finishes up the list, that is.

Now there's an idea to get my house straightened up. Too bad this Rent-a-Husband is in Maine. The Rent-a-Husband business is apparently doing well, with regular appearances on the *CBS Early Show* and a new book (see *www.rentahusband.com*).

That said, let's hit the nail on the head and get to the lawsuit itself. Rent-a-Husband is a franchise, and the incorporation of the company, the franchise documents, and the book deal that came out of the company were all handled by a Maine lawyer who took stock in the company as part of his fee for the work.

Not happy with the lawyer's work, Rent-a-Husband sued for malpractice. The lawyer declared bankruptcy to avoid the liability. Nevertheless, the lawyer tendered the malpractice claim to his insurance carrier, which promptly denied the claim, arguing its "business pursuits" exception precluded coverage. The carrier reasoned when the lawyer took an interest in the company, it amounted to a "business pursuit," not the rendering of legal services. Both the lawyer and Rent-a-Husband sued the lawyer's insurance company, American Guarantee & Liability Insurance Company, and won. The court ruled that the stock taken by the lawyer was more of a fee than it was his participation in the business.

The lesson here? Don't do business with your lawyer. Just let your lawyer do the legal work and write a check. Otherwise, either check to see if you're in Maine or read the policy first.

❧

After reading about all this litigation, you might find yourself reaching for a stiff drink. That's no problem—unless you're trying to order your favorite vintage from a distant winemaker.

Alcohol may pick you up a little bit, but it sure lets you down in a hurry. —Betty Ford

We Will Ship No Wine before Its Time

Shipping wine between states is unnecessarily complicated. There's a mishmash of conflicting state laws about what wines can be shipped from one location to another. It's a nightmare.

You're better off sending a gift certificate.

Recently, a New York court upheld another ban on shipping wine from New York. Add to this complicated mess the fact that a federal agency taxes exported wines.

According to the Volcano Winery (no, I'm not kidding) in Hawaii, they can ship to "reciprocal states." Just in case you wanted some lava wine.

Not sure what a reciprocal state is? You'd better believe your favorite winemaker knows. They have to know: simply by shipping a bottle of their finest to the wrong location, they're committing a federal felony. After Prohibition became yesterday's news, every state set up their own rules regarding wine taxation. The result—a logistical nightmare. Desperate to not miss out on any tax dollars, states have severely limited the export of wines—exporting, despite the fact the wines never left the country. If you live on the West Coast, then chances are you reside in 1 of the 13 states that has a reciprocal agreement with some other state—but the vast majority of the country is simply out of luck.

My head hurts trying to sort through this mess of laws. I think I'll have a drink. Thank goodness I live on the West Coast!

⚬⚬⚬

If you're seeing ghosts, goblins, and green-faced witches around, then it's possible that getting wine shipped to your door may be the least of your problems. Or it may be that you live in the vicinity of a costume shop.

Are those people wearing colorful costumes outside the shop actually signs? Or are they simply people wearing costumes? Only the court knows for sure.

I see my face in the mirror and say, "I'm a Halloween costume? That's what they think of me?" —Drew Carey

Custom-Made Conflict

Just in time for Halloween, Raleigh, North Carolina, determined that kids dressed in costumes outside a costume store constitute a sign for the store. That's right, take a look at Part 10 (comes right after Part 14 in the code), Chapter 2, Article E, Section 10-2083.2. See if you can figure out how a kid dressed in a Halloween costume fits into this ordinance.

Here are the categories that qualify as signs:

- Announcement signs
- Awning, marquee, and canopy signs
- Changeable copy signs
- Community watch signs
- Directional signs
- Directory signs
- Ground low-profile signs
- Ground signs for double frontage lots
- Ground medium-profile signs
- Ground high-profile signs
- Landmark signs
- Product and information signs
- Projecting signs
- Temporary signs
- Tract identification signs
- Wall signs
- Windblown signs

I can't, and I'm a lawyer. I don't see the words "kids dressed in costumes" or anything even approaching those words. Perhaps it's because I'm not licensed in North Carolina, and I just don't understand how they do things in Raleigh, just up the road from Mayberry. I used to live south of the Mason-Dixon line, in Virginia, but I still don't quite get it.

For that matter, neither does the mother of the kids, Louie Bowen, who also owns the allegedly offending costume shop, Hughie & Louie's. Her kids, 13 and 9, were dressed as Mrs. Claus and an elf. They earned a $100 ticket from Raleigh's zoning department for failure to have a permit. The editorial staff of the local paper, the *News & Observer,* is behind Mrs. Bowen, and has called on the town's mayor to intervene.

Meanwhile, the zoning department has threatened a $500 fine for a repeat violation. Of the sections on the list above, the product signs category looked like a possible fit, but that definition requires a sign of at least 32 feet. At 13 and 9, it's doubtful that the kids are that big. I wonder how Raleigh would treat "headvertising," where you get paid to plaster an ad on your forehead.

News & Observer writer Josh Shaffer quoted Larry Strickland, Raleigh's inspections director, who interpreted the sign ordinance for us. "It could even be a person. If she's in the costume business and she's got people in costume out there, that could be a violation," the inspector claimed. The reporter goes on, "Bowen's violation note reads: 'The display of portable sign(s)/banner(s)/ pennant(s)/ balloon(s) at the above location is a violation of Raleigh City Code Section 10-2083.2, which allows for the display of such signs only after the issuance of a thirty (30) day special event sign permit." An inspector scribbled an addendum: "This includes people dress up.'"

In protest, Ms. Bowen donned her own costume: a crushed velvet cape and faux-gold tiara and scepter. As the Halloween Queen, she's going to fight city hall.

It seems to me that if you have a scepter, then you can overrule city hall.

Seriously Now: Lessons Learned

This chapter covers labor relations, defamation (libel and slander), intellectual property (patents and copyrights), franchise agreements, insurance, and compliance with government statutes.

Some of what I've written about in this chapter could have been avoided with a contract. Not just any contract, however, a written contract—a *well-written* contract.

A verbal contract isn't worth the paper it's written on. Someone famous said that, but I can't remember who. For a lawyer, nothing could be further from the truth. So many of the cases I've litigated are the result of either no contract at all or poorly written contracts that clients have found online or in self-help books. If you're preparing contracts by yourself or hiring a lawyer to help you, then hiring a good one is worth every penny, even if you can't afford it as you're starting up your business.

So many things can sink a start-up—or even a well-run business. From labor and contract disputes to failure to comply with government regulations and even something mundane enough, such as the wrong kind of insurance—just about anything can get a business owner into legal hot water.

A good lawyer will help you avoid problems—and you'll never know which ones you've avoided because they will never have occurred. That's part of the reason I wrote this book. So many self-help books out there tell us how to do it right, I thought some more practical examples of how to do it wrong would make the point better.

The long and short of it is this chapter is designed to show you one thing: the value of having a lawyer help you with the legal side of your business. Which side is that, you ask? Just about everything you do in business has legal consequences down the line. Sometimes, it's the one you don't think you need any help on that blows up the worst.

If you have any doubt, then ask. Most lawyers are pretty good with business advice. The more I'm in court litigating business disputes, the more I've learned about how to avoid getting into those disputes in the first place and what business owners can do to avoid the pitfalls of litigation.

Oh, and one more thing. If you're going to sign a contract, please read it first—all of it, even the fine print. There's an adage lawyers rarely share: the big print giveth and the small print taketh away. Reading a contract may seem entirely logical, but you'd be amazed at how many times people don't read the whole thing. If you don't want to read it or don't understand what you're reading, then send it to a lawyer. That's one of the things we do.

Chapter 3

Commit a Crime

If you're in a hurry and have a great need to find yourself in a front of a judge, then committing a crime is the way to go. It's the single, most effective way going to secure an appearance in court—so effective, in fact, that it even works for those folks who committed a crime and didn't even know it.

In this chapter, we examine some highlights from criminal court, from a camp group leader who lost her taste for s'mores to a bank robber with a gift for retirement planning.

⌘

Now you might not have a lot of compassion for the common criminal. After all, they've opted for the easy way out, choosing to break the law rather than obey, the way the rest of us do. You do, don't you?

In this case, however, you might find your heart melting. A septuagenarian in Illinois discovers that this whole bank-robbing business is a lot harder than it looks.

If only God would give me some clear sign! Like making a large deposit in my name in a Swiss bank. —Woody Allen

It's Not Easy Getting Old and Robbing Banks

Once you hit 70, you've got most things figured out. You'd think, too, that a 70-year-old, once-convicted bank robber would have a leg up on the rest of us on how to rob a bank.

I mean the stocking-over-the-head thing probably should be passé for this guy.

But nooooo.

Small-town Versailles, Illinois, is the scene for the attempted caper by 70-year-old Gordon A. Bryant. He showed up at the Farmers State Bank, wearing a stocking mask over his head, at the front door, but not yet through the vestibule. He wanted to be buzzed in.

The bank, however, had installed a buzzer door entry system to foil would-be robbers after a successful robbery some months earlier.

According to news reports, alert (how alert would you have to be?) bank employees refused to let the unusually clad gentleman in. Go figure.

Frustrated, Bryant drove away. Presumably after removing his stocking mask. But again, "alert" bank employees called the sheriff, who managed to catch Bryant. With typical understatement, Brown County Sheriff Jerry Kempf commented, "When you're going into a bank, you usually don't wear those in there. It's not Halloween. He's 70 years old; you would hope he would have learned by now."

Bryant could be in his 90s before he gets out of jail. Maybe by then he will have learned. It only took one time for the bank to figure out what to do.

⊸❦⊷

On the other hand, there are what we like to call natural-born students. They're avid learners, always eager to improve their skill set and become more knowledgeable. Consider the following case, where a would-be, big-time criminal learned everything he needed to succeed—except for the bit about getting caught.

Even if you were to be able to reverse engineer the encoded material what you'd get is nonsensical to you. —Mark de Visser

You Can Learn a Lot from Television

Maybe you can even learn a few things you shouldn't, too. Take, for example, the case of Michael W. Hobbs, 36, of Waco, Kentucky, who pled guilty to five counts of burglarizing homes.

He learned how from watching the Discovery Channel. The TV channel features a show called *It Takes a Thief,* hosted by two ex-cons who explain to everyday homeowners like you and me how vulnerable we are to theft, and what to do about it.

Apparently Hobbs watched the show frequently enough to learn how to exploit those vulnerabilities. He followed the ex-cons' advice, and kept nothing of what he took in his own home, according to police.

Police Major Steve Griggs told the Associated Press, "He didn't hold onto any of the property. He had no physical evidence at his residence whatsoever. When we entered a couple of times, he said, 'Come on in, look around. I've done nothing.'"

Hobbs was ultimately tripped up because police managed to tie him to the successive burglaries. He would show up asking homeowners whether they needed gutter work. Enough victims remembered him that police tied him to the crime spree, and Bob's your uncle, the police arrested him.

Once convicted, he was sentenced to twelve years in prison.

Let's hope he doesn't have cable in there. No telling what he'll learn next.

⌘

Even so, you would think some things wouldn't have to be taught. That some facts were so obvious, so fundamental, so patently clear that to miss them would be like missing the nose on your face. That doesn't mean they can't be missed, just the same.

He's got a little bit of a swagger. That's good to see. You like guys like that. He's got that makeup of a guy that you like playing in the secondary. —Herman Edwards

Where Does a Bank Robber Put Her Stash?

You're a bank teller behind some bulletproof glass, and a woman walks in, dressed to the nines. Slightly overweight, but still dressed to the nines. Sensible, strappy, glittery gold pumps with a perfectly matching handbag.

Blonde, tightly curled hair to boot, with a cute, dark-brown, leopard-print, calf-length dress with a solid black, scoop-neck collar. Makeup applied just right. Well, maybe a little heavy on the eye makeup and foundation, but still, she tried.

Then she hands you a note: "Give me all your money," it says, or words to that effect.

What do you notice? Remember now, you've been trained for this—and you know you're going to have to give police a detailed description after it's all over. Without looking back up at my description, can you do it?

Our Central Islip, Long Island, Citibank teller did, but it was one thing that stuck out the most.

It was her pencil-thin moustache and goatee. Yep, you guessed it. She was in fact a he, and for all his other efforts, he had forgotten to shave.

Aston Barth, who has a prior conviction for bank robbery, was held on $1 million in bail after a tipster turned him in to police based on the teller's description.

The strappy sandals were nowhere to be found. There was a little too much bread loaf in those shoes. And they pinched.

⌘

Going to jail takes some time. You've got to go through your trial, sentencing, and then the long, hurry-up-and-wait process of being transported to a facility and finally incarcerated. It can take forever—unless you're this next guy.

It is better for you to be free of fear lying upon a pallet than to have a golden couch and a rich table and be full of trouble.
—Epicurus

It Makes for a Shorter Trip to the Cell

Stealing from a jail, that is. That's right. Aaron Martin of Columbia County, Wisconsin, allegedly tried to take a wooden pallet from a secured area behind a jail. Deputies noticed a suspicious truck and went to investigate.

Now think about this for a moment. Our hero is aware of his surroundings. He knows exactly where he is. He's at the county jail. Martin claims to work for a pallet manufacturing company that holds a contract with the county. If so, then presuming the pallet belongs to his company, he's out of dutch. But that really isn't his main problem. It's what's inside that counts, especially when you voluntarily give officers the right to search your vehicle. As most of us know from watching police and lawyer shows on TV, the police can't search your vehicle without either your permission or a warrant, unless there's something in plain sight. Or, you've been placed under arrest for a crime and your truck is impounded. Then, it's open season.

Unfortunately, our hero apparently gave permission for the search.

Now, he'll have to deal not only with the pot pipe officers found in his truck, which resulted in a drug paraphernalia charge, but also the additional charge of attempted theft of the pallet. Not a good day, overall.

He was escorted to a nearby cell after his arrest. He didn't even pass go. He was too close to the jail.

❧

Sometimes you can be too smart for your own good. In the following instance, a would-be businessman had a great way to keep inventory costs down. There was only one problem, as you'll see.

New York's such a wonderful city. Although I was at the library today. The guy there was very rude. I said, "I'd like a card." He says, "You have to prove you're a citizen of New York." So I stabbed him. —Emo Phillips

They Come with Sensors, Too.

Craigslist.com (no relation) is a wonderful source for apartments, housing, odds and ends, and just about anything else you used to find in the want ads.

It's also a great place to find inexpensive, used DVDs.

Thomas Pilaar apparently thought so, too. He allegedly sold inexpensive used DVDs on Craigslist until one recipient noticed something odd about the DVD she ordered from him.

It had a library sticker on it.

A librarian bought the DVD, and she noticed the sticker. She turned him in to police, who arrested him. The police claim Pilaar obtained at least seven library cards under different names and may have had as many as 2,500 DVDs at a value of more than $45,000.

According to CBS4 Denver television reporter Brian Mass, librarians said of this theft, "Just like any other system, it's possible to abuse it. And this guy, if he is who he claims to be, shows up at some of the libraries and developed very quickly a pattern of just not acting like an ordinary patron and checking out way too many DVDs."

That's one library card per person, and no more than one book or movie at a time, please.

Oh yes. One more thing: shhhhh.

~~∞~~

Libraries may be where you find teachers, but sometimes they take field trips. S'mores are classic campfire food, one of those traditional favorites that every kid enjoys. Not just kids—more than a few adults enjoy the taste of graham crackers, warm chocolate, and hot marshmallows.

Hope Clarke, however, is not one of those adults. At least not anymore. It's hard to enjoy the sticky, gooey treat when creating one of the campfire goodies puts you directly into the long arms of the law.

Life is like a box of chocolates…you never know what you're gonna get. —Forrest Gump

The Marshmallow Warrant

You're camping with your grade-school teacher in Yellowstone National Park. Sitting around the campfire, she gets out hot chocolate and makes s'mores.

A few ghost stories and it's time for bed, kiddies.

One little mistake, though, but luckily no serious harm, unlike the poor fellow in the last story. Teacher forgets to put away the fixin's. Ranger catches her, issues a $50 ticket. Expensive lesson, very expensive s'mores.

Time ticks by, say a year or so. Teacher Hope Clarke travels from her hometown of Riverton, Wyoming, to Miami to take a vacation, and goes on a Carnival Fascination cruise. Nice, relaxing trip.

Until she returns to Miami from Cozumel, Mexico. Then, she's hauled out of bed at 6:30 A.M., taken from her cruise cabin, hand-cuffed, leg shackled and detained for nine hours. (Yup—count 'em—that's nine hours, longer than most people's workdays.) Only then is Clarke dragged before a federal magistrate to answer for the Yellowstone ticket. For a marshmallow violation.

That's right. The ticket she paid a year ago. The copy of the ticket that the magistrate had (I'm guessing here that the copy came from the customs agents who arrested her on an allegedly outstanding warrant from the supposedly unpaid ticket) showed that she had, in fact, paid the ticket.

Amidst her sobbing, Magistrate Judge John J. O'Sullivan apologized and demanded that the customs agents answer up. Other than the standard "we thought we were doing the right thing," the agents had no real answers.

The lesson here?

Be careful kiddies, it's a jungle out there, and marshmallows can lead to a life of crime. Better to nip it in the bud now—and leave those s'mores at home.

∼◈∼

Hope Clarke might have started sliding down crime's slippery slope, led astray by some tasty s'mores—but others have taken the trip all the way to the bottom of the slide. In this next case, another culinary treat—this time of the pickled persuasion—landed our defendants in hot water.

My mum, a strange creature from the time when pickles on toothpicks were still the height of sophistication.
—Bridget Jones

Quit Jerkin My Gherkin

In the small town of Niles, Michigan, slightly North of South Bend, Indiana, Bobby Lee Bolen and his friends, Jody Lee and

J. W. Romanski, III, were hanging out at Jody's house. It was just a guy's night in, shooting the breeze and having a few beers.

Well, maybe more than a few. In the process of consuming large quantities of alcohol (according to Bobby Lee's attorney, Robert Lutz) Bobby Lee got hungry and raided the pickle jar in Jody's refrigerator.

Apparently not feeling too charitable about Bobby Lee's uninvited choice to eat his food, Jody told Bobby Lee he couldn't afford to feed everyone in the world and to stop eating his pickles.

Bobby Lee didn't take kindly to Jody's rebuke and left in a huff, yelling and swearing at Jody. Somewhere outside the door, however, he reconsidered his frustration. Bobby Lee returned yelling, "Here's your damn pickles" and started throwing pickles at Jody and J. W.

As if I needed to say it, a melee ensued.

During the scuffle, Bobby Lee was so frustrated that when Jody grabbed the phone to call 911 for help, Bobby Lee picked it up and beat Jody over the head with it. Ultimately subdued, Bobby Lee was charged with two counts of assault, home invasion, and cutting phone lines.

According to the *South Bend Tribune*, Judge Scott Schofield was none too pleased with the situation. "If this is not the silliest case I've ever seen in my courtroom, it certainly is among the top ten," Judge Schofield groused. "The fact that it's silly doesn't mean that it's not serious," the judge continued. He then sentenced Bobby Lee to time served while awaiting trial, crediting him with some 54 days the pickle-thrower had already spent in the pokey, but added on $1,150 in fines, $270 in restitution, an anger management course, a substance abuse evaluation, and a year's probation, according to *Tribune* reporter Debra Haight's story.

In a Vlasic case of understatement, Bobby Lee denied allegations he was pregnant. He may have been pickled, however.

༺☙༻

Alcohol played a role in this somewhat infamous pickle case, but that lubricant is not always the culprit. As you'll see in the next case, some people are just guilty, first and foremost, of criminal stupidity.

All that ever came before me are thieves and robbers: but the sheep did not hear them. —The Bible, John 10:8

Every Once in a While, Criminal Stupidity Pays Off

After allegedly trying to rob a Washington Mutual Bank branch in Miami, Florida, Luis Martinez is now charged with armed robbery, use of a firearm in the commission of a felony, and numerous counts of false imprisonment.

He ran into the bank flashing a semiautomatic handgun and yelling and cursing, according to reports. He then told the bank customers to lie on the floor, instructed everyone not to call the police, and demanded $50,000.

An alert teller hit a silent alarm, and within 90 seconds officers patrolling just four blocks away had the bank surrounded.

After collecting money from the teller in the interim, Martinez discovered the police presence outside while trying to head out the door. Now angrier that he had been on his way in, he turned and demanded to know who had ratted him out. "He wanted to know who called the cops," said bank customer Carlos Ardeaga. "He said they ruined his life and if he was going down, he wasn't going down alone."

Luckily for the tellers and bank customers, Martinez's semiautomatic handgun turned out to be a replica BB gun. At the time of this writing, he is in custody pending trial.

And locked up in a real jail, not a replica.

⌘

If a Plant's Roots Are too Tight, Repot.
—*New York Times* gardening article headline

Mistakes 1, 2, 3, and 4—Membership Card Revoked

You really have to wonder whether we're evolving backward. According to the Associated Press, one of our illustrious species in Clarkstown, New York, is allegedly guilty of four mistakes:

1. Impersonating a police officer
2. Making a traffic stop

3. Stopping an off-duty state trooper
4. Driving without a registration or insurance

While you may get away with three out of the four mistakes, number 3 will really get you into trouble. Even so, Shalom Gelbman, 22, of New Square, New York, made all four mistakes, state police said.

Gelbman, with a strobe light on his dashboard and his high beams flashing, allegedly pulled over a car one Wednesday night on the Palisades Interstate Parkway, police said. Inside the pulled-over car was New York State Trooper Seamus Lyons, who instead of getting a ticket, arrested Gelbman.

Gelbman was not clear with investigators about why he pulled over Lyons's car. One investigator said Gelbman told officers he wanted to scare the driver and get him out of the way.

Gelbman was charged with reckless endangerment, criminal impersonation, and was cited for having unauthorized equipment in his car, a dark blue Mercury Grand Marquis with tinted windows. At least he tried to look like a cop. He was released on $5,000 bail after being arraigned in Clarkstown Justice Court.

This guy's fifteen minutes of fame are up, along with his membership card in the human race.

～∞～

Gelbman's fame may be a thing of the past, but the fame you get on the *Jerry Springer Show* lasts forever—or at least as long as the show's in syndication. The low-brow, trash-talking, confrontational show has its share of dedicated fans.

Just as many people, however, don't like the show. Some folks think we should opt for better, classier, more enlightening entertainment, like *Nancy Grace*, while others just don't like the sleazy nature of the topics covered.

Still others don't like the way their *Jerry Springer* appearance went, when it was their turn in front of the camera for their close-up. Sort of like this guy.

A TV show is never any better than the stupidest man connected with it. —(with apologies to) Ben Hecht

Tell Me It Ain't So, Jerry Springer

Here's one for the I-coulda-told-ya-so category. Maybe it should be filed under the no-kidding category, too.

The Courthouse News Service gives us this little tidbit: "In state court in Chicago, a man who appeared on the *Jerry Springer Show* filed suit against another guest who assaulted him onstage. The show and its production company were also named as defendants."

This isn't the first time that Jerry's been sued. There was also that lawsuit over the death of a woman who admitted on the show that she had secretly remarried and was killed by her ex-husband immediately after the show aired. The suit was later dropped.

I don't know. Call me silly. If you're a contestant (not the right word, I know) *née* guest, on Jerry's show, then I think there's a high likelihood you are going to be punched. Or called names. Or booed.

Kinda goes with the territory. In the law, we call it "assumption of the risk." It's a defense theory to injury cases that essentially means "you should know better." In other words, if you're a guest on a *Jerry Springer* episode, then you know it's highly likely someone's going to take a swing at you and some nasty rumor will likely turn out to be true.

Of course, Jerry wouldn't have it any other way.

꼭

Luckily, in America's institutions of higher learning, you don't have to worry about running into any of the chaotic nonsense that is part and parcel of the *Jerry Springer Show or Nancy Grace*. After all, these students are the leaders of tomorrow. Devoted to their studies, they keep their noses to the grindstone and their eyes on the prize.

OK, who am I kidding? Partying and revelry is a long-established part of the American collegiate tradition—almost as well established as the legal consequences that follow.

My green thumb came only as a result of the mistakes I made while learning to see things from the plant's point of view.
—H. Fred Ale

A Little Early for Easter

The Gamma Phi Beta sorority sisters don't exactly have a green thumb, but they have great fashion sense. Because you can't really have a great party without decorations, the sisters went in search of palm fronds to add a tropical flavor to their festivities one Saturday night.

Unfortunately, they may have gone a little too far. The sisters apparently cut palm fronds from several palm trees on private property extending up and down the street from the sorority house, and did a very poor job of it, risking charges of trespass, theft, and destruction of property.

Here's the best part, though. The "mutilation" of the palm trees was discovered Sunday morning—presumably after the party was just winding down. When contacted by the police, one of the sisters told them, "Now is not a good time to talk about the palm fronds." Apparently, some parents of sorority pledges were at the house, perhaps along with some sisters who were sporting headaches.

Not to be put off, the police offered the sorority sister "other options" for a better time to talk with them about the palm fronds. Reconsidering, eight sisters thought that an immediate discussion was their best option, and admitted to cutting the palm fronds.

It's not like there isn't plenty to do at Cal State University–Chico. Just as one example, instead of cutting palm fronds, the sisters could have attended the "Burning Spear with Mystic Roots" music presentation at the college. Don't ask me, I have no idea. Given the choice, I might have considered the fronds, too.

⟡

At least the girls in the previous story were smart enough to make it to college. The fellows in these cases are in no immediate danger of collecting any academic honors.

There are people who believe in leprechauns, Santa Claus, aliens in our midst, the innocence of O. J. Simpson, and that weight makes a difference in the outcome of a horse race. An idea…is not responsible for the people who believe in it. —Don Marquis

Leprechauns or Window Cleaning: You Vote for the Least Likely Defense to Win an Acquittal

Ask any criminal lawyer, judge, or prosecutor and you'll find they hear several standard defenses to just about any crime:

- "It wasn't me, man."
- The SODDI defense ("Some Other Dude Did It").
- "I didn't get my Miranda warning" or, "I take the fifth."
- "I was set up," or another variant, "It was entrapment."
- "They didn't have a search warrant."
- "I didn't mean to _____ [insert name of any crime here]."

None of them typically works. Most of the people involved with that end of the system know the somewhat sad joke criminal defense attorneys make—when you're charged with a crime, you're guilty until proven innocent.

Some creative defenses, however, just might get you off the charges.

Let's first take leprechauns, for example. As first reported by WLWT-TV, out of Cincinnati, Ohio, Mr. Kim Leblanc was in custody for "a variety of charges." And what a variety it is. Mr. Leblanc broke into a parked car and promptly fell asleep in the backseat. The car's owner found Mr. Leblanc in the morning and called police.

The cops arrived and not only found Leblanc in the car, but also not wearing any pants. When asked how he got in the car, Mr. Leblanc responded that leprechauns let him in.

Leprechauns indeed.

Mind you, this crime was committed in Ohio, not Ireland, and Mr. Leblanc's family heritage is likely French, at least one continent and ocean away.

Nonetheless, he pulled the leprechaun excuse out of his hat, so to say. The excuse just might have worked, however, until he explained why he thought the leprechauns let him in the car.

He admitted to doing drugs the night before. Right, like that excuse is going to work.

Remember, you heard it here: if you're going to pull out the old "leprechaun excuse," then don't admit to taking drugs. Judges tend to lose their sense of humor when you make admissions like that.

Next, in Portsmouth Crown Court, in England, Jason Marshall was on trial for breaking and entering into a cop's house, *while the officer was at home.*

That takes some nerve. But not as much nerve as his excuse.

After forcing the front door open, Marshall started sneaking around, looking for loot. But the ever-alert Sergeant Abdul Haque came downstairs and found Mr. Marshall on the prowl.

Marshall quickly summoned up as much gumption as he could muster and told Sergeant Haque he had come to wash the windows. According to the *www.metro.co.uk* site, the sergeant responded in true British fashion, "Not here you're not. You're nicked."

If you guessed neither leprechauns nor window-cleaning worked as an excuse, then go to the head of the class. You're right on both counts.

The moral of the story: Breaking and entering is bad news—and against the law—here and in England. Breaking and entering a cop's house is just plain stupid. Neither leprechauns nor bad excuses will likely get you out of a jam.

⌘

Here's another from the excuses-that-just-don't-work file. You've got to give the guy credit for chutzpah, though. How many of you would have tried this excuse?

Let me say for the record, I am not a gangster and never have been. I'm not the thief who grabs your purse. I'm not the guy who jacks your car. I'm not down with the people who steal and hurt others. I'm just a brother who fights back. —Tupac Shakur

What Seems to Be the Problem, Officer?

If you have to ask that question, then you're likely in a car, pulled over alongside the road with the blue uniform staring down at you behind a pair of dark sunglasses as your fingers tightly grip the steering wheel.

And you better think quick.

Quicker still if you've got an outstanding warrant for your arrest *and* you're driving a stolen car. Twenty-nine-year-old Vincent Estrada, Jr., was in just that situation and came up with perhaps one of the lamest—or most creative, depending on your level of gullibility—excuses ever offered to the Geneva, New York, police.

It went something like this: "I stole this car, officer, because I wanted to drive to the station and turn myself in on my family court warrant."

Right. My foot's out a yard.

Instead, police took him back to the town where the car was stolen to face that charge first. Eventually, he'll make it back to Geneva on that town's outstanding warrant.

He'll have plenty of opportunity in the meantime to come up with a better excuse. Next time, I suspect he'll take the bus.

It could probably be shown with facts and figures that there is no distinctly American criminal class except Congress. —Mark Twain

Eye in the Sky Law Enforcement

He didn't even look back. Too bad he forgot to look up.

A 40-year-old Janesville, Wisconsin, resident spotted a brick-sized electronic object outside a home and stole it, carting it off to his apartment, apparently hoping to fence it. What you'd do with a piece of electronic equipment that had no immediately discernable use, I have no idea, but this bright bulb of the human species thought he did.

So did others. Apparently, it was a tracking device for a prisoner on house arrest. You know, the kind that won't let you travel more than a few hundred feet without notifying the local SWAT team.

When the home prisoner notified the prison that the device had been stolen, the prison guards did what they were trained to do. They flipped a switch.

That switch activated an electronic beacon, and a trail of red dots appeared on the guard's monitor screen, leading right to an apartment. The very same apartment where our hero was planning how to cash-in his ill-gotten gains.

Needless to say, our hero was immediately arrested and charged with theft.

Yep, a true story—reported by the Associated Press. I don't even have to try to make these things up. Real life is too good.

ⲟⲅⲟ

Maybe our electronics thief shouldn't feel all that bad. He's apparently not unique, despite the fact that you wouldn't think more than one person would realize that people were watching him act badly.

In this next case, you'll find proof positive that's not the case.

Art can never exist without Naked Beauty display'd.
—William Blake

Pass the Garden Hose, Please

"Mom, there's Fred taking a shower outside again."

That's pretty much the money quote for this case.

Again, right out of the article, first posted at *www.metro.co.uk*: "According to police, 49-year-old Fred Michaux of Vineland, New Jersey, was seen by a mother and her two young daughters as he showered himself with a garden hose on his front lawn at around 4 o'clock in the afternoon."

There are outside showers, and there are outside showers. Apparently Fred has a penchant for three things: no clothes, outside, and a garden hose.

That penchant landed him a charge for lewdness.

The Web site reports he told police he didn't think anyone was watching him.

That's a great defense.

I can see it now. "But your honor, if a tree falls in the woods and no one's there to hear it, it doesn't make a sound."

And in response: "Guilty. That'll be forty lashes with a…"

Yep, a rubber garden hose.

ⲟⲅⲟ

Here is another from the clearly-not-a-good-idea file.

I'll have one for the road. —Something you don't hear anymore

Maybe He Was Looking for Another Drink

So, you went out and partied last night. Of all the places to go the following morning, where do you think you should avoid?

If you were Robert Gulley, then one of those places would be the Vancouver Police.

Apparently, he wanted a job with the police.

Unfortunately, he was a little bleary-eyed and allegedly drunk. He claims only to have had one Long Island iced tea.

Instead of a job application, he went away with a DUI ticket.

As far as we know, Gulley didn't get the job. Not surprising. When you want a job, and you want to do that job well, it pays to research the position. In Gulley's case, it wouldn't have taken much work to discover that showing up intoxicated at the station was not the most brilliant plan.

The fellow in this next story was hoping that the power of research would work for him. And it did—just not in the way that he expected.

If you're robbing a bank and your pants fall down, I think it's okay to laugh and to let the hostages laugh too, because, come on, life is funny. —Jack Handy

Bank Robbing Advice

It's difficult to rob a bank. Do you wear a mask? Stocking? Which method do you use? Calmly walk in? Rush and run? Then there's the whole question of whether to use a weapon, and if so, then what kind of weapon? Do you use a note or just ask the teller for money?

If you just can't handle all of those questions, then what should you do? One unemployed Japanese man decided to ask the expert: a bank teller.

During what can only be described as an attempted robbery.

That's right. He just walked up to the teller and said, "Any idea how you rob a bank?" The alert teller told another teller, who then asked the man to leave. He complied. I guess the options were just too many to deal with.

As she escorted him out, she noticed a knife sticking out of his trousers and that his leg was bleeding.

According to Reuters, police then arrested the man for illegal possession of a weapon.

⌘⌘⌘

You can hurt someone with a knife. Knives, guns, weapons of mass destruction—all of these items can show up as part of the standard kit for bank robbing.

Office equipment, on the other hand, seldom gets pressed into duty this way. That may mean there's not a first time for everything.

I feel like I've never really played all that well at Staples, and I'd like to change that. —Lindsey Davenport

This Is a Stickup. Give Me All Your Money or I'll…Staple You to the Wall

No kidding. My sides just hurt when I finished reading the news report of the following story. Here's the setup. We're in The Ice Cream Shop, in Ashland, Kentucky. A masked man rushes in, demanding all the money in the cash register.

He flashes…a chrome-plated stapler. The cashier hands over the money, exit stage left for our robber. Police rush to the scene.

Witnesses in the ice cream store tell police where the robber went, and moments later they arrest Gerald A. Rocchi, 32, chrome-plated stapler and $175 in hand.

Police charged Rocchi with first-degree burglary, but only because first-degree stupidity isn't a crime.

⌘

Maybe you've changed your mind. After committing your crime and finding yourself embroiled in the legal system, you've decided that this option wasn't that much fun anyway. The shiny new infatuation you had with the courtroom has faded, and you just want to go home.

Sometimes that means proving your innocence. Other times, it means making the best plea bargain possible. Still other times, you're out of luck, and you'll be getting your mail at a new home for a while.

Just don't select this next option—I guarantee you won't like how it turns out.

To a warden, Utopia is an escape-proof jail. —Gregory Nunn

Into the Lap of Justice

It seems like those who want to escape justice may just find themselves sitting in the very lap of it sooner than they thought. Ben Rogozensky, a Decatur, Georgia, inmate found himself in a precarious position recently during an escape attempt.

Apparently, while in the courtroom and waiting for his hearing to begin, Rogozensky met with his attorney in an empty jury room with a deputy standing guard outside. During the meeting, Inmate Rogozensky excused himself to the adjacent restroom and attempted to escape from the cart hose through a ceiling crawl space.

Unfortunately for Rogozensky, he found out that the ceiling wasn't quite as reliable as he had hoped. In the midst of his escape route, he fell through the ceiling tiles into State Court Judge J. Antonio Del Campo's chambers, and was captured by a technician working on the judge's computer while the judge was out.

That's one of the more unique ways to cut through a busy judge's long docket.

⌘

It's one of the tenets of this country that no one is above the law. We're all held to the same standard: Don't do the crime if you can't do the time.

Unless, of course, you didn't *mean* to do it. In this case, we look at three officers of the law who apparently had no idea what they were doing was illegal.

Cops and robbers resemble each other, so there's not a lot to learn in terms of learning the logistics of committing the crime or investigating the crime. —Andre Braugher

Cops Make the Best Criminals

Be careful parking your car in Albany, New York. More specifically, be careful about making enemies there, especially if your enemies write those parking tickets. You just might find your car towed away.

Three parking officers wrote a lot of tickets, and most were issued to a particular group of alleged offenders. They targeted their enemies.

Well, that's one side of the story.

The other side: if you're the cop writing tickets to your enemies, then you get fired. The real question, however, is why they were only terminated, and not prosecuted.

Let's ask Albany Police Chief Turley. According to him, the three ticket writers were not charged because "it appears that they had no criminal intent…I felt termination was appropriate."

Criminal intent. What does that mean? Does it mean these three parking officers didn't mean to write the tickets? They didn't mean to target their enemies?

It seems pretty clear that they meant it. After all, they wrote the tickets.

It also seems pretty clear that the city isn't telling us the whole story. According to the *Albany Times Union,* "City officials had initially refused to release any information about the scam. They turned over payroll records and an electronic list of all tickets written this year after the *Times Union* filed a Freedom of Information Law request."

But we still don't know why.

We may not know the thinking behind the Albany Police Department, but Timothy J. Bowers's thought process is crystal clear. Faced with what he felt to be an insurmountable challenge and with his golden years approaching, Bowers formed a creative plan.

Note that I didn't say a good plan. Only that it was creative.

My occupation now, I suppose, is jail inmate. —Theodore Kaczynski

The $80 Retirement Plan

It's not a financial plan I would recommend, and I doubt anyone else would, either. But it made sense to 63-year old Timothy J. Bowers. He was a delivery man for a company that went out of business in 2003, and could only find odd jobs after that. He couldn't find a full-time job, and felt employers discriminated against him due to his age. He didn't have tremendously marketable skills, but he apparently had watched a lot of TV.

Here's his plan: he robbed a bank. While that part appears designed to get money to help make ends meet, the next part may not make any sense to you, but bear with me for a moment. After the teller handed Mr. Bowers $80.00, he then turned around to the guard, and said, "It's your day to be a hero," and gave the guard the money. Then he waited for police to arrive.

That's not how it's supposed to work you say?

Well, Mr. Bowers had a different plan. His Social Security wasn't due to kick in until he was 65, so he decided to plead guilty and then asked the judge for a three-year sentence. Yep, a cot and three squares a day until Social Security kicks in.

According to the Associated Press, his lawyer was quoted as saying, "It's a pretty sad story when someone feels that's their only alternative." The prosecutor couldn't agree more: "It's not the financial plan I would choose, but it's a financial plan."

Seriously Now: Lessons Learned

You're probably not reading this book if you're thinking about committing a crime, or if you've already committed one. I'm not sure how to pass along advice about how not to commit a crime, but I think it's easy to put into one word: Don't.

Nothing about the criminal justice system is designed to be a pleasant experience for a criminal defendant. It's expensive to hire a lawyer, it takes a long time (especially if you're convicted of the crime), you have to show up in court regularly and "rights" are not something the criminal justice system provides to criminal defendants, despite what you may have heard about the Miranda warnings.

It's best just to stay away from that side of the law. If you somehow haven't been able to avoid it, however, then give some thought to the purposes of the criminal justice system. It's designed to deter, punish, and rehabilitate, and to compensate the victim.

So, to deal with a criminal charge, just reverse those purposes. Demonstrate compliance with the law, express remorse, pay your victim back, as well as the criminal justice system itself (you didn't think all those people work for free, did you?), and show the court that you're willing to accept the consequences of your actions.

I have a typical pitch I use in my law practice about accepting responsibility, which can go a long way with the district attorney and the judge. It's a bit hackneyed, perhaps overgeneralized and sometimes offends members of one political party or the other, but if you can look past all of that to the moral of the story, I think you will agree it makes sense. Here it is: Richard Nixon refused to accept responsibility for his actions. Shortly thereafter, the House Judiciary Committee introduced articles of impeachment and he resigned, essentially forced out of office in disgrace. On the other hand, Bill Clinton accepted responsibility and apologized for his actions, and remained in office.

In my experience, criminal defendants who accept responsibility and apologize generally don't suffer the same consequences as those who won't and don't.

Chapter 4

Go to Work

Do you live to work, or work to live? No matter which side of that line you fall on, chances are you devote a good chunk of your life to work. The average American puts in close to 50 hours a week in the workplace, with many putting in extra hours on weekends or evenings.

All that time spent in the company of coworkers and colleagues inevitably leads to conflict—and conflict typically brings in the lawyers. It's no surprise that so much litigation has its origin in the workplace.

In this chapter, we take a look at cases born in the office. Some lawsuits come directly from having to put up with a petty annoyance one time too many, while others involve errors of an unbelievable magnitude.

꧁꧂

I got a chain letter by fax. It's very simple. You just fax a dollar bill to everybody on the list. —Steven Wright

The $1.5 Million Fax

Tired of receiving junk on your fax machine? After receiving more than 1,000 faxes in a three-year period, travel agent Sherman Gottlieb was, and he decided to do something about it. He sent by fax instructions to Carnival Corporation, the parent of Carnival Cruise Lines, asking the company to remove his facsimile numbers from its fax machine dialer, but they didn't follow his instructions.

Then he invoked the Telephone Consumer Protection Act (TCPA) and sued the offending sender, Carnival Corporation, in addition to several other companies.

Carnival fought back and alleged that Gottlieb didn't have diversity or subject matter jurisdiction as a private attorney general to bring his case in federal court in New York, where Gottlieb lived. Carnival is a Panama corporation, with offices in Florida. Carnival argued and won in the trial court that Gottlieb had to proceed in state court. On appeal to the Second Circuit, however, Carnival lost. Gottlieb can now prosecute his federal and state claims in federal court. The case is currently pending.

If he wins, then Carnival is arguably subject to pay $500 for each of the 1,000 faxes Gottlieb received from Carnival, and possibly treble damages if Carnival acted knowingly and willfully under the federal law. (Under a parallel law in New York, the Second Circuit notes he can recover another $100 for each fax under his separate state law claim.)

Though Congress may have thought that the TCPA would typically avoid federal jurisdiction because the amount in controversy was less than the $75,000 threshold to invoke federal jurisdiction, it was Carnival who brought disaster on itself. Gottlieb's 1,000 faxes translate into damages of $500,000, and possibly as much as $1.5 million, well over the jurisdictional limit.

That's an expensive travel agent fax campaign for a cruise line.

◦⊶⊷◦

The previous case, it could be argued, centers around a small mistake: failing to remove one phone number from an auto-dialer list. It could be argued that this was a type of spam—the junk advertising we all hate. In the next case, we're going to consider another kind of spam: the kind that comes in a can.

Processed pig is white trash meat. Some people call it SPAM.
—Scott Weiland

In Defense of SPAM?

SPAM is loved by many the world over, but is also the butt of many jokes. See? I couldn't even get past the first sentence without hamming it up. Puns aside perhaps apocryphal, Hormel holds

75 percent of the market in canned meat and claims to have sold more than 5 billion cans of the stuff.

SPAM has been immortalized on Broadway in Monty Python's *Spamalot*, but apparently the executives at the Hormel Corporation couldn't stomach a Muppet imitating SPAM. In response to the *Muppet Treasure Island* movie, the company sued Jim Henson Productions for infringing its trademark through a character called Spa'am.

Hormel argued consumers would be confused and, consequently, SPAM sales would suffer if the product became linked with Spa'am the movie character. The company argued Spa'am was "evil in porcine form" as a wild boar and presented in the movie in a threatening manner. The appellate judges observed: "Spa'am, however, is not the boarish Beelzebub that Hormel seems to fear."

Henson offered the court an expert in children's literature, who testified that although Spa'am was not "classically handsome," Spa'am ultimately became a positive character who befriended the Muppets, helping them escape from Long John Silver, the film's villain. (No word on whether the fast-food chain by the same name felt threatened.) The court decided in favor of the Muppets, and against the canned SPAM.

Perhaps Hormel forgot to consider how most of the rest of us who don't eat SPAM feel: "It is the product of less-than-savory ingredients," the court pointed out, and then went on to quote a columnist who joked, "SPAM contains all five major food groups: snouts, ears, feet, tails, and brains." Given all this unfavorable publicity, "one might think Hormel would welcome the association with a genuine source of pork," the court said somewhat tongue-in-cheek.

Perhaps it's time to start talking about the Other White Meat® (Registered trademark of the National Pork Board), which is one of my favorites.

As you can see, a big case can be built around a small blue can of meat and meat by-products. This next case, however, is a little bigger in nature.

How big?

Well, the average railroad car is well over 10,000 pounds empty and is dozens of feet long—not the type of thing you'd misplace easily.

At least, you wouldn't think so!

A man who has never gone to school may steal from a freight car; but if he has a university education, he may steal the whole railroad. —Teddy Roosevelt

Now Where Did I Put That Railroad Car?

The contract cases on apparent and ostensible authority in law school are hundreds of years old, commonly referred to as *black-letter law* because the definitions are so well known. Why, then, would CSX Transportation, Inc., litigate a case involving the apparent authority of someone with a corporate e-mail address who welshed on a debt?

Because it involved the Internet, where the law is as undefined as the 'net itself.

Let's review the facts. CSX received an e-mail message from Albert Arillotta, who claimed he worked for Recovery Express and used the e-mail address *albert@recoveryexpress .com* (no longer active), which would appear to most people as someone associated with Recovery Express, Inc. (REI). It turns out, though, that he actually worked for Interstate Demolition & Environmental Corporation, who shared office space with REI.

The court gives us the pleasure of reviewing the e-mail, and it is reproduced here—harrendous grammer and all:

From: Albert Arillotta [albert@recoveryexpress.com]
Sent: Friday, August 22, 2003 4:57 PM
To: Whitehead, Len Jr.

Subject: purchase of out service railcars

lynn this is albert arillotta from interstate demolition and recovery express we are interested in buying rail cars for scrap paying you a

percentage of what the amm maket indicator is there are several locations i suggest to work at the exsisting location of the rail cars. we will
send you a brocheure and financials per your request our addressis
the following:

interstate demolition/recoveryexpress
180 canal street 5th floor boston mass 02114
phone number- 617-523-7740
fax number 617-367-3627
email address albert @recoveryexpress .com
thank you for your time

Mr. Arillotta apparently gained access to REI's computers and
sent an e-mail message to CSX offering to buy railroad cars for
scrap. Because that's one of the things that REI does, CSX bit, and
bit hard. They set up a deal with Mr. Arillotta, who showed up at
their railroad yard with check in hand, and hauled several cars
away.

Mr. Arillotta's $116,000 check bounced, and CSX sued REI
and IDEC, believing that one of the two companies had reneged
on their end of the deal.

The court's opinion ruled in favor of REI and IDEC, reasoning that a mere e-mail address, even with a proper domain
name, does not confer apparent authority on Mr. Arillotta.
Judge William G. Young said it was no different than someone who showed up with a business card or company vehicle,
or used letterhead, each of which, taken alone, is insufficient
to establish apparent authority. For that matter, if he ruled
in favor of CSX, then the judge thought he would have been
conferring on everyone at the corporation who had an e-mail
address the authority to enter into a contract, all the way down
to the janitor.

CSX can't find the railroad cars taken by Mr. Arillotta, and to
pursue him in litigation would only add insult to injury.

⚭

The previous problems could have been avoided, if only a few people asked a few more questions. In this next case, however, asking
the wrong question can get you into trouble.

The best way to appreciate your job is to imagine yourself without one. —Oscar Wilde

Want More Money? Kiss Your Job Goodbye!

You've at least thought it, if not said it outright to your boss. No, it's not "take this job and shove it." It's, "I want a raise," or said slightly differently, "You're not paying me enough."

Presumably, that's what Jorja Fox and George Eads did when they went to the producers of *CSI*. The story is about contract disputes.

According to news reports, the two actors were fired for asking for more money.

"How could that be?" you ask. After all, you've probably done the same thing. Well, it's Hollywood. Need I say more?

Technically, it likely works something like this. They're in their fifth year of a seven-year contract. They ask for more pay. It's likely those demands were each a breach of their respective contracts. Kind of like a counteroffer to an existing contract, which the employer had no obligation to accept. But more likely, there was a provision in the contracts that prevented increased demands—the "greed provision," as it's more commonly known.

In other words, take your demand and shove it, the studio said, and fired them.

Later episodes of *CSI* reveal that the studio and actors worked it out. After all, it's Hollyweird. Eads and Fox survived this contract dispute and stayed with the show (Fox remained on the show until the beginning of the 2008–2009 season), but actors never get paid enough. For that matter, neither do writers, eh, kaplan?

⁓◦◉◦⁓

Sometimes, people find the perfect job. An avid gardener lands a position in a nursery, raising and selling plants. A talented baker opens a cake shop, capitalizing on good pastry skills. Jobs like this are often matches made in heaven, bringing people's natural attributes and passions together in the workplace. These workers have a deep and complete understanding of their task, which makes them the ideal employee.

In this next case, the worker in question surely had a deep and complete understanding of the problems he was supposed to be addressing. Yet, somehow, it turned out that he was far from the ideal employee.

A vacation is over when you begin to yearn for your work.
—Morris Fishbein

Letting the Fox Guard the Henhouse

This is one case where they surely picked the right employee to keep track of employee absences.

Here you've got an employee surfing the Internet and an employer warning said employee to stop goofing off and start working. The employee disregards the warnings. The employer then disciplines the employee, and the employee appeals the discipline in an administrative hearing.

As if the surfing itself weren't enough, and just to top it off, the employee admitted in the hearing that he disobeyed the employer's orders to stop using the Internet for personal reasons. Insubordination typically is more than a sufficient reason to fire someone. Inexplicably, though, the New York Administrative Law Judge (ALJ) let the employee get away with it, and ruled that the employer can only reprimand him for surfing the Internet. ALJs notoriously favor employees, and employers regularly lose cases at that level, hoping to appeal and restore some level of fairness to the proceedings in regular court proceedings.

The employer introduced evidence at the hearing that when the employer asked the employee why he was surfing so much, his one word response was "reading."

I would have never guessed.

Just in case you're wondering, here's what he was reading: the Lonely Planet Web site, Google, www.renewnyc.com, www.humanesociety.com, www.chinaadviser.com, www.cnn.com,

Air Canada's Web site, www.cbsnews.com, www.escapeartist.com, and www.islandsun.com. The employee also admitted to "regularly" visiting travel and government scholarship sites. You can look, too, but I don't advise "reading" any of those sites at work.

To add insult to injury, let's add these facts into the mix. Over the course of a year and a half, the employee was AWOL from work for 33 days, arrived late to work 49 times, and left work early 23 times. Given those absences, and the allegations of Internet surfing, I'm betting the only thing he had time to do at work was surf the Internet.

Apart from his absences, the employee took his allowed vacation. Not only did he take his vacation, but here's a guy who also bought his vacation tickets before he put in a request to approve that specific time off, apparently assuming that it would be approved without question. I have to wonder if he also bought the tickets while at work.

To put the icing on the cake, the ALJ ruled that the employee's absences weren't excessive. If that's true, then I'd love to have the ALJ's work schedule—he probably thinks working one day a week is too much.

Don't get me wrong here. I like vacations as much as the next guy, but I think this ruling is over the edge. That's just my humble opinion.

Oh, one last thing: the guy who was reprimanded is an analyst with the Division of Human Resources for the New York Department of Education. His job includes the task of keeping attendance records for New York schoolteachers. Go figure. I guess that's the difference between government employment and private sector employment, but should it be that way?

⌘

There are a few other differences between public sector and private sector employment. In the private sector, if you do a great job, then you're generally rewarded. On the other hand, doing that great private-sector job might land you in trouble with the public-sector regulators.

In this next case, we take a look at how the relationship between the public and private sectors can be troublesome at times—and expensive at others!

Government's first duty and highest obligation is public safety.
—Arnold Schwarzenegger

Putting Uncle Sam out of a Job Can Be Expensive

What's wrong with this picture?

Consider this: A meatpacking company in Kansas wants to test every cow it slaughters for mad cow disease, but if it does, the USDA has threatened to institute criminal prosecution proceedings. That's right. Go back and read that first sentence again. A private company wants to do more than it's required to do to protect consumers, but the government won't let it.

According to Kansas meatpacker Creekstone Farms, its Japanese customers insist that every cow be tested for bovine spongiform encephalopathy, or BSE, which we know commonly as mad cow disease. The company cites a December 2005 poll by the Kyodo News Service, in Japan which found that more than half of Japanese consumers want U.S. beef to be tested for BSE. The company also said, "Creekstone simply wants to satisfy its customers," according to its press release.

Somewhat surprisingly, the USDA has for two years refused to allow Creekstone access to the BSE test kits, claiming that it has exclusive authority to conduct testing. The testing would add about ten cents to each pound of beef sold, or $20.00 per cow.

To fight back, the company, Creekstone Farms Premium Beef, LLC, filed suit in Washington, D.C., challenging the USDA's ban. The USDA Web site has no immediate response to the lawsuit, but did post a press release about its visit to Japan asking the Japanese government to reopen its borders to American beef.

The USDA reports, "Japan reopened its market to U.S. beef on December 11, 2005, but halted U.S. beef imports on January 20, 2006, after receiving a shipment of U.S. beef that posed no food safety risk but did not meet the specifications of the U.S. export agreement with Japan."

Am I missing something here?

Let's recap. We know that Japan wants all of its imported beef tested for BSE. All of it. All the time. Every single cow. Because it's not, Japan banned U.S beef imports.

In response to that ban, two things happened. First, a U.S. beef exporting company voluntarily offered to test for BSE, but the USDA won't permit it. Not only will the government agency not permit the testing (which would also make beef safer for U.S. consumers), but the USDA has also threatened to criminally prosecute the U.S. company if it tries to test in order to comply with its customers' demands.

Second, and somewhat incongruously, the USDA has dispatched a team of negotiators to Japan to convince the Japanese government that importing U.S. beef is safe. The only clue we have about this apparent disconnect on the government's part is a thinly-stated position that the USDA has prepared a "thorough report" showing the safety of U.S. beef. Not even a claim that the Japanese have agreed in a treaty to allow the sporadic level of testing we have now.

According to the Associated Press, a U.S. District Judge ruled that the USDA does not have the authority to regulate the mad cow test, and cannot prohibit individual meat producers from testing their products. Later, the USDA threatened to sue Creekstone over its behavior, and no immediate resolution of the issue is in sight.

༖

Every job has its downside, those less-than-wonderful tasks that have to be done in the course of a day's work. I'd like being a lawyer much better, for example, if there wasn't so much tedious paperwork involved. But I deal with it, because it's part and parcel of my profession. It comes with the territory.

In this next case, however, the territory associated with a particular job veered distinctly in a dangerous direction. See what you think about this:

The only thing worse than a liar is a bad liar.
—Lucy Liu, on *Sex and the City*

Read That Job Description Carefully

Every once in awhile you run across something unbelievable, but then again, it takes all of us to make a village, even a village idiot. It's just troubling to figure out which ones were the real fools here: the boyfriend, girlfriend, several unrelated women who "worked" for the couple, or the police.

Here are a couple of ground rules. Sex for pay is, well, *prostitution*. There are exceptions, but they're mostly in Nevada, from what I'm told. When someone files a complaint with the police that people are engaged in prostitution, the police generally hop to it. The crime is an easy one to recognize, and consequently solve, which makes the police look good. Sometimes, that is.

Let me explain.

A woman and her boyfriend in Palm Springs, California, convinced several women living in the area that performing sex acts on the boyfriend constituted legitimate sexual therapy. Let's stop here for a moment and reread that last sentence. We have, on one side, a boyfriend and girlfriend. On the other side, we have other women not involved with this primary relationship. They are, in other words, not the girlfriends of the boyfriend.

The couple advertised for "caretakers" and offered good pay. The girlfriend then "convinced" the women to take part in a "rehabilitation" program for her boyfriend. She told the other women (the non-girlfriends) he had an alleged spinal injury. The other women accepted the pay and performed the sex acts. One of the other women refused to play along, however, and turned the matter over to the police.

The police took two years to solve this crime, and ultimately the boyfriend and his girlfriend were arrested, but not after just a few more sex acts in the ensuing two-year period.

Two years?

❧

On the other hand, maybe those ladies weren't as gullible as I'd first thought. After all, the trend toward sex-as-therapy seems to be going global.

It is chiefly through books that we enjoy intercourse with superior minds, and these invaluable means of communication are in the reach of all. —William Ellery Channing

Swiss Mix Massage, Sex for Disabled. You Can Volunteer, Too

We're going to examine the Palm Springs case from a different perspective—in fact a different continent, different culture, and one perhaps a bit more liberal than our own. In Switzerland, everyone is entitled to sex. That's why Basel, Switzerland-based Welfare Group for Disability and Sexuality is recruiting volunteers to provide erotic massages and full sex to those with disabilities.

The group's founder, Ahia Zemp, says it's completely natural. "It's a big taboo that needs to be broken. Having sex is a basic human need, like eating and drinking, and we have to fight for this right for the disabled," Zemp claims as part of her campaign, as reported to Ananova, Ltd., a U.K. news Web site.

Others charge she's just creating a legitimate cover for prostitution.

Zemp rejects the claim outright: "The big difference between the assistants and prostitutes is that the assistants show tenderness and are conscious of the needs of the disabled, rather than rushing and just taking the money."

On the other hand, *volunteer* may not be the right choice of all the words available. You can substitute your own here: _____.

∽∾∘∾

In the previous cases, all involved were adults, even if they didn't exercise adult judgment. The same can't be said for this next vignette, and it's a pity.

You would think, however, that we could expect adult judgment and clear thinking from the bench. If so, you just might be wrong, as evidenced by the following decisions.

In America sex is an obsession; in other parts of the world it is a fact. —Marlene Dietrich

How Old Is Your Girlfriend?

It's amazing to realize the things that you can do and not lose your real estate license.

Having sex with a minor is a surefire route to trouble. You'd expect that this type of behavior would come with pretty stiff penalties, and by and large, you'd be right. Beyond the criminal charges and subsequent jail time, it's a safe bet that your reputation would suffer, your professional credibility would be shot, and that you'd find yourself unemployable.

Unless, of course, you're a real estate agent.

A California ruling in 2005 held that even though a real estate agent had had a sexual relationship with a girl who was underage, that in and of itself was not sufficient cause to revoke his real estate license.

Unbelievable. Yet California courts are not the only ones to rule that way. The Oregon Supreme Court also ruled in favor of a real estate broker who admitted to using illegal drugs and pornography to engage in inappropriate sexual contact with a 16-year-old boy.

If I were a betting man, I'd be willing to bet the reason the Oregon Supreme Court didn't think it was a big deal was because the sexual contact was between two males, but the stated reason given was that despite the fact that the broker's admitted prior behaviors might raise concerns that might be reasonable in the abstract, there was no "factual support" for the view that such risks actually exist in the future.

If the courts don't find that type of behavior violates professional standards, then one has to wonder what behavior would?

⌘

Drivers make up a sizable portion of the workforce—from long-haul truckers to taxi drivers, delivery boys, and chauffeurs. These professionals are already subject to a dizzying array of rules and regulations, but now there's a new law on the books.

Apparently, it's necessary to point out that you shouldn't try sleeping and driving at the same time.

The lion and the calf will lay down together, but the calf won't get much sleep. —Woody Allen

Forget Drinking and Driving: Try Sleeping and Driving

New Jersey has criminalized driving while tired. The legislation is dubbed Maggie's Law for the 20-year-old who was killed by a truck driver who admitted to driving for 30 straight hours.

It's the first law of its kind in the nation. Other states, including Illinois, Kentucky, Massachusetts, Mississippi, New York, and Washington, have similar bills pending. There's an attempt to create a federal version of Maggie's Law, too.

No, they don't plan on pulling you over if your head is leaning too far forward and then snaps upright. Maggie's Law says that the district attorney has to prove that you've been up for more than 24 hours.

The New Jersey law, introduced by State Senator George Geist, had eleven cosponsors. The National Sleep Foundation supported the bill, and is glad to see action being taken.

"We are so accustomed to being fatigued and tired and sleepy that it's part of our daily life and we think nothing of getting behind the wheel and driving despite the horrible ramifications of that act," said Marcia Stein of the National Sleep Foundation, a nonprofit research organization.

I can't imagine how the law can be effectively enforced. It's not like there's a version of the field sobriety test for sleeping or drowsiness. How tired do you have to be?

If you keep quiet, then how are they ever going to know unless someone else turns you in? It will be a dead giveaway, however, if you put your head down in the police car and start snoring.

It gives a whole new meaning to being arrested.

⚭

Certain professions come with certain obligations. For example, if you consult with an attorney or a medical professional, then that professional must keep the substance of your discussions confidential. It's an obligation of these trades.

In this particular case, a physician learns that he might have an obligation that one might have suspected belonged to a giant pharmaceutical company.

I love drugs, but I hate hangovers, and the hatred of the
hangover wins by a landslide every time. —Margaret Cho

Who Wants to Be a 1L?

We're going back to first-year law school here. Remember torts (civil wrongs) class? I know, it was a long time ago for those who are lawyers and a foreign language for those who aren't, but bear with me—I'll explain it. Specifically, let's take a moment to look at the "learned intermediary" rule.

The rule deals with the sufficiency of warnings. In this instance, it deals with side effects and injuries that result from taking prescription drugs. Drug manufacturers warn doctors, and doctors are in turn obligated to warn consumers. Or so you would think.

Because doctors prescribe the drugs, the doctor is the intermediary between the patient and the drug company. As educated professionals, doctors are learned, and especially so because the drug companies warn the doctors about the side effects of their drugs. Thus, the "learned intermediary." The "rule" part of the theory provides drug companies insulation from claims by patients.

One consumer, Robert Larkin, took drugs manufactured by Pfizer. After taking those drugs, he contracted toxic epidermal necrolysis and Stevens-Johnson syndrome. He sued Pfizer.

Pfizer had warned Larkin's doctor of the possibility of both of these side effects. The company defended the case on the basis of the learned intermediary rule, and claimed that it wasn't their responsibility to warn Larkin, it was the doctor's.

Larkin lost. The Kentucky Supreme Court held for Pfizer, and endorsed the rule by a four-to-three vote.

It was a close one, but still a win for the manufacturer. Now, I assume, Larkin will sue the doctor, who likely doesn't have as deep a pocket as Pfizer.

⚬❦⚬

We started this chapter with a discussion of faxes, and in the interests of symmetry, we end it the same way. Junk faxes aren't limited to the cruise and travel industry. One of the biggest offenders is *www.fax.com*, as you'll see below.

The wireless telegraph is not difficult to understand. The ordinary telegraph is like a very long cat. You pull the tail in New York, and it meows in Los Angeles. The wireless is the same, only without the cat. —Albert Einstein

A Paler Shade of Gray: Toner for Your Fax Machine

Fax.com has gotten into some hot water, having been fined nearly $6 million by the U.S. Federal Communications Commission (FCC). What is only slightly funny is that the FCC has a fax-on-demand (dial 202-418-2830) for the press release of its fine issued against Fax.com. What is even less funny is that *fax.com* still operates today.

I'll be the first to admit it: I detest junk faxes almost as much as junk mail. At least with junk mail, it costs me only time. Junk faxes use up toner and increase wear and tear on my fax machine. Don't even get me started on junk e-mail; that's another story.

Fax.com has a public service of locating missing children. Admirable, but I suspect the number of missing children faxes pales in comparison to the number of commercial faxes it sends out.

Fax.com claims it is being hounded out of existence. The Web site of watchdog group Private Citizen lists its campaign against *Fax.com*, and notes that the company has folded but reemerged under a different name to do the same thing.

Don't you just love it?

Apparently, *Fax.com's* fight isn't over yet, though, so don't get your fax machine's hopes up. Seems as though the company has started to fight back. It is suing those who sue it, and hounding lawyers who represent businesses that receive junk faxes by "turning them in" to the state bar. For what, I'm not exactly sure. Last time I checked, it was *Fax.com* who was in trouble, not the lawyers suing them.

One solution, if you find you're troubled by junk faxes: you can just hook your fax machine up to your computer, and turn your computer into a fax machine, and then set the software not to print out any faxes. Then, you just hit the delete button.

Zap!

Seriously Now: Lessons Learned

Getting up in the morning and going to work is some serious stuff, and, as I've shown above, can get you into some serious trouble. The company you work for hasn't written that employee manual just to humor itself.

Generally the best way to stay out of trouble at work is to, well, work and not goof off. Surfing the Internet and downloading some version of porn, games, or music to your work computer can get you fired, despite the example I've given you above.

Some of us are self-employed and others work in companies of varying sizes, from the very small to the monolithic, multi-national behemoth firm. All of the laws that apply to us in our everyday lives outside of work apply equally to us at work, and then some.

Many of the cases I see coming out of the workplace revolve around two main themes: pay and sexual harassment. Occasionally there will be others, like the cases I've written about above, but like the rest of life, sex and money usually take top billing.

Sexual harassment is an easy one to avoid, but hard for most of us to understand because it's not what we think that matters. You see, sexual harassment is a lot like the concept of beauty. It's in the eyes of the beholder. In other words, it's not what *you* may think constitutes sexual harassment that matters, it's what the person who hears or sees it thinks. That's right, the world revolves around what other people think—here, the person who's claiming she or he has been sexually harassed. It's how that person views the comment, action, or visual event.

So, the easy way to avoid sexual harassment is to not engage in any form of it at all. It's extreme advice, but because everyone sees and hears things differently than you and I do and it's what they perceive that matters, "nothing" is the safest method of dealing with it.

Pay, on the other hand, can be a real minefield. Each state has its own wage and hour laws, and a discussion of those is beyond what I can explain in this short space. The laws vary even for professionals, management, staff, and laborers. There's no one piece of advice I can offer that will make sense in all situations, so you're on your own on this one. If you have questions about how it works in your state, you know my standard advice: Call your favorite local lawyer.

Chapter 5

Live on Earth

Environmental law is one of my specialties. There's a lot of litigation revolving around the planet and its protection. From endangered animals to air, water and groundwater contamination, there's a constant battle to protect and, preserve the environment.

The planet can be saved in a number of ways. Some people recycle, while others work at reclaiming contaminated building sites. Still others stand in front of bulldozers and chain themselves to giant trees to prevent them from being cut.

Other people fight their battles in the courtroom, taking polluters to task and trying to force social change via litigation. Some cases are clear-cut issues of right and wrong, while others are far more complicated. A few are just mind-bogglers, especially when definitions and standards change every time the wind blows.

In this chapter, we take a look at a few notable cases tied to Mother Earth. After all, we all live here. Alternative housing is in short supply! And if that means that everyone on the planet has a chance to get involved in a lawsuit at some point, whether as a plaintiff or as a defendant, then so be it. Sometimes, it's good to be a lawyer.

Let yourself be open and life will be easier. A spoon of salt in a glass of water makes the water undrinkable. A spoon of salt in a lake is almost unnoticed. —Buddha

Take It with a Grain Of…

You put it on your food, it's likely on your kitchen table, you sweat it out of your body, and if someone associates it with you, then you've received a compliment. Crystals of it form when ocean water evaporates, and it's spread on some roads and sidewalks in the winter to melt snow and ice. It helps make great homemade ice cream, and at least one company refers to one of its qualities in its motto: "When it rains, it pours."

The last thing you'd think of it—salt—would be to classify it as a pollutant.

But many publicly owned treatment works do through their city and county permits. The U.S. Environmental Protection Agency limits the discharge of salt.

That regulation, however, suffered a little-known setback in a federal district court ruling in New York. The ruling holding that salt was not a pollutant under the Clean Water Act (CWA) was overruled on other grounds, but nonetheless, the ruling, issued in late January 2004, appears to be intact given the decision of the Second Circuit Court of Appeals.

The case, *Alliance for Environmental Renewal, Inc., v. Pyramid Crossgates Co.,* stands for the proposition that salt is not a pollutant, but the Court of Appeals overruled the district court's opinion on the basis of standing, a procedural technicality.

Nonetheless, the Second Circuit did not overrule the district court's ruling that salt fell outside the category of pollutants regulated by the CWA. What can you take away from this ruling? Though it seems ridiculous that salt is listed as a pollutant, too much of anything can be a pollutant, and that's the point here. In small quantities, salt is necessary for your body to operate. In the sewer, too much of it can overwhelm water pollution treatment plants.

⁓⊱⊰⁓

Bet you'll look at those golden, salty french fries a little differently now. Sometimes a little knowledge can change our perspective.

On the other hand, sometimes bringing differing perspectives into alignment can be close to impossible. Consider the following case, which brings nature lovers into direct conflict with four-wheeler fans.

Float like a butterfly, sting like a bee. —Muhammad Ali

Butterflies or Buggies?

It's a fair bet that we're not going to run out of dune buggies or off-roaders anytime soon. According to environmentalists, however, we are going to run out of the Sand Mountain Blue Butterfly, which has a life span of about a week. Back in April 2004, the environmentalists filed a petition to designate the Blue Butterfly as endangered, but the U.S. Fish & Wildlife Service did nothing in response, allegedly due to a lack of funds. After a twelve-month study, it decided not to list the Sand Mountain Blue Butterfly as endangered.

The Center for Biological Diversity (CBD) and a coalition of other environmental groups filed a complaint against the Fish & Wildlife Service to force listing the Blue Butterfly as an endangered species and designate the Sand Mountain Recreation Area in western Nevada as critical habitat.

The off-roaders counter that off-road space is just as endangered. Associated Press writer Scott Sonner asked Richard Hilton of Reno, a board member of the Friends of Sand Mountain, a group of off-road enthusiasts, who replied, "If it did become listed, no telling what type of restrictions they could do out there," reported the *Desert Morning News.*

According to environmentalists, critical habitat designations don't have any effect other than requiring those who want to use the designated area to consult with federal agencies regarding the consequences of use of the area. While technically that's true, it ignores the practical result: after a critical habitat designation, there is limited or no use of the designated area.

In a CBD press release on the complaint, Daniel R. Patterson, desert ecologist with the CBD who formerly worked with U.S. Bureau of Land Management (BLM), said,

> This attractive blue butterfly lives only at Sand Mountain, BLM is un-
> ethically letting its dunes habitat be destroyed by off-road access, and
> the Bush administration won't even follow the law to read our petition
> and consider protection. The Sand Mountain blue and other dunes
> endemics are a beautiful part the Great Basin Desert, and only the
> protections of the Endangered Species Act will ensure their survival
> and recovery.

In this case, the butterfly resides in the Kearney Buckwheat shrub, which covers about 1,000 acres of the 4,795-acre recreation area. While it may seem that distinction would allow off-roaders to co-exist on the remaining 3,795 acres, a critical habitat designation may just encompass the entire site. Sometimes, though not always, the Fish & Wildlife Service requires as much as a four-to-one designation to protect a species. That means there would be 795 acres left for off-roaders.

That reduction leaves off-roaders to claim they're the ones that are becoming endangered. The CBD claims that Nevada dunes are not the only ones that need protection. California's Tolowa Dunes State Park contains critical habitat for the snowy plover bird that will be damaged if off-roaders are allowed back on the land, according to the group.

Who wins? In this case, it appears that the dune buggies win: The U.S. Fish & Wildlife Service has ruled that protecting the Sand Mountain Blue Butterfly was "not warranted."

❧

Californians apparently have a special regard for butterflies, as evidenced by this next case.

There is science, logic, reason; there is thought verified by experience. And then there is California. —Edward Abbey

Welcome to California. Pass the Twigs, Berries, Nuts, and Honey, Please

I grew up back East, studied in the Midwest, and moved to the Left Coast to practice law. For the most part, I've made the transition pretty easily. I don't miss the snow or the humidity, and certainly don't miss the bugs.

I just can't get used to some things about California, however. Perhaps the hardest is the sunset. It sets over the ocean here.

Where I came from, it *rises* over the ocean. The whole concept of a sunset over the ocean is foreign to me, and I get bollixed up with directions as a result. Sometimes west just doesn't seem...well, West. Especially in Southern California where we have South-facing beaches. Just when you get used to the idea the waves are coming from the South instead of the East, the sun sets over the ocean.

See what I mean?

One thing that is not hard to get used to, however, is the twigs, berries, nuts, and honey.

Everyone is so Oliver Wendell Holmes here out on the Left Coast. You know, he was the one who said, "The right to swing your arm ends where the other person's nose begins." Unlike small towns in the East and Midwest, no one here knows or cares about your business.

It's fairly straightforward. It's your business, and not anyone else's.

So when I read about Pacific Grove's municipal code protecting butterflies, I wasn't surprised. The whole laissez-faire attitude doesn't just extend to you and me; it extends to the twigs, berries, nuts, and honey.

And butterflies.

So it won't surprise you that in 1952, the little town of Pacific Grove (pop. 15,000), located near Monterey, enacted this municipal code:

11.48.010 Interference with prohibited.

It is declared to be unlawful for any person to molest or interfere with, in any way, the peaceful occupancy of the monarch butterflies on their annual visit to the city of Pacific Grove, and during the entire time they remain within the corporate limits of the city, in whatever spot they may choose to stop in, provided, however, that if said butterflies should at any time swarm in, upon or near the private dwelling house or other buildings of a citizen of the city of Pacific Grove in such a way as to interfere with the occupancy and use of said dwelling and/or other buildings, that said butterflies may be removed, if possible, to another location upon the application of said citizen to the chief of police. (Ord. 210 N.S. § 8–3060, 1952).

Think about it. You have to ask the chief of police to move a butterfly.

Only in California.

✂✄✂

Technological progress is like an axe in the hands of a pathological criminal. —Albert Einstein

Let's Pave Over Paradise, Too

As I stated previously, I am, among other things, an environmental lawyer. Both sides, actually, but typically for businesses. So, you may be a bit surprised about this one: I'm for the tree.

Let me explain.

Seems that there's a drug problem down in Fort Walton Beach, Florida. While that's not too surprising, the proposed solution is.

Cut down the tree.

Huh?

Apparently, drug dealers gather under a big, shady tree. So rather than police those under the tree, the police want to cut it down.

My grandmother would say that's like throwing the baby out with the bath water. The tree had nothing to do with the crime, but those in Fort Walton Beach want the tree to do the time.

Here's my solution: let's arrest the criminals, and leave the tree for the next generation to enjoy.

Otherwise, my guess is that the drug deals will simply move to another tree, and pretty soon, well, Florida will really worry about hurricanes.

✂✄✂

That tree made it, but others weren't as lucky. Consider the following case, where a homeowner decided a little guerilla landscaping would improve the scenery.

Nothing's beautiful from every point of view. —Horace

Can You Move That Cot a Little to the Left, Please?

My law firm tends to get its fair share of view cases, typically caused by overgrown trees blocking the view of mountains, oceans, or other scenery. After all, we're in sunny Southern California, and some of the views from people's homes can be absolutely stunning.

While we don't have a state law in place that guarantees the right to a particular view, there are several ways you can be assured your view will be preserved, including restrictive deeds or city or county ordinances.

Feng shui, otherwise known as geomancy, is not one of them. This omission is despite its prevalence in many Asian cultures.

But like most everything else, an extreme approach may just land you in hot water. In Taiwan, Lo Pu-yi was a respected feng shui priest, and he likely knew how to adjust living areas to maximize success and energy flow.

In fact, he was so sure that his neighbor was blocking energy coming toward his home that Lo went over the fence and cut down 40 trees and arranged his surrounding environment to be at peace with it. He thought the neighboring banyans, willows, and bamboo trees blocked the flow of air and undermined his ability to make a living.

In response to the tree-cutting spree, Lo Pu-yi got to contemplate his inner peace from the inside of a jail cell for four months. He was convicted by a Taiwanese court of illegally cutting down the trees.

Lo Pu-yi wasn't alone in his quest for a view. Let's zip over to the observation deck of 60-year-old Douglas Hoffman, of Henderson, Nevada. He had a lovely view of the Las Vegas Strip from the back of his home, but was none too happy that his neighbor's trees blocked his view.

So he, too, cut down or poisoned some trees. He killed them off or cut them down over the course of a year to restore his view and cover his tracks. He cut down nearly 500 of them. He caused $242,000 in damages, according to court records, and after being convicted of seven felony counts and three gross misdemeanor counts of malicious destruction of trees on the land of another, the court fined him $250,000 and gave him the inside of a jail cell to look at for the next five years.

There's a view for you.

~ঔ৯~

Not all of Florida is in immediate danger of being paved over and not all of either Nevada or Taiwan is losing trees. The earth may be wondering, however. Along part of the U.S. coastline, engineers want to create some more natural, open space.

Creating a natural area has the quixotic effect of putting wild-life in danger, however. What can be done? No one's sure, but we're keeping score.

I have the world's largest collection of seashells. I keep it on all the beaches of the world. Perhaps you've seen it. —Stephen Wright

USACOE: 3, Turtles: O

In addition to the devastation it wreaked in New Orleans, Hurricane Katrina wiped away some of Florida's coastline. And, in addition to the U.S. Army Corps of Engineers' efforts to refortify the dikes in New Orleans, the Army is also restoring beachfront in Destin, Florida. Beachfront homeowners were upset because the beach replenishment plan would create a public beach in front of their previously private beach. The plan was to add 80 to 100 feet of beachfront along a five-mile stretch, including where the private homes are located.

The Army met with some stiff resistance from a citizen property owners group made up of these beachfront homeowners, but the Army eventually won the right to dredge the seabed and pump the sand onto the Destin beach in Walton County.

In the course of dredging the seabed, the Army apparently has killed three endangered turtles, and dredging is now suspended. The Army issued advisories about turtles in the past, but it's not been a high priority recently. There's been nothing about protecting sea turtles posted in the Army's newsroom of press releases for the past five years. The National Oceanic and Atmospheric Administration issues marine take permits, and it appears the Army has such a permit for this project. The dredging will resume when the permit renews and the "takes" can recur.

Maybe this year's hurricane season will shift sand to the beach, and avoid the Army's dredging. Otherwise, the citizens of Florida will have to choose between building up beachfront property and preserving sea turtles. Alternatively, perhaps the Army can truck the sand from an inland location and dump it on the beach, or leave Mother Nature to her whims.

New Orleans can't keep the water out, and Florida can't bring the sand to the beach.

What's the message here?

I'm a lawyer, not a botanist. That means I can't look at a plant and tell you where it came from. Like many people, I just assumed that Kentucky bluegrass was grown in Kentucky. Actually, it comes from a lot of places other than Kentucky.

That's the smallest part of the story, however. Do you know what grass really is? You might think it's the green stuff in front of your house you have to mow on a semiregular basis. There's more to the story than that, as this next case shows.

Farming looks mighty easy when your plow is a pencil, and you're a thousand miles from the corn field. —Dwight D. Eisenhower

Kentucky Bluegrass in Idaho, Not Iowa

First, you're going to have to get over the fact that Kentucky bluegrass is grown outside of Kentucky. Actually, it's grown in Idaho, by farmers.

Let me say that again: Idaho, not only in Kentucky. In fact, Kentucky bluegrass is really from Europe, Asia, and more specifically Algeria and Morocco.

Sacrilege, you say? I just report 'em; I don't make this stuff up.

OK, with that warning aside, you're ready for the rest of the story.

Seems that an environmental organization, Safe Air for Everyone, was unhappy with the Idaho farmers' practice of burning straw in the fields that is leftover from bluegrass seed harvesting.

So, like all red-blooded Americans, they sued.

But, they sued under Resource Conservation and Recovery Act, the Solid Waste Disposal Act, claiming that the bluegrass residue (aka straw) was a solid waste, and had to be disposed of properly, and not burned.

Seems the Ninth Circuit didn't agree. They think grass is, well, grass. Not waste.

In the lawsuit, the farmers argued that they reuse the straw, returning nutrients to the soil, which allows them to grow more and better bluegrass in the future. That argument was the one the Ninth Circuit bought. The court disagreed that the straw was actually waste, subject to regulation under our environmental laws.

I lived on a farm in Iowa (no, not Idaho; Iowa). The farmers' argument was the same pitch I heard there in my little town, Hudson. Except the farmers there didn't burn straw, they gathered it into hay bales and sold it to livestock farmers.

But not in Kentucky, of course.

꧁꧂

The best intentions can have the strangest results. Witness this effort at environmental protection.

Have I got a deal for you. —Anonymous

Forget Buying Bridges, How about an Ocean?

A real estate hustle? How about buying some ocean?

I don't know if you'd call it oceanfront or under the ocean, but the next big bid for land by environmentalists is buying up the ocean to protect it. Check out the newest California fad: 2004 Senate Bills 1318 and 1319. Environmentalists are asking the state to buy land under the ocean, ostensibly as a means to prohibit fishermen from taking fish from the water above the land.

Fishermen are upset. They think their livelihood and recreation will be taken away. The whole thing is an obvious takeoff on the land-banking efforts of The Nature Conservancy and other similar groups, who buy up land to preserve open space. It's a well-regarded program to ensure not every speck of land is developed. Sometimes the groups will hold conservation easements on land, which limit uses of the land to open space or minor development.

Land-use battles sometimes take the form of objections to neighboring development (Not in My Backyard—known more affectionately as NIMBY). Buying the open space limits or eliminates those battles and keeps land in its pristine state.

So, when environmentalists become concerned about the effects of alleged overfishing, the choice is an easy one: buy the ocean. But this tactic didn't work, and the California legislature didn't buy it.

Too bad. I know a bridge in Arizona that's for sale.

⌘

Moving right along, we'll leave the ocean behind. Now it's time to talk freshwater, specifically the water that comes out of our taps at home. Drinking water is obviously a prime concern in any community, and luckily we have a top-notch government agency keeping track of water quality and safety.

Or maybe we're not so lucky after all.

Never go to a doctor whose office plants are dead. —Erma Bombeck

Water Figures Are All Wet

The agency we have come to rely on (just kidding) to determine what to clean up and how much of it to clean up apparently can't get its data straight.

The U.S. Environmental Protection Agency (EPA) is responsible for the purity of our water and to keep pollutants out of it so we can drink it. Drinkable water is important to all of us, and we look to the EPA to keep us informed about how things are going. Most everything that comes out of the tap can end up in a glass that goes right to our lips. Purity is an imperative.

So, to assure us everything is fine, the EPA has told us that 91 percent of our nation's drinking water is pure. And some of us believed them.

Turns out that it's not true. What a surprise.

Remember, this is the same EPA that's fighting with fourteen other states to prevent them from enacting stricter air standards than the EPA wants, but that's another topic and another story. Let's get back to the water purity percentages.

Turns out they're way off, but nobody really knows by how much. According to the Associated Press,

> "The [EPA] reported meeting its annual performance goal for drinking water quality even though it concurrently reported that the data used to draw those conclusions were flawed and incomplete," the USEPA's Inspector General office said in a report this week. "EPA's own analysis, supported by our review, indicated the correct number was unknown but less than what was reported."

Wow. Flawed data. Incomplete figures. We don't even know where the right information is.

The EPA's water office says, "We are aware of the data's shortcomings and have been diligent in flagging those to key audiences, as well as to the general public."

I think they're all wet.

One of the most common problems you run into with water is when there's just not enough of it to go around. Droughts are serious business, adversely affecting agriculture, municipal drinking systems, and just about everything else in the dry zone.

Still, there's not much you can do about it—after all, the weather's one of those things still beyond man's control. Just don't try saying that in Georgia.

If I were running the world I would have it rain only between 2 and 5 A.M. Anyone who was out then ought to get wet.
—William Lyon Phelps

Georgia Governor Sonny Perdue Lobbies God for Rain

That headline has a corollary: The Georgia legislature has banned the children's song "Rain, Rain, Go Away." Suffering through one of the state's worst droughts in 2007 and predicted to extend into 2008, Georgia faces the possibility it will run out of drinking water.

The typical precipitation range for the state is 16 inches, but the actual level is well below half an inch. Everything is dry as a bone. It's so bad that once-floating docks are now resting on dry lake beds.

Consequently, Governor Sonny Perdue and his wife, Mary, gathered some 250 of the state's faithful on the capitol steps and led a state-sanctioned prayer vigil, asking God for rain.

Not surprisingly, some cried foul, despite this generally accepted step in the Bible belt.

The Atlanta Freethought Society (AFS) claims the governor's rally violates the principle of separation of church and state. While technically true, it's doubtful a Georgia court would uphold the challenge, and more likely it would be dismissed as moot. Think about it. It's Georgia, not Vermont. At least the AFS had the foresight not to file a lawsuit over it. They held a peaceful rally instead.

Even so, no one disagrees the state needs rain. It's just how to get it.

Maybe AFS would support cloud seeding, a scientific but perhaps no more effective remedy than prayer. Georgia could try an Indian rain dance, which works just about as well as the two prior suggestions.

Perhaps they could get the coast guard to tow an iceberg down—while they last.

My suggestion? Charge all the state's lightning rods to attract the thunderclouds. I know a guy who will do it cheap.

~∞~

While grass may not be a solid waste, other things most certainly are. One of these is sewer sludge—so why is Georgia letting farmers use it as fertilizer? Something stinks here, and it's not just the headwind.

To avoid criticism, do nothing, say nothing, be nothing.
—Elbert Hubbard, who probably did

Whistleblower Scientist Saves the Family Farm? Not This Time

Here's a lovely thought: the EPA denied a petition to prevent the use of sewer sludge as fertilizer. In lawyerspeak, that means it's OK to put sewer sludge on family farms in Georgia.

One problem, though.

Georgia state agencies found the sludge was so corrosive that it dissolved fences and emitted toxic fumes that could sicken cows. Mmm, mmm, good. Yuck!

It gets better. Turns out that the EPA terminated a 32-year employee for blowing the whistle on one small fact: when it allowed the sludge to be used on the basis that the heavy metals in it were within tolerance limits, it allegedly *knew* the data were "completely unreliable, possibly even fraudulent," according to Georgia officials and the whistleblower.

Whistleblower David Lewis, Ph.D., testified before a House subcommittee, and reported that nearly three million tons of sludge were allowed to be dumped on Georgia farms as a result of the EPA's ruling. Lewis's contract with the EPA wasn't renewed and his allegations were dismissed as junk science, which Lewis contests. Treated sludge continues to flow, but lawsuits have been settled alleging violations of toxic sludge dumping.

༺༒༻

Let's make a quick turn, going from the brown and yucky to the brown and yummy. Just about everyone loves chocolate, and research tells us that it might even be good for us.

But maybe there's something more to the picture. Are there sinister ingredients in your favorite snack?

I stand by my misstatements. —Dan Quayle

Is Your Chocolate Heavy?

Is there more than just naturally occurring lead and cadmium in your candy bar? One group wants us to think that the question is still up in the air. Maybe, instead, it was never a problem in the first place.

According to *Prop 65 News*, the nation's major candy companies settled a Proposition 65 warning lawsuit with American Environmental Safety Institute for just $20,000. Prop 65 is a California creation, designed to require warnings to consumers and others when levels of toxic chemicals might cause cancer, birth defects, or other reproductive harm.

According to this article, the allegations were very serious, and the Safety Institute claimed that lead was "clearly" in the chocolate. When all was said and done, though, *Prop 65 News* reported, "No penalties or attorney fees were awarded and the deal, which was the result of an 'offer to compromise,' did not require the companies to warn customers of lead or cadmium exposures."

Maybe the allegations were all a mistake. Or maybe they were just designed to get money. You be the judge.

But before you make up your mind, you might want to consider this: the California Attorney General had this to say: the Safety Institute's claims "lack merit."

∽⧯∼

If you move to the big city, then you might expect to see certain things: taxi cabs, subway trains, and crowds at rush hour. The same would hold true, one would imagine, if you moved to the countryside: the scenery would be different—the view, the sounds—perhaps even the smells.

And that might just be a problem. Luckily, some country folks have a creative solution to help would-be residents get prepared for the reality of the situation.

Very few people who have settled entirely in the country, but have grown at length weary of one another.
—Lady Mary Wortley Montagu

Smell That Fresh Country Air—Ewww!

Yep. I used to live on a farm. A real-life hick. In Iowa. On a gravel road, about half a mile from a paved road we called "blactop."

My neighbor to the north raised pigs. I could tell because of the downwind smell. Especially when he used the honey wagon (euphemism for manure spreader). I knew it was part of living there. But not so anymore.

City dwellers who move to the country are now fighting back—with lawsuits. The concept comes from what is known to us lawyers as "coming to the nuisance."

Generally speaking, when the offending smell is there before you are and you then buy a home within smelling distance, you have no one to blame but yourself. It all got decided long ago, in the seminal 1972 case of *Spur Industries v. Del Webb*. Homeowners moved in next to a cattle feedlot and started to complain about the smell. Though the homeowners were successful in putting an end to the nearby cattle yards, they got the worst end of the deal. The developer had to pay to move the cattle lot.

As if they haven't learned their lesson, homeowners are still suing to move offensive smells, sounds, and sights out of the way. Just like the neighbor who sued the farmer whose tractor kept the neighbor from hearing his television. Or the nuisance lawsuit over the smell from a hog farm.

Having had the experience myself, the reaction is understandable. But, you have to be prepared for what you're getting into when you move to the country. Farmers get up early and work late into the night. Tractors and combines are loud and slow on the highway.

I haven't yet seen a tractor that was aerodynamic like a Porsche.

And hogs stink. Really bad.

So much so that Michigan's rural Ottawa County is trying to prepare city dwellers ahead of time. Not by offering reruns of *Green Acres*, but by providing real-life descriptions and smells. The scratch-and-sniff brochure idea has caught on: Counties in Indiana are considering copying the brochure for new would-be rural residents.

You got it, a manure scratch-and-sniff brochure. Now that's creative.

But I'll pass on the manure smell. I've never forgotten it.

Seriously Now: Lessons Learned

Environmental issues abound, from the big ones like global warming all the way down to a butterfly that flaps its wings in your backyard and causes a typhoon in Asia. But I'm not talking about chaos theory here. How do you and I, dear reader, have any effect on this big environment around us?

Reducing and reusing doesn't take much. Taking your used chemical containers to the county's hazardous waste site instead of throwing them in the landfill will help you avoid violating at least ten different laws you've never heard of (yet).

When I was a little boy, my grandfather used to tell me to take the leftover oil from changing the oil in his car's gearbox and pour it into the sandy soil in the back of his house. "It came from the earth," he used to say, "and the earth can clean it."

We now know it doesn't work like that, and the future will prove wrong many things we think today. But we do know at least a few things, and we know that environmental and other laws at least try to do some good.

Chapter 6

Have Children

Wealth and children are the adornment of life, the Koran tells us, as opposed to what others think that book might say. They're also the two things that provoke people's passions the most strongly, inspiring them to acts of greatness—or to bitter battles in the courtroom.

In this chapter, we look at cases involving children. Things in this area of the law are far more complicated than they were a few generations ago; science has changed how we create kids, how we define paternity, and what we have to teach our children and who does that teaching.

All of these changes have opened up new areas for litigation. Some of the results will leave you shaking your head, and others will have you wondering how in the world they could have come about in the first place.

❦

You've heard of marriage vows? Changes in technology have contributed to the creation of what I call divorce vows. When all of the promises unravel, you've got some things to do to protect your best interests.

The birth thing was just insult added to injury. —Barry Toiv

The DNA Divorce Vows

If you're a dad when you get divorced, then you might want to consider this vow, recommended by the Florida Court of Appeals: "Test now, or forever hold your peace," even if you think you are the father. It could end up costing you years of child support payments for a child you didn't father.

According to a *www.law.com*[2] article written by Carl Jones, Florida residents

> Richard and Margaret Parker were married in June 1996, and Margaret gave birth to a child in June 1998. In December 2001, the couple agreed to a divorce settlement, obligating Richard to pay $1,200 per month in child support. Throughout the marriage, Margaret told Richard the child was his, and repeated that claim in front of the judge during the divorce proceedings.
>
> In June 2002, Richard filed a petition in Broward Circuit Court seeking relief from his child support obligations, based on alleged fraud by his ex-wife. He claimed she had an affair with another man and that she always knew the child was not his.
>
> Judge Rene Goldenberg dismissed Richard's petition, finding that the divorce decree established paternity and that any challenge must be filed within a year of the decree.
>
> In 2003, Richard had a DNA test performed on the child after Margaret alleged that he was behind on child support payments. The test revealed he was not the father of the child.

Ouch. To add insult to injury, when Richard petitioned the court to end his child support payments, the court denied his request as too late.

In fact, this vow appears to be of value not only in Florida, but also in Pennsylvania. In that case, a father who waited eight years to seek a paternity test waited too long. The court there denied his request, too, in the case where the child is now nine.

Now when you get divorced, in addition to resolving issues over property, spousal support, and bank accounts, you may want to consider including DNA tests for you and other family members.

⤟⥼⤠

---

[2] Reprinted with permission from the December 6, 2005, edition of *www.law.com* © 2008 ALM Properties, Inc. All rights reserved. Further duplication without permission is prohibited.

Sometimes the problem's not getting out of the paternal relationship. In fact, it turns out you can do too good a job looking out for your kid. At least that turned out to be the case for Brian Woods, who found himself in trouble after going to bat for his son.

I was never ruined but twice—once when I lost a lawsuit, once when I won one. —Voltaire

Out-Lawyering the Lawyers: You Can't Beat a Dedicated Dad

Maybe he should take the bar exam. Adjunct Professor Brian Woods of Cuyahoga Community College in ohio was upset that his son was not receiving care in school. Brian argued that his autistic son, Daniel, deserved more care, but wasn't getting it. So Brian sued, and the school hired a team of lawyers. Brian won, and won big. In addition to numerous concessions, he also won $160,000 for his son. Brian, however, is not a lawyer.

When the Cleveland Bar Association found out about it, they sued Brian, too, for the unauthorized practice of law. While you might think the suit was a vendetta, the bar thought it was taking a preemptive strike to protect others in the future. You see, after his victory, Brian was helping other parents who couldn't afford or obtain legal help.

The U.S. Supreme Court is about to hear a case involving a similar issue where parents sued on behalf of their son, also autistic. The decision is pending, but a stay in that case prevented dismissal because the parents didn't have a lawyer for their son. Pressure from *The Plain Dealer* and the yet-unresolved case forced the bar to back down, and back down a bit apologetically.

The federal courts are split on the representation issue, thus the intervention by the Supremes. Parents argue that they can't afford to pay attorneys fees and costs to secure their children's rights. Bar associations argue that laws prevent nonlawyers from representing others, which would preclude parents from representing their children.

Tell that to Brian Woods.

Children are the closest we get to immortality. There's a bond between parent and child that's supposed to be stronger than anything going—the type of relationship you simply can't walk away from.

Or you'd like to think so, anyway. Apparently, the courts had to point out that some things truly are forever.

Children begin by loving their parents; as they grow older they judge them; sometimes, they forgive them. —Oscar Wilde

Parents Can't Divorce Children

Though I don't practice family law, every once in a while a case comes along that takes my breath away. Kristin and David, aka Mom and Dad, but not Mr. and Mrs., tried to allow Dad to divorce Seth, their child.

They stipulated in court to the "divorce," if you can call it that, in return for David's one-time payment of $6,500, or up to $9,000 by wage garnishment if the first amount wasn't paid in a timely fashion, to Kristin.

What is more shocking, however, is that the ruse got by the trial judge, whose name (thankfully) is not in the appellate opinion. The Department of Child Support Services correctly filed an appeal challenging the parents' attempt to avoid child support through this stipulation. The appellate opinion struck down the attempt.

What's almost just as shocking to someone who doesn't practice family law is that it takes a statute to define who are a child's parents: Section 7601 of the Uniform Parentage Act defines "parent and child relationship" as the "legal relationship existing between a child and the child's natural or adoptive parents, incident to which the law confers or imposes rights, privileges, duties, and obligations. The term includes the mother and child relationship and the father and child relationship."

Excuse me, but I thought what it took to qualify as a parent was fairly obvious, at least to what it took to get into that position (no pun intended).

∽✖∾

Millions of parents live on this planet, and each and every one of them has his or her own opinion about child-rearing. After all, deciding what to teach your children is a fundamental part of forming their identities and world view—it's one of the ways parents help form the next generation.

But parents aren't the only ones who influence children. Among other things, children go to school. It's there they pick up on some other life lessons, including some perhaps you'd rather they never heard about.

Quite frankly, teachers are the only profession that teach our children. —Dan Quayle

Who Teaches Your Children about Sex?

You're a parent, and though you dread having the inevitable birds-and-bees discussion with your third grader, you've psyched yourself up and you're ready to go, euphemisms at the ready. Until your child instead tells you what he or she learned in school today from the teacher.

That's right, the Palmdale School District beat you to it. They had schoolchildren answer ten questions about their thoughts about sex as part of the teacher's master's thesis.

Some parents were upset enough that they brought suit against the school, claiming that they had exclusive province over the subject area of sex, to the exclusion of the school and its teachers. The parents claimed the school "robbed" them of their "basic constitutional right" to govern the upbringing of their children, including their right to privacy and a host of other constitutional claims, invoking practically every amendment in the Bill of Rights.

Upholding an earlier lower court ruling, the Ninth Circuit held that no such rights exist in the Constitution, strict constructionist or not.

⌖

Maybe the kids from the previous story would have better luck understanding this next case. After all, they've already answered nearly a dozen questions about sex.

Things just aren't the same anymore. Those birds and bees have picked up a few tricks, creating children in ways that were never previously possible. This new-fangled biology, of course, creates potential for problems and court cases like the next one.

Women have more to offer this world than just a fallopian tube. Nothing is going to change until you quit looking at us as just sperm receptacles.
—Barbara Hall, *Northern Exposure*

New Biology, Weird Outcomes

Here's the deal. Husband contracts cancer. Husband freezes sperm. Husband dies. Wife is fertilized with frozen sperm—you'll forgive me if I don't go into the details. Wife (technically now a widow) has dead husband's twin babies ten months after he's in the ground. You count the months.

So far, so good, except it gives me the willies.

Then, wife gets the idea to apply for survivor's benefits. Huh? The new babies weren't surviving at the time the husband died. That is, of course, unless you consider them on an existential or metaphysical level.

Biologically, at the time the husband died, each baby was only half of a whole.

The Ninth Circuit didn't see it that way. They ruled that the babies are entitled to have our tax dollars support them. OK, to be honest, the decision is based on Arizona's definition of "dependent," and the twins apparently fit that legislative definition. Now we get to pay back seven years of two sets of survivor's benefits after we've finally reached the end of the case.

It just sounds too weird to me. The courts are catching up with technology?

But to round things out, Massachusetts Supreme Court says that an after-death conceived baby can inherit from the deceased parent.

Will it ever end?

⁓⊙⊱

Conceiving children can be difficult, but as we've read, people will go to tremendous lengths—even beyond death's icy grasp—to bring more progeny into the world.

Not everybody is eager to expand their family. In fact, some women do everything possible to ensure that they won't find themselves in the family way. Imagine how pleased they are when it turns out they're pregnant.

They're not nearly as pleased as the doctor in this next case is, I imagine.

Whoever called it necking was a poor judge of anatomy.
—Groucho Marx

All the Cost without Any of the Fun

OK, I'll bite. A woman in Colorado is suing for what may be the first lawsuit on wrongful pregnancy because of a botched sterilization.

She is suing the doctor for the cost to raise her child. If the Colorado doctor looks at the precedent set by an Australian court, then he might be feeling a little nervous right about now. Unlike United States and United Kingdom courts, Australia's high court parted company with other world precedent and there held doctors liable for failing to ensure a woman's two fallopian tubes were addressed. Even though she informed the doctors her right tube had been removed and the doctors properly cut the left tube (not checking on the right tube), the doctors had to pay $105,000 AUD toward the unexpected child's upbring.

Here's another case from the doing-anything-to-have-a-child contingent. Science now makes it possible for two people of the same gender—with a little anonymous help—to create a child. That's all well and good, until the same-sex partnership dissolves.

Then you get a situation like this one.

Most quarrels are inevitable at the time; incredible afterwards.
—E. M. Forster

Eggs Gone Mad

It had to come to this.

K. M. donated her eggs to her then–lesbian partner, E. G., who, presumably with the help of a sperm donor, became pregnant and had twins nearly a decade ago.

At the time she donated the eggs, K. M. signed a waiver of parental rights, but then proceeded to parent the twins for the ensuing eight years.

Then K. M. and E. G. broke up. When E. G. presumably denied access to the twins, K. M. filed a petition to establish parental relationship in Marin County, California, just North of San Francisco. The have land of twigs and berries, fruits, and nuts.

In the trial court, the commissioner rejected K.M.'s petition, according to Courthouse News Service. Commissioner Randolph E. Heubach ruled that K. M. was no different than a sperm donor who gave up his rights to the sperm after donation.

K. M.'s argument is that her eight years of parenting should amount to something, and her position was supported by a brief filed by amicus curiae National Center for Lesbian Rights. Ultimately, the California Supreme Court ruled in favor of K. M. and allowed her to assert a claim of parentage.

This case is apparently the first time that a lesbian has attempted to assert parental rights to children based on donating her own eggs.

∽⊙∾

Experienced parents will tell you that all the years of diaper changing, burping, and teaching the kids how to walk are actually the easy years. The real trouble starts when the kids hit their teenage years.

You try to teach them right from wrong, and then send them out into the world to do the best they can. Of course, with decisions like this next one, the best they can do might just not be good enough.

On the highway, beware of rolling stoned. —Anonymous

Sure, Search My Car. I Want to Go to Jail!

Given this decision, I'm glad my kids aren't teenagers any more. If you have teenagers, then read on. You'll want to know who your kids travel with now more than ever.

The U.S. Supreme Court decided the case of *Maryland v. Pringle* and ruled that police officers can arrest everyone in a car if no one admits to ownership of contraband (drugs, guns, use your imagination) found in the car. In this case, the contraband in question was a small amount of cocaine.

Great. Now you don't just need to worry about what your kids are up to. Their friends are now your headache as well.

Chief Justice Warren Rehnquist wrote, "We think it an entirely reasonable inference from these facts that any or all three of the occupants had knowledge of, and exercised dominion and control over, the cocaine. Thus, a reasonable officer could conclude that there was probable cause to believe Pringle committed the crime of possession of cocaine, either solely or jointly."

So, if your son or daughter piles into a car, gets pulled over, and the police officers find marijuana, then get out the bail money. You'll probably need it.

In this much-anticipated ruling, the *Christian Science Monitor* has been doing its best to warn parents. Get to know your children's friends and acquaintances. It's not enough to rely on others anymore.

Knowledge may be changing, but the law's pretty well set. If you have children, then you may want to educate them.

The advocacy group FlexYourRights.org recommends that you and your kids refuse police searches if they ask. There may be a way out of the wrong place at the wrong time.

It's 11:00 P.M. Do you know where your kids are? Let's hope they're not in jail.

Vigilant parents know that danger lays in wait for their children around every corner. One of the few places where they can relax is when the kids are at school. After all, with the teachers keeping watch, what can happen?

The next case might make you rethink those feelings of security.

I have often wanted to drown my troubles, but I can't get my wife to go swimming. —Jimmy Carter

Swimming and Diving in 3/4 Time

Usually, California courts hold that the assumption-of-the-risk doctrine prevents claims arising from sports injuries.

In an unusual departure, the California Supreme Court determined that a high-school swimmer might be able to hold her coach liable for instructing her to dive in the shallow end of a racing pool. An inexperienced swim-team member, Oliva Kahn, followed her coach's instructions, started her race with a dive into the pool, and hit the bottom, breaking her neck.

Most of the time in sports cases, the assumption-of-the-risk doctrine is a killer, and puts a quick end to these lawsuits. That didn't happen here, probably because Olivia was an inexperienced swimmer.

The opinion seems largely founded on the majority's factual-specific determinations: the coach had previously promised she didn't have to dive, she was inexperienced and the coach didn't train her, and, finally, the coach broke his promise during the meet, threatening to throw her off the team if she disobeyed him.

In her concurring opinion, Justice Joyce L. Kennard raised an interesting question: Why distinguish coaches from shop instructors who teach students how to operate a power saw or repair a car, and then end up injured?

※

How do you pick your child's name? There are dozens of baby name books on the market, not to mention Web sites where you can search lists of names sorted alphabetically, by ethnicity, popularity, meaning, and more.

But that's for the first name.

When it gets around to the baby's last name, things usually aren't so complex. You get Dad's name most times, with Mom's standing in on other, fairly well-defined occasions. So how can a baby wind up with a last name that belongs to neither Dad nor Mom?

Here's how.

I am calm. My surname is not a burden for me. It might be for others, but not for me. —Diego Maradona

What's in a Name? The Court Knows

Not many children can claim that an appellate court judge assigned their name. I say "assigned" because the parents couldn't agree on the child's last name for the first seven months of the child's life, which led to a trial.

With that clue, you've likely figured out that Mom and Dad were not married, but Mom was married before. Here's what happened: Several years ago, this case started its way through the Oregon court system.

Dad won at the trial level, but Mom appealed, and the decision was issued two years after the child was born. Two years is a long time to go through life with your last name up in the air, but the court system is notoriously slow. That's why there are turtles under the columns and lamps throughout the U.S. Supreme Court. They symbolize "The slow and deliberate pace of justice," according to wags at the Court. But I digress.

Mom, Christy Wizner, had three other children in her first marriage. She divorced, but kept her former husband's name. She and Chad Doherty (Dad, in this case) had a child without being married to one another, and the child's birth certificate shows Wizner as the child's last name. Chad sued to change the name to his own last name, among other things.

Surprisingly, the parents rather quickly settled the issues of paternity, child support, custody, and visitation rights. Any family law lawyer will tell you that those things are typically sticking points to any settlement. It's not something you hear every day, but fathers and mothers are apparently up in arms over naming rights. Christy wanted her previous married name and Chad wanted his last name.

His rationale? "She has no blood of Wizner in her," Chad testified at trial.

Christy, on the other hand, argued for practicality: "I just think it would be a whole lot easier on the children. . . [for all four] to keep the same last name."

And with that, the courts got involved, and we get treated to the history of Anglo-Saxon naming customs and rituals, starting in 1066. It's fitting, I guess, that the court started with the year of the Norman Conquest in the Battle of Hastings. It's an interesting history, and one that makes this court opinion an entertaining read.

The appellate court then proceeded to lay out a slew of factors to determine how to decide which name this baby gets. Here is the abridged version of the tests relied on by the court (in the opinion, they come complete with citations):

- The identity and preference of the custodial parent
- The avoidance of embarrassment, inconvenience, or confusion
- Identification of the child as being part of a distinct family unit
- The age of the child and the length of time the child has used the surname
- The preference of the child
- The effect of a name change on the relationship between the child and each parent
- Parental misconduct [none here, other than involving the court, which is my personal commentary and not in the opinion]
- The level of support for and contact with the child
- The motivation of the parent seeking the name change or the parent seeking to oppose it
- The community reputation associated with the names at issue
- Assurances of the custodial parent that she or he will not change hers or his own surname or the child's surname
- Important ties to family heritage, ethnic identity, and cultural values

So how did the court reach its decision? The important factors for the court were both practical and the reasonable request of the custodial parent—Mom in this case. Like it or not, Chad lost on appeal and the baby now gets Mom's last name.

The Oregon Supreme Court declined to take the case, allowing the appellate ruling to stand intact. You may ask whether the outcome would have been different if the parents were married. That's the easy question, and perhaps the one Chad should have thought of first.

∞◈∞

If you've got a daughter, then you may have tried to mentally prepare yourself for the inevitable battle over attire: "No daughter of mine is going out wearing THAT!" Chances are, however, you didn't expect to have a fight over your child's appearance while she was in elementary school—or that your adversary would be the school principal.

Leprechauns, castles, good luck, and laughter. Lullabies, dreams and love ever after. Poems and songs with pipes and drums. A thousand welcomes when anyone comes. . . . That's the Irish for you! —Irish saying

Not So Lucky Leprechauns

Self-expression is one of the keys to individuality. Consider leprechauns, for example. Two of them, Jaclyn Timmering and Kurisa Suhr, put on some Irish outfits (what else?), dyed their hair green, and went to John H. Eader Elementary school, in Huntington Beach, California, on a certain March holiday. The two eight-year-old third graders had planned their St. Patrick's Day celebration for weeks, wearin' plenty o' green and even T-shirts that read "Be Lucky" and "Good Luck Girl."

Unfortunately, their St. Patrick's Day celebration turned into a dud.

Their principal, Cynthia Guerrero, was none too happy with their temporarily sprayed green hair, applied willingly by Jaclyn's mother. When the green-clad and green-maned girls arrived at school, the principal gave the girls three choices: wash the dye out, spend the day in the principal's office, or go home. The girls were crestfallen. What had planned to be the "best day" of their lives turned into the worst. The girls' school district in Huntington Beach has a policy that discourages dyed hair.

The problem with the policy, however, is that it can only be unevenly applied. Many Irish folks that I know, including their children, have red hair. As a Welshman, I have brown hair (yes, I know it's got more gray in it, but stay with me here). In the summertime, my hair starts to turn red from the sun. When I was younger, say, for example, eight years old, my hair could easily go from brown to substantially red, pretty much on its own. My daughter's hair is blonde, and she can turn it more blonde overnight. Perhaps surprising to us all, many blondes are not true blondes, and many other hair colors may not be completely natural.

If you're a principal—not a hairdresser—then how do you know for sure?

Green hair, and perhaps a few others, like blue or magenta, are easy to spot and punish. But I'm willing to go out on a limb here and bet that the Huntington Beach School District does not evenly enforce this policy among its students, and especially among its high school students.

Beyond the unequal treatment (we lawyers would call it arbitrary and capricious), it's a celebration, for God's sake. Let the kids have some fun for a day.

A little digging on the Internet revealed a few things about the principal's background, which leads me to ask, what should we expect from a principal whose choice of a "historical figure to have dinner with" is Oprah Winfrey? I suggest we instead send the principal to a day of sensitivity training, and let the little leprechauns dress up and have a good time.

Seriously Now: Lessons Learned

Kids. What can you say? They're bound to get into some trouble now and again. With luck, it won't be the kind of trouble that lands them in the courts.

But, if you're in need of some guidance, then may I suggest the State Bar of California's *Kids & the Law: An A-to-Z Guide for Parents*. You can download it for free on the state bar's Web site at *www. calbar.ca.gov/state/calbar/calbar_generic.jsp?cid=10180&id=1398* or *http://tinyurl.com/38kyd5*.

Because it discusses California laws, it's not going to have direct applicability to all states' laws, but it's a great guide that offers practical advice, regardless of where you live. If you have questions about laws and kids in your state, then you know what to do: Call a local lawyer.

Chapter 7

Enjoy Yourself

Everyone likes to cut loose now and again and have themselves a little bit of fun. Normally that's not a problem—until your fun impedes on someone else's. Conflict on the golf course, over the restaurant table, and around the waistband of your favorite jeans have seriously cut into some people's good times. These cases are the result.

⚬⚬⚬

I'm an addicted snowboarder—I snowboard about 110 days a year.... I mostly snowboard out west—I'm a champagne snowboarder. —Montel Williams

Skiing or Snowboarding? You Decide

Skiing is a particular passion of mine. I hit the slopes whenever I can, even if the white stuff is only artificial. Usually I can't wait to strap on my skis, but reading this particular case gave me pause. I've been skiing since college, and previously qualified as an almost-official ski bum, having taught my way through school and on-and-off since then, when I can get away.

No, I don't snowboard, and yes, they whiz by me almost as fast as I whiz by them—but only in self-defense, of course! There are always two thin, long planks tied below this skier's feet, now somewhat shaped to add some depth to those carved turns. When I stop and watch those crazy snowboarders, though, I sometimes think of the attendant liability associated with skiing and snowboarding, especially when the two collide. It's the bane of being a lawyer. I see risk where others ignore it.

Every season, the obligatory appellate case(s) come out and remind us that skiing and snowboarding are dangerous sports. They each cite the general rule that you assume the risk of injury unless the resort does something grossly negligent to increase your risk. In other words, those waivers on the back of your lift ticket actually work. Most ski resorts do nothing of the kind to increase your risk, and consequently, the plaintiffs who bring I-was-injured-on-your-slopes-so-you-owe-me-lots-of-money cases frequently lose.

I haven't conducted a scientific survey, but since I've been a lawyer, I've read most of these cases because of my interest in skiing. I feel confident saying that something like 95 percent of them are losers for the plaintiff. Yet the cases keep coming each year. So when I read a recent case involving Mammoth Mountain, I was surprised that the plaintiff won, but actually not too surprised after reading the facts.

The case turned on one fact: the courts ruled for the plaintiffs, and sent the case back to the trial court to determine whether the snowboarder's conduct was so reckless that there was no assumption of the risk.

In the case, a snowboarder ignored his coach's instructions, went on a steep run he'd never skied before, "raced" against his friends, didn't pay attention to where he was headed, and at the last minute smashed into a skier standing alongside the run, and hit the skier so hard that they both flew 50 feet in the air.

Here's how the court put it concerning the resulting damage:

[The standing skier] suffered severe injuries. The impact shattered her ankle and broke her lower leg into 16 pieces. Her right tibia and pelvis were fractured, the muscles and tendons in her thigh were torn, and she was bruised throughout her body. The surgeon who operated on her equated her bone fractures with those suffered in a car or motorcycle accident.

The snowboarder was unhurt.

Is it hard to imagine why snowboarders are held liable?

❦

We move now from the snowy slopes to the fairway.

It's one of the facts of golf that not all players are equally gifted at the game. In fact, some golfers are really, really poor players. They're so bad at the game that they might want to consider another sport entirely.

At least that's what I'd do, if I was this next guy.

It took me seventeen years to get 3,000 hits in baseball. I did it in one afternoon on the golf course. —Hank Aaron

What's Your Handicap?

According to an article from the Courthouse News Service, "A bad golfer has been sued for negligence in New York State Court. The defendant allegedly 'aimed and struck the ball so inaccurately' that it was 'beyond the scope of reasonable risk' when it whacked and injured the plaintiff."

Keep me off the course.

❦

It's not enough that there are bad golfers on the course. Some bad golfers don't even warn you that they're attempting to play through.

They call it golf because all the other four-letter words were taken. —Ray Floyd

Do You Have to Yell "Fore"?

It's one of those burning golf questions: Are you required to yell "fore" on the golf course?

The mystery has been solved. Now you know. *Fore* is a term of etiquette, not a mandatory warning when you slice or hook one on to the next fairway. At least on Hawaii golf courses, that is.

Hawaii is fairly (no pun intended) far away from the home of golf, the Royal & Ancient, in St. Andrews, Scotland. There, *fore* is considered a warning, first derived from military use, according to the Rules of Golf. As if it were as simple as just that.

How misguided the rules are. Apparently, the rules have yet to run into the Hawaii Supreme Court.

There in Hawaii, Andrew Tom was playing golf on the Mililani Golf Course. Like most of us, what Andrew was playing may not have exactly passed for golf.

Unfortunately, Ryan Yoneda got hit with one of Andrew's golf balls—in the eye. Ryan subsequently lost vision in his eye.

He sued Andrew for failure to warn—specifically, failure to warn with a "fore." Ryan believed that had Andrew done so, he would have ducked and avoided the injury. But Andrew didn't yell "fore."

According to the Hawaii Supreme Court, "the ball, however, took flight in an unintended direction. The ball hit the left side of the fairway, bounced into the rough, bounced again on the dirt area, then bounced onto the cart path, sending the ball towards the golf cart in which Yoneda was seated."

And with that, along with some law focused on assumption of the risk, the Hawaii Supreme Court ruled in favor of Andrew, determining that when Ryan stepped on the course, he understood that he was in harm's way, and also that Andrew had no obligation to warn Ryan of Andrew's errant ball. The term *fore* is simply a matter of good golf etiquette, according to the court.

Whether the justices have ever played golf is an open question. On the other hand, maybe they understand all too well the differences between a straight drive and a hook or a slice, or a dribbler, as Andrew apparently hit.

⁂

Let's leave sports behind for a while. Most people like to go out for a bite now and again. Somehow, the food usually tastes better in restaurants, and there's something to be said for being served your dinner and never having to worry about cleaning up.

As most of us have learned, however, not all restaurant meals turn out to be pleasant. If you're less than pleased with the food and service received, then do you have to leave a gratuity indicating your thanks for both?

One group of diners said no. The restaurant disagreed. In this next case, we see what the court had to say as a consequence of the inevitable dispute that arose between the two.

The tipping custom originated in England when small sums were dropped into a box marked T.I.P.S.—To insure prompt service. —Author Unknown (apocryphal)

Here's a Tip: You Don't Have To

Humberto A. Taveras went out for pizza to Soprano's Restaurant and Italian Grill, in Great Neck, New York.

Like some of the rest us have done from time to time, he took a big group. Unfortunately, the food wasn't good, and the service wasn't much better. So, Mr. Taveras didn't leave a big tip. He left less than 10 percent.

Consequently, he got arrested—for not leaving an 18 percent tip. Technically speaking, for theft of services. A misdemeanor crime, all for voting with his wallet. He left a tip, but not the kind the restaurant wanted.

Seems that Soprano's had a requirement that if you brought a large party, defined here as more than eight, then you had to tip 18 percent. But, neither Taveras nor anyone in his party knew that. They didn't see it on the menu, and although Soprano's claimed that the waiters told the party, Taveras and his group said they didn't know.

This story has flown across the world because we are all confused on the issue, and don't want to have a restaurant with bad service and bad food tell us how to tip. That, in itself, is a license to steal.

It seems to me that if anyone should have been arrested, then it was the restaurant personnel for not delivering what was promised. But that, too, would have been wrong.

So what happened to Mr. Taveras? The New York District Attorney saw it the same way you and I do. A tip is just a tip, and it is discretionary, not mandatory.

Even if the restaurant says otherwise, then you'll be glad to know.

⤳⤳⤶

After dinner, you might like to go for a few drinks. But don't have too many, or you might wind up like this next guy.

The King shall cut off the hands of those robbers who, breaking into houses, commit thefts at night, and cause them to be impaled on a pointed stake. —Guru Nanak

What Was Your First Clue?

In Lubbock, Texas, 23-year-old Ross Baker stumbled into the wrong house and set off the alarm. According to TV station KCBD news reports, "his mother, Teresa Baker, said." 'He was walking home so he wouldn't drink and drive, like we taught him, and he accidentally got in the wrong house. That's what I want people to understand. He was not a burglar.

Unfortunately, homeowner, Charles Mire didn't know that. He fired a warning shot and when the intruder didn't leave, shot again, killing Baker. Baker had entered through a side door and set off the alarm at 3:45 A.M. Baker was a Texas Tech student who lived nearby.

At some point in our lives, most of us have imbibed a little too much. Some even have to admit to having way too much. It happens everywhere, but thankfully not with such disastrous consequences. Take, for example, what recently happened in that well-known town of Gasselternijveen, in the Netherlands.

Our 53-year-old hero was unable to get his key to fit in the front door lock, so he broke into his home. Once inside, however, he couldn't find his dog and he noticed his furniture was different.

But when someone came knocking at the door, he was the perfect host and greeted the newcomer with a drink. After all, our hero was pretty far along, so why not share the wealth?

As you have likely guessed, it turns out our hero was in the wrong house. He actually lived just two doors down.

He likely missed the number on the side of the house, especially easy to misunderstand because it was written in Dutch. At least it would have confused me.

He was arrested for trespassing, and being the hero that he is, he's offered to repay the damages to the home's actual owner.

∞⊕∞

Here's another case illustrating that there comes a point when even the most practiced drinker needs to put the glass down. If this seems even vaguely like a good idea to you, then you've clearly already had enough.

I heard what sounded like a train wreck. I looked up and saw the tree falling on top of the car. I thought she saw it and had stopped, but she kept driving. —Billy Jackson

Don't Try This at Home

Waving down a train isn't high on my list of things to do in my life, but 54-year-old Debra Thompson, of Live Oak, California, thought she'd give it a go.

Though her attempt didn't work too well, at least she's alive to talk about it. That's right, the train hit her.

Or perhaps it's better stated the other way around: she hit the train and then flew 25 feet in the air, ending up in the hospital banged up with a broken thigh bone and head injuries, but alive. According to reports, she thought she could get out of the way, but she was too slow.

Maybe it had something to do with the fifth of whiskey she drank. She said she was just "being silly." She was hospitalized, but thankfully survived the incident.

Next time she won't confuse a train for a cab, I'll wager.

∞⊕∞

I like a good movie as much as anyone—and if it's one of my favorite films, then more than some people! But there's a time and a place for everything. Driving a car is not the time to watch a film. You might have thought that was obvious.

Apparently, it wasn't obvious for everyone.

The only factor becoming scarce in a world of abundance is human attention. —Kevin Kelly

Watch the Road or Watch a Movie?

You might want to think twice when installing an in-dash DVD player. Apparently, it can be installed bypassing the safety feature requiring your foot to be on the brake when watching it.

That's what prosecutors in Alaska claimed. They believed that a pickup swerved across the highway and killed the two occupants of an oncoming car. The authorities believed that the pickup driver was watching his in-dash DVD player instead of the road.

The pickup's driver, Erwin J. Petterson, Jr., denied using the DVD player as he drove north along Seward Highway on October 12, 2002, and contended he was only listening to music from a compact disc.

The National Transportation Safety Board discourages the use of in-dash units because they distract drivers. I couldn't find much about the issue via the Consumer Electronics Association. They just seem happy that sales are up.

There's no law against in-dash units yet, but you can expect that Alaska may lead the nation in putting one on the books.

∽≈∾

Driving while watching isn't the only problem with vehicle-mounted media systems. There's also the issue of what you watch.

I love the script, but I can't be in it because I can't be a porn star again. Everyone will judge me. —Heather Graham

Let's Take This Show on the Road

The Supreme Court says of pornography that they know it when they see it. Apparently, Fort Worth, Texas, police use the same test.

Cameron J. Walker, 24, of Irving, Texas, was driving down the road in his relatively new car with big, ten-inch flat-panel TV screens, when a policeman noticed a movie showing "multiple naked people" on the screens inside the car, around 2:00 A.M., near a nightclub.

The cop pulled him over, and issued misdemeanor citations for an obscene display, not having a driver's license, and having an open container of alcohol.

No word on whether Cameron will soon be starring in his own video.

∽✵∾

Travel is a favorite pastime for many. Seeing the world is a wonderful thing, especially if you can take the time to enjoy the sights and get to know the people.

Being in distant locations and enjoying yourself is one thing. Getting to those locations, especially if you need to take a plane to get there, is another. We've all heard the airport horror stories—but seldom do we hear the tales in which the passenger actually wins.

Here's one case that might make you smile.

The scientific theory I like best is that the rings of Saturn are composed entirely of lost airline luggage. —Mark Russell

Fight for Your Flight

Picture this: It's the holiday season, and your plans include going to grandmother's house, so over the river and through the woods you go. Like all the other modern travelers, you're planning on taking an airplane flight.

Of course, you're dreading it. You know what the holiday crush is like: canceled flights, misplaced baggage, long lines, and the added thrill of having your underwear X-rayed by the Transportation Security Agency. Let alone the crowds of surly passengers, crying babies, and understaffed, almost bankrupt airlines whose pilots or mechanics or flight attendants are planning on going on strike right before your flight departs.

Rethinking your plans yet? Well, never fear, the courts are sympathetic to your plight.

Take the case of Thatcher A. Stone, of Akerman Senterfitt, LLP, an aviation lawyer and law professor at the University of Virginia who went through much of what I described, decided he wasn't going to take it anymore, and sued Continental Airlines.

Thatcher, who is divorced, planned to take his daughter to Telluride, Colorado, for a week-long ski vacation between Christmas and New Year's Day. After checking their bags and clearing security, they arrived at the Continental Airlines gate in Newark, New Jersey, when they were "bumped" on an otherwise oversold flight, and presented with the option to leave from Newark on the day before they were scheduled to return from Telluride. Thatcher refused the offer, if you can call that option an offer.

To add insult to injury, the baggage handlers had transferred their bags to the plane departing for Telluride, but refused to pull the bags off. All of their winter ski clothes went to Telluride. Thatcher and his daughter were officially bumped, and went home to Manhattan, where Thatcher lives and practices. Their bags returned from Telluride four days after the bags left on the Christmas-day flight.

Not to be dissuaded because he didn't get to spend much time with his daughter, once their winter clothes returned, Thatcher went to Stratton, Vermont, but could only get there for one day.

Judge Diane Lebedeff understood his frustration, and awarded $3,110 to him against Continental Airlines. She issued a thirteen-page opinion and cited a law review study that "since 1990, an average of 900,000 domestic passengers a year are bumped. The U.S. Department of Transportation says 96 percent of those passengers accept the airlines' compensation offers, leaving about 36,000 bumped passengers who may be entitled to sue."

If the proposed Passenger Bill of Rights becomes law, we may see the end of cases like this. The proposed language can be found at *www.thetravelinsider.info/2005/draftpassengerbillofrights*. htm or *http://tinyurl.com/yu4hov*.

So there's hope for the 36,000 of us who have enjoyed the same experience as Thatcher. At least we know a good plaintiff's lawyer.

◦➾◦

Even though Thatcher had problems with the airline, one of them was not a poor sense of direction. The pilots know, pretty much, where they're supposed to be flying to. The same can't be said of the following wayward driver.

We are not retreating. We are advancing in another direction.
　—General Douglas MacArthur

Go to the Pier, Take a Left, and Swim 3,462 Miles

Before bloggers busted Google, its map service provided those directions if you tried to drive from the United States to London, England. Google has since removed that "Easter Egg" from its maps, but it was an entertaining option, allegedly set to reappear with the next update.

In Sweden, these kind of directions almost got one driver into a head-on collision with a train. He relied on his Norwegian GPS for directions, and during a snowstorm where four inches of snow covered the road, he took one wrong left turn—onto a set of railroad tracks.

He got stuck and called authorities, unsure of where he was. The authorities knew based on his cell phone's GPS feature, and they asked just how far he'd travelled on the train tracks. He didn't realize he'd even turned off the main road. They immediately halted all surrounding railroad traffic and rescued our harried traveller from what might have been a very unpleasant experience.

The moral of the story? Stop and ask for directions the old-fashioned way. Unless you're a guy. In that case, just jump off the pier and start swimming.

On the other hand, if you're a GPS manufacturer, then maybe you'll want to consider adding a disclaimer: "Do not rely on this device for directions" or something like that. Otherwise, you may end up with a lawsuit on your hands. For more disclaimer examples, flip to the end of the book.

⌘

Watching movies is fun. For some, paying for movies is not so fun. That's why so much time and energy has gone into developing technology to illegally copy and share movies. Of course, the movie industry isn't thrilled about these developments, and the courts are on their side.

On the other hand, it might just be an exercise in futility. You decide.

Napster and music is the first big battleground for digital media on the Internet; clearly it's a preamble to what will happen... *with movies.* —Jim Long

Go Forth and Copy No More

The California Supreme Court issued its long-awaited decision in *DVD Copy Control v. Bunner* in 2003 and ruled that Hollywood can stop those who decrypt the technology that allows DVDs to be copied.

The court resolved the issue of whether free speech controls over trade secret law, and held for that good, old-fashioned capitalist mentality (which, I have to admit, writes my paycheck). Trade secrets won out, and cash registers will continue to cha-ching with the sales of DVDs. The Napster revolution stumbles once more.

That is until the next Web site posts the code to decode DVDs.

If you're not watching a movie, perhaps you're checking out pretty girls. A favored way to spend time, starting when there were first pretty girls to look at and continuing to the present day. The trend has changed somewhat, with the advent of more, shall we say, provocative clothing.

This trend has raised eyebrows across the nation and the ire of some legislators in Louisiana. Can you imagine reading these briefs?

I don't trust FEMA any more than the agencies in the state of Louisiana. —Tom Tancredo

No More Crack! The Art and Science of Thongspotting

The fashion police are rearing their heads in Louisiana. Admittedly, I do not have the body type that would allow low-slung jeans. Plumber's pants are not part of my inventory. But, I have had to "have a chat" with my kids before. I may not have to worry much longer, though.

If one Louisiana lawmaker has his way, then it'll cost you $175 if your underwear shows. Louisiana Congressman Derrick Sheppard introduced a bill to fine youngsters if their thongs or tighty-whities were visible above their outer pants.

How is he going to deal with the Victoria's Secret Fashion Show? I mean, come on. They don't call it trainspotting any more. It's thongspotting.

Perhaps fortunately, perhaps unfortunately, depending on your perspective, Congressman Sheppard was heckled, booed, and shouted down with catcalls by other members of Louisiana's Congress.

His bill didn't pass. Thongs are safe once again.

❧

Fast women appeal to some, but fast driving appeals to almost everyone, even if they've never set foot on a race track. The need for speed breaks through all social barriers. Gray-haired grannies get pulled over for excessive speed nearly as often as teenaged drivers.

There's something exhilarating about the wind rushing through your hair and the responsive purr of a high-powered engine that makes luxury automobiles irresistible. The only thing that might keep you from enjoying one of these joy machines is the six-figure price tag they command.

If you pay that much money, though, then you're practically assured of a good time, right?

Not necessarily! Read on.

I play the harmonica. The only way I can play is if I get my car going really fast, and stick it out the window. —Stephen Wright

Out, Out, Damned Spot, but I Can Still Drive 185

You spend $128,000 to buy a Maserati GrandSport, and beyond the fact that it's fast, you figure that it's probably pretty well put together. Apparently, Christopher Cefora, of Manhattan, New York, disagrees.

He was a bit distressed with some defects in his car, which Maserati, he claims, refused to repair. According to Courthouse News Service, Mr. Cefora has problems with: "a. Defective paint, b. Scratch on window, c. Headlight washer detached, [and] d. Any and all other defects."

Yep, you guessed it. That refusal to repair led to a lawsuit. Now, Mr. Cefora wants his money back, along with punitive damages. In federal court, it didn't get any traction with the judge—case dismissed.

I don't know about New York, but in California, he'd better keep making his car payments. Our lemon law probably wouldn't help him out. Generally speaking, the defect has to relate to a safety problem. Maybe the headlight washer would qualify. Then again, probably not.

Seriously Now: Lessons Learned

Sports and risk go hand-in-hand. If you're engaged in a sport, then you've assumed the risk inherent in the sport unless someone else has done something unreasonable to increase the risk involved with the sport. So be careful kiddies, it's a jungle out there.

Driving while intoxicated will land you in a whole lot of trouble, and it's certainly something I don't need to explain here. Driving while sleepy likewise may land you in trouble, so use the easy remedy: Pull over and get a room.

If you're flying, then you'll want to know your rights. Each airline has its own set of rights, and some states, including New York, have passed their own. We have yet to see a federal Passenger Bill of Rights, but it may not be far off, depending how airlines continue to treat flyers.

This chapter also briefly discussed product liability, a tort (civil wrong), which arises sometimes when products have unintended consequences from their use. Sometimes products behave unintentionally. Sometimes we use them unintentionally—or at least in ways not intended by the manufacturer. When the use of a product causes injury, we usually see the results in a lawsuit seeking damages. Hopefully there's insurance to cover the damage.

We also talked about copyrights. The recording industry is on a campaign to shut down illegal copying of music and Hollywood is shutting down copying of DVDs, and they're doing it one household at a time. It's safer not to copy; just rent or buy, instead.

Chapter 8

Indulge a Few Vices

Saints walk the Earth, I'm sure of it, but most of us don't qualify. We all have a few vices. Some of us indulge in the occasional cocktail, while others light up a fine cigar after dinner. Every now and again, some people indulge in adult entertainment or place a bet on the ponies. It happens.

Even though it does happens some people don't like it. They don't participate in such behaviors, and they're bound and determined that you shouldn't either. It's a conundrum, and there's only one way to resolve the situation: litigation.

In this chapter, we look at cases and legislation borne out of mankind's desire to stamp out vice—except those vices that the stampers themselves, enjoy, of course.

❧

A fine wine, a sparkling cocktail, an ice-cold beer on a hot summer day—all of these are enjoyed by many, but the prudent among us know you don't indulge before you have to drive.

In an effort to reduce the number of intoxicated drivers on America's streets, activist groups introduced a program that turned hundreds of years of legal precedent on its head by assuming everyone's guilty until proven innocent, technically speaking.

Want the details? They're here.

Do not allow children to mix drinks. It is unseemly and they use too much vermouth. —Fran Lebowitz

Drinking: DMV, DUI, Duh!

Forget gas prices. We soon may need something else to run our cars. Cars of the future may require your breath to start. If you've got a record of driving under the influence, you may need to blow into a Breathalyzer in order to get the car engine to kick over.

You heard it here second. First in *USA Today*. Add about $1,000 to the cost of cars to include this device, and some irritation to blow into it if you're not a drinker. Thank MADD if you're happy about it. Get mad if you're not.

·⚬❀⚬·

You can take a presumptively punitive approach to preventing drunk driving, or you can reward drivers who play it safe and stay sober.

I wish the bald eagle had not been chosen as the representative of our country; he is a bird of bad moral character; like those among men who live by sharking and robbing, he is generally poor, and often very lousy. The turkey is much more respectable.
—Benjamin Franklin

Don't Get Stuffed in This California Town and You May End Up with a Turkey

Make it sober through the long Thanksgiving Weekend in Salinas, California, find the mystery sobriety checkpoint between 6 and 10 P.M., and you'll get a free turkey for your trouble. Failing that, you'll be the one that gets stuffed—in the back seat of a California Highway Patrol (CHP) cruiser and eating crow, instead.

All available CHP officers patrol the city streets, highways, and byways over the long, holiday weekend to cut down on what resulted in nearly 50 deaths and nearly 5,000 accidents across the state on the fall weekend.

Mothers Against Drunk Driving and several other community organizations teamed up with the city to hand out the free turkeys as both a reward and as a means to generate awareness of the consequences of drunk driving.

For once, it'll be the police that will give you the bird—which is always better than a getting a ticket for DUI.

⁓⊛⁓

Driving isn't the only behavior that should be avoided after having a few too many drinks. Consuming too much alcohol can impair all kinds of abilities, including the ability to make reasonable fashion choices.

For her fifth wedding, the bride wore black and carried a scotch and soda. —Phyllis Batelle

If You Drank One Shot of Scotch Each Night in Succession from Every Distillery in Scotland, Then How Long Would You Have to Remain There?

The answer to that question puts your stay at well over a year-and-a-half. If you've been to Scotland, then you've likely had a taste of Scotch whisky (without the *e* if it's Scottish, and with the *e* if it's Kentucky *whiskey,* thank you very much) and you also likely know the effects it has on its drinkers.

Sometimes, you do foolish things. Take, for example, statues that wear kilts. Let me explain.

Somewhere in Scotland, there's a wee kilt on the lam. It shouldn't be too hard to spot; it's been outside on a statue of the Mad Hatter for over a year. Likely it's a bit tattered.

Tommy Roberts runs Back Tracks Music, on Brougham Street, Tollcross, Edinburgh, and has the statue outside his store. He also owns the Mad Hatman, a nearby disco, and someone gave him the statue for his business.

Roberts added the kilt to the small statue to promote Scottish football (soccer) games at his disco. Flustered about the theft, Roberts told the *Scotsman News,* "If someone was to wear the kilt it would barely cover their modesty. I can't believe someone stole it."

The area around Roberts's businesses is frequented by a young Scottish crowd known as NEDs (non-educated delinquents). One of the responsive comments to the story questioned the owner's surprise at the theft, "Not exactly up with nedette fashion is he? A tartan belt would not be out of place on Lothian Road on a weekend night."

It brings to mind a drunken Scot stumbling from pub to pub wearing nothing but a child's kilt, covering not much more than a belt.

Wouldn't ever happen in Scotland, would it?

Whether across the pond in Scotland or here in the States, people who drink too much tend to do stupid things. Sometimes funny things. Sometimes illegal things. But it's usually not too funny ending up in jail—especially with a hangover.

Scotland's NEDs might have an explanation for the missing wee kilt, but I bet even they'd be stumped when faced with this next case.

This is the most fun I've had without lubricant. —Leigh Whannell

I Can't Make Up Stuff This Good

You may occasionally wonder whether I make some of these stories up. Nope. I'm just not that creative. Don't believe me?

I submit as Exhibit A this opening paragraph from a recent United Press International story: "Police arrested a Texas airport passenger for public intoxication after he was found sitting on a jet bridge covered in salad dressing and missing a shoe."

Not only was our 27-year-old gentleman (and I use that term loosely) covered in salad dressing, but so were the walls of the jet bridge. You have to wonder what was going on before the police got there, and whether anyone else was covered in salad dressing. If I'm remembering my college days correctly, I'd hazard a definite maybe.

Before you reread those paragraphs though again hang on a moment—it gets better. Our apparently drunken hero questioned police—in slurred speech of course—about why they wouldn't let him board his American Eagle flight. At least we can thank God he wasn't the pilot.

I'm about to rest my case here, but before I do, I'll throw in one more tidbit about our hero, as if I need to. He couldn't even stand up. Police had to assist him to get him to his feet and keep him there.

Perhaps not too surprising, our hero admitted to drinking vodka in an airport restaurant, which was apparently one of the sources of his problem. The other one was too short of a security line, which obviously gave him too much time in the restaurant.

I am troubled by two nagging questions however. Where did he get that much salad dressing? where was his co-conspirator?

⚬◈⚬

One question naturally leads to another, and if you're looking for a great question, I think you'd be hard pressed to top this next one.

Don't use an axe to embroider. —Malaysian proverb

Can the Police Detain a Man with an Ax Riding a Bicycle at 3:00 A.M.?

That question is posed by one of California's best jurists, a dear friend of mine, Justice William Bedsworth, who sits on the Court of Appeals. In addition to writing some of the clearest appellate opinions, he writes a well-known column and blog of the same name, *A Criminal Waste of Space*. He's just "Beds" to those who know him.

Beds demonstrates the beauty of the law in the fifteen words of that headline question. It's all about framing the issue—asking a question so there can be only one possible answer. But it's his choice of words and real-life treatment of typically arcane law that make his writing interesting reading, something not generally seen in stodgy appellate opinions.

Let me get to the setup.

Beds starts out with the facts in a short, five-page opinion. "A Huntington Beach policeman approached Robert Francis Foranyic when he saw him standing astride his bicycle, to which was attached a large ax, at three in the morning. The officer ordered him to dismount, explaining that he 'wanted to put some distance between him and the ax.'"

And rightly so. The rest of us surely would have, too. Beds has a penchant for plainly describing the obvious.

When the cop detained Foranyic, he also found a baggie of methamphetamine taped to his belt, and noticed Foranyic was drunk. Foranyic was arrested and charged with public drunkenness and possession of a narcotic. Foranyic's lawyer tried to suppress the evidence of the methamphetamine, arguing there was no probable cause for the cop to pull over Foranyic in the first place.

Beds makes short work of that argument: "This incident did take place during the hours of darkness—stygian darkness. No one who has ever worked a graveyard shift can underestimate the significance of any bicycle traffic at that hour, much less lethally armed bicycle traffic," writes Beds in classic prose.

He continues,

> Nor can we ignore the long history of the ax as a weapon. While no one refers to a "gun-murderer" or "knife-murderer" or "crowbar-murderer," the equivalent usage with regard to an ax is well ensconced in American usage. The ax, like the machete and the straight razor, is an implement whose unfortunate utility as a weapon sometimes overshadows its value as a tool.

Wrapping it up in inimitable fashion, Beds says,

> We conclude that a reasonable police officer, considering the totality of the circumstances, would reasonably suspect criminal activity might be afoot upon viewing someone on a bicycle, with an ax, at three in the morning. Certainly we would expect a diligent officer to investigate such unusual behavior through the relatively unintrusive means of a detention. This is so even though no recent "ax crime" had been reported.
>
> For while Foranyic insists there was nothing about him which suggested criminal activity, he is unable to suggest, and we cannot conceive of, much in the way of non-criminal activity which is accomplished with an ax in the dead of night. The officer could reasonably

eliminate firefighting and lumberjacking from the list of possible pursuits Foranyic might have been engaged in.

Apparently, Foranyic's lawyer argued that carrying an ax was not unusual, which met with a swift rebuke in the opinion: "The more cogent point is that there is some activity which is so unusual, so far removed from everyday experience, that it cries out for investigation. Such activity will justify a detention even when there is no specific crime to which it seems to relate."

The lawyer tried another tack, arguing it was not at all unusual to be out riding an ax-armoured bike at three in the morning. Not too surprisingly, Beds counters, "We consider it equally unusual to be abroad at that hour on any errand that requires an ax."

Overruling the lawyer's attempt to suppress the evidence of the methamphetamine based on his argument that the cop had no reason to detain Foranyic, Beds puts it simply, "Some things cannot be ignored."

We'd all want the cop to stop someone wielding an ax at 3:00 A.M., whether on a bike or not.

After all, what good could you be doing with an ax at that hour?

⁕

Fewer people are smoking than ever before. This downward trend makes government health workers happy, of course. Fewer smokers means a healthier citizenry, placing less of a burden on limited health care resources.

The tobacco industry isn't happy about the declining number of smokers, of course. Especially since they're funding the media campaign designed to persuade people to kick the cancer sticks.

It has always been my rule never to smoke when asleep, and never to refrain when awake. —Mark Twain

Taxing Tobacco to Tie Tongues?

Is it legal to tax a business and then use that tax money to discourage people to buy from that business?

Apparently so.

California has a tax that takes money from the $0.87 per-pack tax from R. J. Reynolds and Lorillard Tobacco Company, and then uses that tax money to run antismoking advertisements.

The tobacco companies don't like the government spending their money to advocate quitting smoking. They claim it violates their First Amendment rights. But the Ninth Circuit didn't agree. "The implication of the tobacco companies' argument is that industries subject to an excise tax are entitled to a special veto over government speech funded by the tax," said Judge Raymond C. Fisher. The three judge panel of the court split, and ruled 2–1 in favor of the state of California.

The dissent in the case started its argument with a quote from Thomas Jefferson. The quote read: "To compel a man to furnish contributions of money for the propagation of opinions which he disbelieves is sinful and tyrannical." The tobacco companies agreed with dissenter Judge Trott.

You're right. This isn't the end of the story. You can be sure they'll be an appeal to the Supreme Court, challenging the Ninth Circuit's ruling.

Tobacco wants to regulate the government's speech, and the government wants to regulate tobacco's sales. What do the rest of us want? Some want to smoke, and others don't want to—and don't want others to smoke, either.

The First Amendment says I can say what I want—and I usually do in my blog, May It Please the Court. But instances abound of the government limiting what can be said. Now the Supreme Court will have to determine whether the government can use our money to argue against our own speech.

Next thing you know, the government will use my tax money to write a book.

◦◦◦

Obscenity is one of those things that is difficult to define, but if the famous quote is any type of guide, then most people know it when they see it.

Of course, some people want to make sure you never have the opportunity to see any adult content and decide for yourself whether it's objectionable. They're behind this latest bit of technology, designed to keep us safe from our baser urges.

I know nothing about sex because I was always married.
—Zsa Zsa Gabor

Editing DVDs—Pornography Controls Gone Mad

There are already parental controls for television, and now a company has come up with a way to filter DVDs and remove what some may deem objectionable content. The question, however, revolves around whether you can edit a copyrighted movie. The directors determine what to cut from the movie and then create the DVD for our viewing pleasure. They're not at all happy with the prospect that someone else can edit their copyrighted work.

Think about the consequences.

If they put those controls on the Chris Rock HBO special, then you'd practically be watching a blank screen. ClearPlay has made possible the technology to essentially edit DVDs.

The federal Family Movie Act may allow parents to buy DVD filters that screen out material they deem objectionable.

The Directors Guild is upset. "You're getting a doctored reinterpretation of the product," said Dan McGinn, a spokesman for the Directors Guild of America. "What they [ClearPlay] have is a new version of the product. It should be licensed."

This technology may also be able to automatically remove commercials from cable and network television programs.

Where do I sign up?

⸙

Changing the technology is one way to avoid offensive content. Of course, in the United States that's a choice: if you want to watch racy movies, no one's going to stop you. In China, it's another story.

The ultimate censorship is the flick of the dial. —Tommy Smothers

Too Much or Too Little? What to Do When You're Caught in the Middle

The motion picture rating system leaves little to be desired in China. If the movie's got a steamy sex scene, then it gets cut out. Unlike the United States, if you believe the Trilateral Commission, China has one national censor, the State Administration of Radio Film and Television (SARFT).

Nothing gets past these guys. Anything censorable ends up on the cutting room floor.

Censoring sex scenes can make for a disjointed movie-going experience, and one fan decided to do something about it. According to the *Beijing Times*, Dong Yanbin, a Ph.D. student at Beijing's China University of Political Science and Law, filed a lawsuit against SARFT for infringing his "consumer rights."

Yanbin seeks 500 Yuan (about $67.00) and an apology, the paper reported, for "psychological damages." His complaint? "Compared to Eileen Chang's original, the incomplete structure of *Lust, Caution* and [its] fragmented portrayal of the female lead's psyche makes it hard for the audience to appreciate the movie's art," Yanbin told the *Times*.

That's one serious moviegoer.

Like the national censor, however, the court will likely cut Yanbin's complaint from its docket. In fact, the court hadn't accepted the complaint when the paper wrote its story, and probably won't.

So, he's probably stuck with the one remedy chosen by many other serious movie fans in China. Travel to sin city, Hong Kong, to watch the full, uncut version.

China might seem far away, but the world is getting smaller all the time. What's happening there, as with this case, is the same as what the Family Movie Act is doing, it's just handled differently. The point is, things could be worse—much worse.

◦◦◦◦◦

Gluttony is one of the seven sins deadly—and if heart attack rates and obesity levels are anything to judge by, then it may be the deadliest. America's love affair with food has some dangerous consequences, but fear not! There are do-gooders out there, determined to save you from your dinner and your fork.

A gourmet who thinks of calories is like a tart who looks at her watch. —James Beard

You Aren't What You Eat

Brace yourself: according to the Associated Press, class-action lawsuits against Coca-Cola are being litigated as this book goes to print. No, it's not the caffeine, the carbonation, the aspartame, or even the food coloring.

It's the calories.

Yep, we used to blame McDonald's for making us fat, but it turns out we were wrong. It's those darn sugar-laden soft drinks, also known as pop, tonic, or soda, depending on where you live. You can be sure that Coke is not the only target of this latest round of finger-pointing. I don't know about you, but maybe it's time to point at our forks—or just put them down more frequently.

The problem is childhood obesity, and the availability of soft drinks to children in school. The attorney who's drafting those suits likens soft-drink dispensers to cigarette machines. Though they put Diet Coke into their vending machines, the argument in return will likely have something to do with low-tar, low-nicotine cigarettes.

The pending lawsuits over the cause of childhood obesity due to the availability of vending machines that dispense high-calorie soft drinks, according the Associated Press article has drawn fire. The American Beverage Association counters by arguing the suits are "trying to paint a bull's-eye on a particular product and pass it off as a meaningful solution to a complicated problem." The Center for Science in the Public Interest, a watchdog group, sued Coke for false advertising, claiming drinking soda doesn't burn calories. I'm no doctor, but just about anything you do burns calories, so I don't get it.

Coke seemingly just can't get it right: After being sued for too many calories, the beverage manufacturer was sued for promoting a product that had a claimed "negative" amount of calories. Sometimes you just can't win!

I thought the solution was to eat less, exercise more. Maybe we need long physical education classes and more sports in school, and less time in the courtroom.

⋘⋙

No one's immune from this new health consciousness, not even those superstars who are known for being larger than life.

There are three stages of man: he believes in Santa Claus; he does not believe in Santa Claus; he is Santa Claus. —Bob Phillips

Just in Time for Christmas, Will Santa Go on a Diet?

Obesity is a big problem in the United States, and consequently everyone's got an opinion about it, A host of obesity lawsuits are trying to blame everything else but the forks in our own hands. The lawsuits filed against McDonald's for causing our obesity got dismissed. It got so bad that some 23 states actually passed legislation outlawing lawsuits against restaurants for making us fat, with 6 more states in the wings.

But it never seems to stop.

Apparently there are those who want to put Santa on a diet and "get him off the sleigh and onto a Stairmaster," according to some quoted by the United Press International.

Just when you thought it was finally safe to have a Griswold-style Christmas and pile more lights on your home, everyone seems to think less is more.

Come on, admit it. You're building a small nuclear power plant next to your home in order to put all those lights up and not blow a fuse.

Excesses aside, child experts don't think a thinner Santa will help in the fight against obesity.

Dr. Andrea Vazzana, of the Child Study Center at New York University, says, "I think the true culprit is probably far closer to home than the North Pole."

Whew. She didn't say anything about more lights. It's safe to go ahead and plan your big light show for the end of the year.

You know you want to.

⌘

A friendly wager's one thing, problem gambling is another. If you can't tell the difference between the two, then read through this next case. If you find yourself nodding in agreement with this woman, then chances are that you too have a little bit of an issue with wagering.

Here's something to think about: How come you never see a headline like "Psychic Wins Lottery"? —Jay Leno

Gambling Problem

Every once in a while you stumble on something so bizarre you can't believe it. Here's the story of a woman who stole up to $6,000 *a day* from her employer to play the New York lottery, apparently hoping to win it big.

In all, she stole $2.3 million.

I don't know about you, but that amount sounds like a winning lottery ticket to me. Apart from the stealing part, I'd be satisfied with $6,000 a day. I could probably figure out a way to live on that kind of change. It apparently wasn't enough for Annie Donnelly, however. She kept at it over a three-year period, taking the money in checks of varying amounts from Great South Bay Surgical Associates.

She faces up to twelve years in prison. The district attorney, with the brilliance only an attorney can muster, said, "She obviously had a gambling problem." That gem comes from Donna Planty, assistant Suffolk County district attorney, according to CNN.

Assuming you worked a regular eight-hour day, where would you find the time to buy 6,000 lottery tickets a day?

✼

Normally, only adults have vices. It's not a word we associate with children. That assumption changes once an ad agency comes into the picture, however.

The best car safety device is a rear-view mirror with a cop in it.
—*Dudley Moore*

Boys Like Cars? Who Knew?

Every few years, we get to watch the Olympics, which means we also get to watch Olympic ads, too. TiVo apparently can't do everything. (Long sigh here.)

Some advertisements are good, others are pretty dismal. On average, they're nowhere near as good as Super Bowl ads.

But, I have to admit that in a recent ad shown during the Olympics Chevrolet had a good one, filmed by Guy Ritchie, Madonna's current husband. So why was there a problem? Apparently, it must have been too good.

Complaints drove Chevy to pull the ad (no pun intended). Freedom of speech and advertising gave way to consumer pressure. It's all about selling cars, not making enemies. It's the one with two young children driving (well, not really) two Corvettes, and winking at each other as they pass each other while "jumping" the cars.

Apparently after watching the ad, some five-year old took his Uncle's Caddy for a stroll, and the ad is now gone.

Where were the parents? Why was the car unlocked? How did a five-year old child conceivably reach the gas pedal in a Cadillac? Inquiring minds want to know.

⁓♾⁓

Now that we've got soda on the hot seat, let's look at all the other things that are making us fat. It couldn't conceivably be our inability to stop putting high-calorie food in our mouths, oh no. Instead, someone else has to be responsible, right?

That is the American way, after all. What could be simpler?

Although golf was originally restricted to wealthy, overweight Protestants, today it's open to anybody who owns hideous clothing. —Dave Barry

McDonalds or Gluttony? Voting with Your Fork

Admittedly, I used to be overweight. OK, fat. All right, obese. Within a couple of points of diabetes.

I readily admit to it. Good news, though, I've lost 85 pounds. Off to a good start. Just a few more to go.

But, as you know from looking around, I'm not the only one. And, there are a lot of plaintiff's lawyers who try to help overweight people blame others—like McDonald's. And, just to prove their point, they sue. But as we've already read, obesity cases regularly get dismissed.

After all, does the responsibility lie with the people that sell us the food, like McDonald's, or the people that put the food in our mouths? Oh. Wait a minute. That's us, heaven forbid.

As a side note here, I guess this argument is not much different than the argument over guns and criminals. If they can't sue McDonald's, then does that roadblock mean they next try to sue the farmers?

It appears that Illinois has legislated solution. No more lawsuits against a restaurant for injury resulting from weight gain, obesity, or any other related health condition. Well, that ought to put the responsibility back where it belongs.

Right on our fork.

But not to worry. The government has seen to it that obesity can be covered by Medicare. At least that benefit takes care of those eligible for that coverage. What about the rest of us?

Never fear. Congress is considering the "Cheeseburger Bill." It's the Personal Responsibility in Food Consumption Act. The act places the responsibility for eating too much right on the plates in front of us. If you don't want to gain weight, then don't eat so much. Despite passing the House of Representatives twice, the Personal Responsibility in Food Consumption Act failed to pass the Senate, and never became law. So far, the Illinois state legislation hasn't seen a challenge probably because lawyers would be embarrassed to bring it. Unless you were a perfect 10 and worked out eight hours a day with an athletic body.

∽≈∾

One's weight might seem like a personal issue—but that's not necessarily the case. Obesity causes health problems, which puts a strain on national health care systems—and governments are starting to fight back.

Is she fat? Her favorite food is seconds. —Joan Rivers

Fat People Banned Worldwide

Yes, the headline is an exaggeration, but it could be true if New Zealand has anything to say about it. There's a law there requiring immigrants to have a body mass index (BMI) of 30 or less in order to cross the border.

To give you an orientation, an average of the ideal BMI is just under 22. To get to that weight, the average six-foot-tall man would weigh 162 pounds and an average five-foot-four woman would weigh about 122 pounds.

I don't know about you, but at just over six feet, I haven't seen the shy side of 162 pounds since I was a sophomore in high school.

Imagine then a BMI of 42. Under New Zealand's law, you're not getting in, and likely for awhile. That rejection happened to 35-year-old Welshman Richie Trezise, who's apparently one of only four people in the world who know how to coordinate linking a certain type of underwater telephone cable between Australia, the United States, and New Zealand. He was just a tad overweight and had to lose some pounds (kilos in Wales) in order to emigrate to New Zealand to work on this project.

If you've consulted the tables, and assuming Richie is six feet tall, then with a BMI of 42 he would have weighed about 309 pounds. To get into New Zealand, he had to hit 227 pounds (assuming he's six feet tall). That's quite an accomplishment, and hats off to him for losing the weight.

But it's lonely Down Under, especially if your wife is back in Wales.

For Christmas, Richie wanted to have his wife join him, so she filled out all the paperwork, packed her bags, and…

Yep, you guessed it. She apparently was eating the same way Richie was before he left for Down Under, and she consequently got rejected, too.

Richie says he's going home if his sweetie doesn't get down to the required weight before the holiday.

So, we may not be talking to New Zealanders anytime soon, solely depending on Richie's wife. How'd you like to have that kind of pressure?

And, with immigration such a hot issue here in the US of A, who knows what the next round of immigration laws will bring? Maybe BMI will be the acid test for securing our own borders.

❧

Personal responsibility keeps most of us from drinking and driving. In fact, it may have been personal responsibility that kept some

Pennsylvanian men from getting behind the wheel after they'd had a few too many drinks.

That decision, however good it was, didn't prevent them from getting in trouble with the law. Now we've got a judicial decision that has dire consequences. That sound you hear? It might be coming from the other side.

"Well, now, hold onta yer horses, there, Frazier. I mean, as a psychiatrist, isn't it your job to, uh, 'seek and uphold the truth'?" —Cliff, *Cheers*

Mr. Ed Rolls Over in His Grave

A horse is a horse, of course, of course,
But the Vehicle Code does not divorce
Its application from, perforce,
A steed, as my colleagues said.

'It's not vague,' I'll say until I'm hoarse,
And whether a car, a truck, or horse
This law applies with equal force,
And I'd reverse instead.

That rhyme is Justice J. Michael Eakin of the Pennsylvania Supreme Court, dissenting to the majority opinion that ruled Pennsylvania's DUI law doesn't apply to people on horseback.

Obviously, he didn't agree.

Three men were arrested for drunken driving, but two of them were on horseback. The prosecutors argued that Pennsylvania's laws applied to them, but the majority of the Pennsylvania Supreme Court disagreed, found that the law was vague, and reversed their conviction for drunken "driving."

Justice Eakin made his point that riding a horse while sloshed isn't the same as driving drunk, but lost this round.

What about the Amish buggies all around Pennsylvania? If the buggy driver is drunk (admittedly a stretch), then does that mean that because they're driving a horse-drawn carriage that the DUI laws don't apply?

This case isn't going to ride off quietly into the sunset.

⌘

In England, however, it's pretty much settled. You can be as intoxicated as you'd like to be—as long as you can stay in the saddle.

You can lead a horse to water, but a pencil must be lead.
—Unknown

In Gloucestershire there may have been a lot of drunks riding around in 1872; witness England's 1872 Licensing Act, which states that it is an offence to be "drunk while in charge on any highway or other public place, of any carriage, horse, or steam engine."

Apart from the unusual grammar, you get the point. In what may be one of the first drunk-driving statutes, you can't drive a horse-drawn carriage drunk.

Before I get too far along, let me introduce the characters in this vignette. First, we have 21-year-old William Royles, and next, we have his horse, Dipstick, a two-year old bay.

With a name like that, you know what you're in for next.

Bill and Dipstick headed home late one evening on a highway in Gloucester. If you're following along, then we so far have three of the necessary four elements required to violate the 1872 Licensing Act.

Let's pause here for a moment and take a trip back in time to somewhere around 1872, and think about how you would go about determining whether the driver of a horse-drawn carriage is drunk.

No cheating now; you can't use a Breathalyzer or a blood test. Those two options just didn't exist.

Now you've found Bill's defense to the charge: you can't prove he was drunk.

Technically.

Before the magistrate's court, Barrister Matthew Harbison, representing our hero, Bill, told the magistrate, "According to case law, the standard of drunkenness in these circumstances is higher than that applied to motoring matters. The person must be drunk to the extent of loss of self-control."

I think that's maybe where the term *falling down drunk* must have come from.

But just in case you're wondering, here's the wrap-up from the BBC News:

> The 134-year-old charge of drunkenness rests only on the allegation of the arresting officer.
>
> [Special Constable] Kirk Ravenhead admitted that he had let Mr. Royles drive the horse and carriage two kilometers home after he had stopped him, with police following behind. "This was the safest course of action to prevent any injury to himself," he said.
>
> Greg Jones, chairman of the magistrates, said: "The bench is of the view that the test for this case is that the defendant must be so drunk that he is deprived of self-control. The officers supported him to drive home. We don't believe that there is a case to be answered."
>
> Mr. Royles was fined £25 [just over $50.00] for not having lights on his carriage.

So next time you're in England, you now know how to beat a drunk-driving charge.

Ride a horse home.

⌘

In this next case, we're talking about what may be one of the most notorious vices. It may not be a vice for everyone: some folks are afraid of planes and others are just too modest.

Still others might be discouraged from "applying" to the club after hearing what happened to this couple during their attempt to become part of the exclusive set.

Women need a reason to have sex. Men just need a place.
—Billy Crystal

Joining the Mile-high Club

You've probably heard of the mile-high club. Heck, maybe you even have a commemorative pin. If you wait until the plane has reached maximum altitude, however, then it's more like the six–mile high club, but let's not be picky here. It's a club, not a law school exam.

Besides, there are some interesting tales of—ah…how should I put it?—the membership requirements to join.

And there are other ways you might want to avoid when you to try to join.

Take, for example, the facts in the indictment of Carl Warren Persing, of Lakewood, California, and Dawn Elizabeth Sewell, of Huntington Beach, California, who were on a cross-country flight and landed in hot water due to their hot time in the air. According to the affidavit detailing the Federal Bureau of Investigation's investigation, things were getting hot and heavy on the ground during the layover in Phoenix, and then continued after takeoff.

But a heavy-handed FA-1 (that's FBI talk for *flight attendant number one*) tried to put an end to it, and finally alerted the captain, who alerted authorities on the receiving end of the flight (no pun intended). Mr. Persing and Ms. Sewell were flying on Southwest Airlines from L.A. to Raleigh, North Carolina, and allegedly tried to make a go of it in the cabin, which apparently offended other passengers. The affidavit is full of titillating details, but suffice it to say that FA-1 alleges that Mr. Persing's head was in Ms. Sewell's lap, and she was smiling.

FA-1 and the other passengers were not.

From what I can tell, the couple violated the most basic requirement for membership in this perhaps mostly exclusive club: discretion. The idea behind joining, apparently, is not to get caught, let alone criminally indicted for the behavior. Perhaps there's a permanent ban from membership for the violators of these tenets. I'll wait for a ruling from you, dear reader. Beyond the exclusion, however, that indictment might turn into a one-year layover in the slammer. Perhaps they should have taken a flight on Virgin Shaglantic (an actual term in the advertisement for Virgin Atlantic airlines).

If you really want to join the club without running the risk of getting caught, then here's one way to do it with the ultimate discretion: be the only passengers on the plane other than the pilot, who's locked on the forward flight deck.

Just a thought.

⌘

The transfer of semen will not be allowed. —Ofer Lefler

Continuing with a theme, of sorts, I present to you this case. I'd lead in with a witty intro, but i'm afraid you'd find it hard to swallow.

Honey, How about Trying U.S. Patent No. 6,485,773 First?

Now here's true romance for you—trust me on this one. The U.S. Patent and Trademark Office issued a patent for a dietary supplement that claims it "significantly improves the taste of male ejaculate." Yep, it's right there in Patent No. 6,485,773, issued on November 26, 2002, right around Thanksgiving (no pun intended).

Right. I presume someone had a white lab coat, clipboard, chart, and some type of numerical scale. Very scientific, not at all romantic. Well, perhaps we should change *romantic* to *sexual*.

You probably guessed the patented formula can be put into a "drink powder, tablet, chewable tablet, or capsule form." No kidding here.

But it gets better.

Again, according to the patent, "These optimal results were discovered only after experimenting with certain freeze-dried fruit and vegetable powders combined with specific spices."

Experimenting? Is that what they call it? Who's that gullible?

So not only does the formula allegedly taste better, it's apparently also good for you, too. Once more, right out of the patent: "Certain vitamins and minerals were additionally added to replenish in the male those nutrients lost via ejaculation."

I never knew.

And don't think there's a do-it-yourself kit. You see, "pineapple juice and broccoli were only slightly effective in improving semen taste, regardless how much of either or both were ingested," the patent reports.

According to the patent application, the formulation was successful in "reducing its generally salty and/or bitter taste while also adding a pleasant flavor that is considered by 98.5% of all customers as very enjoyable."

98.5 percent? How do they know that?

All I want to see is the ad for *that* clinical study. You'll have to read the patent yourself to see the four-step process to maximize (again, no pun intended) the benefits of the formula.

I'm laughing so hard I can hardly type. As my grandfather used to say with a groan, "Oh, my achin' bones."

Seriously Now: Lessons Learned

Alcohol, too much food, smoking, sex, and more drinking can and do get folks into trouble. We've regulated and taxed all of these vices, succeeding mostly in taxing them, not stopping them. Prohibition didn't work, and telling us we're going to die from smoking so far hasn't put the tobacco industry out of business. In fact, it may be just the opposite.

Nothing I suggest here is going to make anyone stop drinking, smoking, or eating too much. My only suggestion to stay safe would be to do it at home, take a cab, or designate a driver. That's so much easier than landing in court for a DUI—or worse—and having to deal with lawyers and judges.

Chapter 9

Own a Pet

Americans love their pets. They love their pets so much that between sales of animals and, increasing, numbers of animal accessories—dishes, leashes, toys, and, God help us all, clothes for animals—they make up a $32.5 million-a-year industry.

Does this mean that we, as a nation, are a little obsessive about our animals? Do we take our pets too seriously? Considering the number of pet-centered court cases I've got to tell you about, I'd say the answer to those questions is an unqualified YES.

⁂

It's not the size of the dog in the fight; it's the size of the fight in the dog. —Mark Twain

Some Pricey Puppies: Hell's Angels' $990,000 Dogs

Sometimes it pays to settle early. Of course, this means the converse is also true: sometimes it doesn't pay to settle early.

In the case of the Hell's Angels Motorcycle Club, however, settling early certainly did pay. After losing rounds in the lower courts, the County of Santa Clara appealed all the way to the U.S. Supreme Court, claiming that their sheriff's deputies' actions were immune from liability, but the court denied the appeal, and refused to hear the case.

The blog *Overlawyered* points out that the city settled for $990,000 to avoid a trial for damages, resulting not only from the deputies' actions of shooting and killing several Hell's Angels guard dogs, but also the Fourth Amendment violations of the Hell's Angels' rights.

There has been a lot of public support for the Hell's Angels. But it seems to me that it's the dogs that get the sympathy. Motorcycle gangs have long fought for their rights, and damages awards of this size rarely occur when just people are involved.

According to press reports, the Santa Clara officers had a week in advance to prepare for the raid on Hell's Angles HQ, and while they knew about the existence of the dogs and had their guns at the ready, they did nothing to prepare for a lesser remedy, such as tranquilizer guns. On the other hand, officers are trained about the Fourth Amendment search-and-seizure restrictions from the very inception of their career, yet violations of those constitutional rights rarely evoke these types of awards.

But the lesson to be learned is not whether people or dogs are involved. It arises, in part, from a realistic evaluation of the potential exposure.

According to CNN, "Officers from the cities of Santa Clara and Gilroy also were involved in the raids, and those cities settled their cases several years ago for a total of less than $50,000, the plaintiffs' lawyer told the *Chronicle*." Then again, hindsight is 20/20.

⚜

Some people have an irrational love of animals. Their passion for their furry friends leads them to overlook a few playful nips from their pets and turn a blind eye when Fido spoils the hallway carpet.

But even the most fervent animal lover might agree that Mr. Yates, the gentleman from the next case, has some definite issues. Someone might want to let him know that things are a little out of whack, because he seems incapable of figuring that out for himself.

He who rides a tiger is afraid to dismount. —Chinese proverb

Here's a Clue: The Rabbit's out of the Hat

A three- to four-pound rabbit is missing from his New York apartment, but that's the least of Antoine Yates's worries. Two years ago, he was mauled by Ming, a ten-foot long "pet" Siberian tiger he kept in his apartment, and was taken to a Philadelphia hospital for treatment of severe lacerations, which included exposed bone.

A friend of mine who is a curator at the Los Angeles Zoo described the relationship of tiger claws and human skin to be roughly the equivalent of human fingernails to onion paper. What may be playful to a full-grown, 450-pound wild cat with leather-thick skin can be deadly to you and me.

Until that fateful day, Mr. Yates apparently didn't appreciate that possibility. He had raised Ming from a cub, along with a hatchling now named Al that turned into a six-foot long alligator. Yates also kept a small rabbit.

After his recovery, Mr. Yates was sentenced to five months in jail for reckless endangerment. He also brought suit against the city of New York for the NYPD's alleged violation of his constitutional rights based on his allegation that the police unlawfully searched his apartment and seized the animals. They still can't find his rabbit, however.

Last time I checked, the Constitution didn't contain either a tiger- or alligator-search clause.

Ming and Al now reside in an animal shelter in Ohio, but there's been no word about the rabbit. U.S. District Court Judge Sidney Stein, who dismissed Yates's claims, noted, "The whereabouts of the rabbit have not been ascertained, but there is no indication in the record that Al the alligator was questioned in that regard. The court suggests he may be more knowledgeable on this issue than he disgorged to date."

꙳

Alligator and tiger bites are fortunately very rare. Dog bites, on the other hand, are extremely common. So common, in fact, that most localities have laws regarding the treatment of dangerous canines.

Of course, if you're a vet, then you might expect that you'll run into some sharp-toothed dogs along the way. Such was the case in this lawsuit—at least until some pertinent details came out.

When a dog bites a man that is not news, but when a man bites a dog, that is news. —Charles Anderson Dana

Give a Dog a Bone, Not an Arm or an Ankle

We out here on the Left Coast have a unique approach to many things, and oddly enough, to dog–bite laws, too. OK, time for disclosure. I'm a defense lawyer, not a plaintiff's lawyer. That said, let's get to the issue at hand.

Seems as though dog owner Nelson needed surgery, and wanted to kennel Mugsey at a vet's during Nelson's time under the knife. Mugsey is a Staffordshire Terrier. That's doublespeak for pit bull. Perhaps not surprisingly, Mugsey was "dog aggressive."

In fact, Mugsey actually had earlier bit Nelson and severed an artery, putting Nelson in the hospital, along with another dog owner Mugsey attacked. Though the recent case didn't go so far to characterize it this way, I'm guessing Mugsey was "human aggressive," too. After all, it was an artery.

But here's the rub. It appears that Nelson might not have been completely up front with the vet who operated the kennel fully disclosing Mugsey's biting tendencies, however characterized. Next, as you probably know by now, Mugsey bit his handler on her ankle during a walk. Yes, as you also have already guessed, our walker, Priebe, sued Nelson.

This is where it gets interesting. The Left Coast has California Civil Code section 3342, commonly known as the strict liability dog bite statute. You own a dog, it bites someone, you are liable. Period, end of story—or so you would think.

What would the law be without exceptions to the rule? And yes, we have two, or at least one, with a variant. It's called the firefighter's rule, and derived from that one, the veterinary variant, announced first in our case.

Basically, it means there's no recovery for people employed to handle the very risk where they may be injured. It's an odd rule that results in odd outcomes. Someone negligently starts a fire, the firefighter gets injured, but the firefighter can't recover from the person who negligently starts the fire. But, if an arsonist starts a fire, then the negligence element is removed, and recovery would be proper for the intentional act of starting a fire.

So, too, here. Our dog walker was employed to walk dogs, and inherent in that job is the risk of a dog bite. Our illustrious court determined therefore that the veterinary variant applied, preventing application of California Civil Code section 3342, the strict liability dog bite statute.

But, that's not the end of the story. Our appellate court also decided that the trial court should have instructed the jury that the occupational assumption-of-the-risk does not apply here because a domestic animal is presumed not to have vicious tendencies even though, the owner knew about it but failed to disclose it.

Remember that Nelson apparently forgot to tell the vet that Mugsey severed an artery in his arm, and put another dog owner in the hospital, too. He will likely get tagged for that failure.

You could say that the court threw Priebe a bone.

I had to say that.

⋘⋙

Can you put a price on love? The romantics among us would say no, of course, but most lawyers aren't all that romantic. Trust me, I've met several other lawyers. The law isn't worried about sentiment, it's worried about semantics—specifically definitions.

In this case, the word being defined is *pet*. In one instance, a pet is property, but in another it's a family member. What does that mean to you? It depends. You have to ask.

I am minutes ahead of my time. —Louis Weinstock

How Much Is That Doggie in the Window?

You can sign a prenuptial agreement for your pet, you can sue for injuries to your pet, and you can even bury your pet in a pet cemetery, but you can't sue for emotional damages when your pet dies after treatment by a veterinarian.

At least in Tallahassee, Florida. But if you're in Miami, then go right ahead.

Go figure.

Robert Burns Kennedy tried to sue his basset hound's vet, Albert Byas, for emotional damages after Fred died on the operating table. The court said no, writing that a dog may feel like family, but Florida law classifies canines as personal property, not kin.

But this new ruling may conflict with the Florida Supreme Court's decision in *La Porte v. Associated Independents, Inc.* In that case, a purebred Dachshund named Heidi was killed after a trash collector deliberately hurled a trash can at her. The court allowed an award for punitive damages, stating that the malicious destruction of the pet provides an element of damage for which the owner should recover.

Confused yet? You can't collect for damages in one instance, but can in the next. It's not an easy concept.

One thing's for sure. Someone might find that they're barking up the wrong tree.

⌘

Dogs doing tricks are nothing new, but a pooch with a gift for litigation? That's worth talking about. Especially since it turns out that the dog should have won.

The dog has seldom been successful in pulling man up to its level of sagacity, but man has frequently dragged the dog down to his. —James Thurber

The Dog Has the Better Case

"It's not a dog-and-cat fight, and I'll show you proof of that," Richard Espinosa said in his opening statement.

Several years ago, Espinosa went to the library with his assistance dog, Kimba, a Labrador. When they entered, the library cat, L. C., attacked Kimba and scratched the dog. Espinosa, who represented himself, sued the county of San Diego, California, for $1.5 million.

In the beginning of the trial, after the judge threw out his federal causes of action for violation of the Americans with Disabilities Act, Espinosa reduced his claim to $15,000.

The judge had earlier denied Espinosa's motion for summary judgment.

The jury didn't award Espinosa any scratch for Kimba's scratch.

To quote the *San Diego Tribune*: "One man, who was not picked as a juror, said he didn't have any reason to be biased in the case but told the judge he had another concern.

"'I wish it was the dog suing the cat,' the man joked. 'We've all used the word *frivolous,* but I think the dog has a real case.'"

Custody battles are some of the most bitter, emotion-filled situations you'll ever encounter in the courtroom. It used to be that people would go to war over their children. Now, they're warring over their cats!

In order to be irreplaceable one must always be different.
—Coco Chanel

Get Your Pet's Prenuptial Agreement Here

Yes, I admit it. I've had both a dog and a cat in the past. There. My kids are grown and out of the house, now, too.

Does that qualify me as a pet lover? Perhaps, but not by today's standards, apparently.

Consider this: A woman bought a cat with her roommate. More than a year after the roommate moved out, the two became embroiled in a custody battle—over the cat!

The woman won a five-figure settlement. "In a historic ruling, the court applied the best-interest standard, which is usually applied only in child-custody cases," her attorney said.

"The judge was sympathetic to animal rights, but didn't want to make a big splash out of it," the attorney said. "I had a 50-page brief in that case, and the last sentence was the kicker: 'You can't treat the breaking of the leg of a table the same way as breaking the leg of a puppy.'"

Ouch.

Now don't get me wrong, here, and I said it above, I've had pets before. But five figures? 50 pages? Get real.

It gets worse. There's the *www.petcustody.com* Web site, where you can fully explore what you need to do to protect yourself from becoming embroiled in a similar situation. You can even download a prenuptial agreement for your pet. No kidding.

I'm still trying to get over the map of the Roadside Pet Cemetery on the Web site.

⌘

For a while, Taco Bell was running an extremely popular ad campaign with a small dog named Dinky, the talking Chihuahua, who mouthed the immortal message "*Yo querio Taco Bell*" (I want Taco Bell).

You might have wondered whatever happened to that little dog. Don't fear for him. He's still working—just on a smaller stage. Right now, he's the main attraction in an intimate venue: a courtroom in Michigan.

If you take a dog who is starving and feed him and make him prosperous, that dog will not bite you. This is the primary difference between a dog and a man. —Mark Twain

Plenty of Dogs in This Fight

Dinky the talking Chihuahua can't sport one of those T-shirts that reads: "If you can't run with the big dogs, stay on the porch." Previously relegated only to TV commercials hawking burritos, he's now starring in a Michigan courtroom.

Two men, Joe and Tom, claiming to have created the talking Chihuahua, sued Taco Bell for ownership of the mascot.

The plaintiff's attorney, Douglas Dozeman, stated, "My clients created a licensed character named 'Psycho Chihuahua,' which was then adapted and used by Taco Bell in the ads." Dinky is the name of the actual dog that played the part of the Chihuahua in the ads.

Dozeman's clients won big. Now they're the ones on the porch.

But not satisfied with the paltry $30.2 million victory, the two men went for the gusto, and ended up with *mucho* gusto. In posttrial motions, Federal District Court Judge Gordon J. Quist awarded an extra $11.8 million in interest on top of the judgment.

Dozeman said, "Sooner or later, Taco Bell is going to run out of issues, and Joe and Tom will finally be able to receive the proper compensation for their intellectual property."

Taco Bell Spokeswoman Lauire Bell responded, "We continue to believe that the Chihuahua character was created independently, and we intend to appeal the jury's verdict."

I'm still waiting to hear Dinky's thoughts, now that the Psycho Chihuahua is running with the big dogs.

Seriously Now: Lessons Learned

Pets keep us company and for many are much more than companions. It's no wonder we spend money on them. When two people own a pet, it can lead to trouble if they split up and can't reach an agreement over who gets the much-loved pet. When a pet dies, we grieve for the pet and that, too, can lead to problems.

Pets, however, can likewise be dangerous, especially exotic pets, which in most places are not only dangerous, but in many cases are also illegal to own. That's what zoos are for.

There's pet insurance to protect Fido and Fluffy when they get sick and pet life insurance to pay for burial expenses. Just remember that pets are property and can't own anything themselves. That's why Leona Helmsley left a million-dollar trust for her dog, Trouble, who's now anything but. She couldn't give the money to the dog if she tried.

Pets are great companions. Planning for future eventualities will solve a lot of other problems before they even come up. See your favorite pet lawyer now.

Chapter 10

Own a Home

A man's home is his castle, and he defends few things more fierce-ly. The same holds true for female homeowners too—when faced with lackluster performance by the insurance company or lousy cell phone coverage, they know exactly what to do.

They head right to court. Here are some of the results.

Until you walk a mile in another man's moccasins you can't imagine the smell. —Robert Byrne

The Tail Wags the Skunk

It's a rare day when I choose to take on a panel of appellate judges, but this one seems an easy task. Here's the pitch, with apologies for the baseball analogies.

Skunk gets under house, homeowner calls insurance company. Strike one. Insurance adjuster sends out restoration company to deodorize the house. Restoration company allegedly uses chemicals and deodorizers, and homeowner gets sick. Strike two. Homeowner sues restoration company, restoration company makes a claim to its insurance company.

Then, of all things, restoration company gets its claim denied. Surprise! Strike three—yer out!

The insurance company says there's an absolute pollution exclusion in the policy. So the restoration company sues. Twice, now, courts have upheld the insurance company's position. Deodorizers are a pollutant, they say.

What?

Let me see here. The policy exclusion says they're not covered if the cause of the injury is an "irritant or a contaminant." I don't know whether the deodorizer used was either, but even if it wasn't, then what happened here?

Let's look at it again. What is the original pollutant?

Right—the skunk smell. What is the deodorizer designed to do? Right again—remove the smell. To make it smell better, less like a skunk.

Nowhere in the Court of Appeals' ten-page opinion do they explain how a deodorizer—that makes things smell better—qualifies as an irritant or contaminant.

It's the exact opposite. Call me silly, but I would have reversed the trial court.

Maybe the judges would have understood the idea better with an actual demonstration of the effects of the skunk smell, followed by the deodorizer. Think about the possibilities. How about a scratch-and-sniff patch in the brief to the court, followed on the next page by the deodorizer? Nothing like reality to drive home a point.

⁓⋙⋘⁓

Part of home ownership, of course, is your yard. Whether it's the front yard, bedecked with flowers and birdbaths, or a wooded backyard replete with a children's play area, people spend hours and thousands of dollars making their yards perfect.

Sometimes that perfection includes lawn statuary. Specifically, gnomes.

GNOME, n. In North-European mythology, a dwarfish imp inhabiting the interior parts of the earth and having special custody of mineral treasures. Bjorsen, who died in 1765, says gnomes were common enough in the southern parts of Sweden in his boyhood, and he frequently saw them scampering on the hills in the evening twilight. Ludwig Binkerhoof saw three as recently as 1792, in the Black Forest, and Sneddeker avers that in 1803 they drove a party of miners out of a Silesian mine. Basing our computations upon data supplied by these statements, we find that the gnomes were probably extinct as early as 1764. —Ambrose Bierce

Gnomes Gone Gwild

Gnomes make easy fodder for poking fun, but perhaps *www. freethegnomes.com*'s recent letter to the U.S. Congress seeking an end to gnome slavery in U.S. gardens makes it the easiest. To quote their letter, "In attacking the Gnome Slave trade, we have kept two objectives in the forefront: First, that we must liberate all enslaved Gnomes, and second break the link between Gnome trading and the accumulation of wealth, because the Gnome Slave trade is a multibillion dollar global trade."

On the other hand, perhaps it's the French Gnome Liberation Front (GLF) who makes it the easiest. Risking charges of trespass and theft, these gnome-supporters truly put their belief in the woodland creatures on the line.

The little, red-capped lawn ornaments have been mistreated around the globe, but French men and women are finally doing something about it. We learn from several Limoges correspondents who report for the *Daily Telegraph* that there's a wave of gnome liberation afoot.

Last year, some 79 gnomes were liberated from their owner's yards. The only telltale sign? Notes appeared in the owners' mailboxes explaining, "Because of the heat wave, they wanted to get some air."

The gnomes were recovered next to a swimming pool. The news report was unclear on whether any skinny-dipping charges would be filed.

Recently, the GLF struck a blow for Gnome freedom again, this time liberating some 86 of the little folk, who were found shortly thereafter in the underbrush, next to a stream. They were found with notes that read, "Gnome mistreated, gnome liberated."

No ransom was requested, and the gnomes were successfully returned to their ghomes.

Just in case you're interested, several groups are working to prevent the world's oppression of garden gnomes. There's the Front for the Liberation of Garden Gnomes (FLNJ), at *www.flnjfrance.com* (French language only). They claim 100 active members throughout France, Canada, Germany, Spain, and the United States. Then there are Gnomes without Homes and Free the Gnomes (FTG) at the Web sites of the same names, and finally this book's hero, John Leckie, who serves as General Counsel for FTG.

Who ever said attorneys don't know how to have fun?

⚬⚭⚬

When you have a problem with your home, you call on your insurance company to help deal with the cleanup. After all, that's what they're for, right? So what do you do if the insurance company throws up its hands and says, "Not our problem?"

You take them to court, of course, and hope for a decision like this next one.

One kind word can warm three winter months. —Japanese proverb

Hot Spots: Cleaning Up Home Heating Oil Spills

With oil prices raising steadily, it looks like winter's going to be rough for anyone who heats with home heating oil. Out here on the Left Coast, though, it's not so much of a worry. I just have to turn off the air conditioning.

My mom, however, isn't happy. She lives on Cape Cod, and will have to spend more than she wants to keeping warm this winter. I think that's why she switched to gas heat.

She's also glad that she doesn't have the problem a woman had in Pennsylvania. But as homeowners, we all celebrate the decision that heating oil leaks don't fall within the pollution exclusion of homeowner's insurance policies.

In this case, Marlene Epstein's heating oil tank ruptured in her basement and the oil leaked onto her neighbor's property. The neighbor promptly sued her, and Marlene's insurer, Atlantic Casualty Insurance Company, denied coverage and, heaping insult on injury, filed a declaratory relief action against Marlene seeking to avoid paying her claim.

Now there's a surprise—an insurance company that doesn't want to pay a claim.

But, righteousness won in the end, and Justice Ronald Buckwalter protected the community of homeowners who have heating oil tanks and ordered the insurance company to pay for the cleanup. And we all sigh with relief knowing oil contamination under our homes will be cleaned up.

Now about switching to gas....

⸘⸘

Hot air aside, cell phones are omnipresent now. You can get coverage almost anywhere. But if you can't, then it might not be your service provider who's at fault. It could be your neighbors. You won't be surprised to learn your neighbors can sue you or prevent you from using your cell phone at home.

Well, if I called the wrong number, why did you answer the phone? —*James Thurber*

Drop Any Calls Lately? Blame Your Neighborhood, Not Your Network

You buy a nice house, live in a nice neighborhood, and life is wonderful.

You get some what sketchy cell phone coverage at your house, but it's not the best. You complain to your carrier, and maybe they put in a nearby cell phone tower.

Not everyone's happy, though, there in mild-mannered suburbia.

Lately, there's been a lot of static over the location of cell phone sites.

The battle cry is NIMBY (Not in My Back Yard). Others, however, like the idea.

Whatever side you fall on, there are those who claim the cell phone signals are bad for our health. From at least this writer's perspective, the jury's out.

The more immediate issue seems to be the view of cell phone towers dotting the landscape. Cell phone companies, understandably, want more towers, we all want better cell phone coverage, but not everyone likes the way towers look. That means complaints to the government, and, of course, litigation.

The San Francisco Board of Supervisors denied MetroPCS's application for a new cell phone site. Not to be dissuaded, MetroPCS sued, claiming discrimination. The case, *MetroPCS Inc. v. City and County of San Francisco*, was upheld by the Ninth Circuit, which upheld the board's written decision, detailing the reasons for its denial under the Telecommunications Act of 1996.

The act requires that the decision must be in writing, based on substantial evidence in the record, must not discriminate between providers of functionally equivalent services, may not prohibit the provision of services, or be based on concerns regarding the environmental and health effects of radio frequency emissions if the provider demonstrates that it complies with Federal Communications Commission regulations concerning those emissions.

Whew, that's a mathful congress wanted to create effective, nationwide wireless networks with sufficient competition to increase innovation, improve customer service, and lower prices. It just took too many words.

When local jurisdictions bann cell towers, they're mandated to make the required findings to overcome the goals outlined by congress. Essentially, the Ninth Circuit said significant gaps of coverage had to exist before it would overturn local jurisdictions' decisions to ban towers in the area, a showing Metro PCS couldn't make. San Franciscans must enjoy some fairly good cell coverage in the area and not suffer from dropped calls.

Meanwhile, as Jimmy Buffet says, "If the phone doesn't ring, it's me."

∽ᕽᣞᣞ∾

Faced with a situation very similar to the cell-tower scenario described in the last case, some Massachusetts companies have come up with an innovation solution. What have they discovered?

They know now that you can never please all of the people all of the time, but if you try really hard, then you can tick off a whole mess of folks all at once.

Neighbors are the strangers who live next door. —Rick Bayan

NIMBY? Try NIMO!

Cape Wind Associates is attempting to build a wind farm in Nantucket Sound. Not all nearby residents are too happy about the plan. A simple Google search will result in numerous articles and organizations both for and against the proposal.

Another company, Winenergy, LLC, has at least fourteen wind farm proposals pending for East Coast oceans.

Oceans aren't the only place where wind farms have popped up—we have them right here in Palm Springs, California, and just outside Livermore too. They're in Minnesota, Ohio, Pennsylvania, and many other states.

The Department of Energy says wind farms are also in Colorado, Hawaii, Iowa, Kansas, Maine, Michigan, Montana, Nebraska, New Mexico, New York, North and South Dakota, Oregon, Tennessee, Texas, Vermont, Washington, West Virginia, and Wyoming. Not surprisingly, they're in Holland, too.

To some, they're an eyesore. But windmills are nothing new to the American landscape. They come from the Old Countries, too. Holland and England's national treasures have inspired individuals, as well.

Many people have installed windmills for themselves. There is much support for this form of individualism; the bibliography for small projects is amazingly extensive. Small projects are generally accepted, but the big projects often meet stiff opposition.

The general concept opposing these large farms is NIMBY (not in my backyard). I think the argument against windmills in oceans will have to be called NIMO—Not in My Ocean.

There are good arguments on both sides. Clean energy and no pollution versus dangers to navigation (in oceans) and scarring the landscape. So far, there's lots of rhetoric on both sides, but we have yet to see a significant court challenge. You can be sure it's coming. I have to ask, though, are we just nothing more than Don Quixote tilting at windmills?

You know I wouldn't have missed that pun.

Finally, we'll finish up with one more insurance story. Sure, they may be slow to pay claims. Yes, having them help you resolve problems can be like pulling teeth. But there's one surefire way to get their attention: stop paying your premiums.

In the opinion of the insurance companies, nothing should interfere with the steady flow of your payments to them. Not even the fact that the home you're paying to protect no longer exists.

So, rather than appear foolish afterward, I renounce seeming clever now. —William of Baskerville, *The Name of the Rose*

We Don't Care If the Ruins Are Still Smoking: Pay Your Bill

You've got to love insurance companies. After houses burned down from the 2003 wild fires in California hills, five insurers wanted to recoup their losses.

They wanted to recoup those losses so badly that they continued to charge full premiums, even though the houses no longer existed, a new, proposed class-action lawsuit alleges. As this book goes to print, the lawsuit is still pending.

The insurers who were sued include Allstate, Farmers Insurance, and Safeco.

Remember, now, you're in good hands.

Seriously Now: Lessons Learned

As my grandmother lay on her deathbed, she reached up and pulled me closer to whisper in my ear and give me what I surely thought would be sage wisdom. I was in my early thirties and could use just about any kind of wisdom, either sage or not. She had been a big influence in my life and I valued her advice. Her parting words would surely provide the guidance I needed for the rest of my life, something I would never forget.

As I leaned over, she said, "Never own a home. Always rent."

Yep, that was it. Eighty years of life distilled down to two sentences. She didn't really mean it; she was expressing her worry that my grandfather would now have to take care of their family home, something she had done for the both of them their whole life. It was then that I understood perspective, perhaps more than ever.

Owning a home can be a big headache for a number of reasons, the least of which is the continual maintenance and the cost of things that go wrong. When they're big things that go wrong, like some of the examples above, our sole resource is the insurance company. That's why it's so important to put this book down for a moment and go find your insurance policy. Make sure it's currently in effect, and you've calendared the time to pay next year's premium.

Look to see if you have the right amount of coverage. Is it high enough to rebuild your home in the event that it burns down or is otherwise destroyed—all or part? See if you have "replacement cost" coverage instead of "actual cash value." Although the coverage forms can vary from company to company and state to state, generally speaking, replacement cost coverage pays to replace your home, assuming you haven't undervalued the coverage. If your home isn't covered up to the true cost to replace it, then in the event of a loss, you'll likely only get that proportional amount of the policy, not the full amount.

On the other hand, actual cash value pays the depreciated value of your home, which is usually insufficient to replace it. And no matter what, to get any payment from the insurance company, you'll have to replace your name. They won't just write a check to you and let you move to the tropics.

You'll also want to check the coverage for liability insurance (the coverage that kicks in when someone else is injured on your property and sues you) to ensure it's high enough for the risks you face. Generally, you want to consider liability coverage at least as high as the amount of assets you own, and then multiplied by, say, three as a minimum.

There's another little-known and rarely considered coverage on homeowner policies called "additional living expenses." This coverage kicks in when your home has been either partially or completely destroyed but you can't stay there anymore. It pays your hotel and extra food bills. The question you want to ask is whether the coverage is sufficient to sustain you while you repair or replace your home, however long that effort may take. Typically, this coverage is nowhere near high enough, based on what I've seen in clients' policies after the house is destroyed, which is too late to do anything about it.

If you've got an oil heater in your home, then you'll want to make sure the liability portion of your policy doesn't exclude pollutants. If it does, then talk to your agent to get the right kind of coverage in place. Also, special types of coverage are available if you own artwork, jewelry, and a host of other small but expensive items that typically aren't covered completely (usually limited to $500 or so) by regular insurance policies. Again, talk to your insurance agent.

Now's the time to look.

If you live in an apartment or otherwise rent where you live, then don't think you've escaped this issue. You still need coverage for the contents you own and the liability you face. Your landlord's policy does not cover your possessions. You'll want your own renter's policy, and make sure that it's enough to pay to replace your belongings and the liability you may face if you damage the landlord's premises. The same analysis above applies to the types of coverage available.

If you have questions about the language and the coverage your insurance agent can't answer, then ask your local lawyer. Better to find out now, when you can do something to fix the problem, rather than later after the damage has been done.

My grandmother will rest easier knowing you've covered all these contingencies.

Step 2

Retain Competent Counsel

Chapter 11

Representation Is Priceless

Now that you've selected a reason to get sued from one of the ten methods outlined in Step One, you're ready for the next step. That's retaining competent counsel.

I have to admit as an attorney, I may be a little biased. There's more than a grain of truth in this little saying: "Lawyers are expensive. Good lawyers are priceless."

If you don't believe me, then see for yourself. Bad things can happen if you opt for less than ideal representation. You can alienate the court, lose your case, and wind up in hot water, just like these folks we're going to read about next.

∽◉∼

Our legal system is adversarial in nature. We have at least two sides in every case: the defense and the prosecution, each aiming to prove his or her point and defeat the other. Still, it never pays to unnecessarily antagonize the other side, as demonstrated in this next case.

I'd insult you, but you're not bright enough to notice. —Unknown

It's Not Nice to Fool the Attorney General

If you do, then you just might end up with your name all over a negative opinion like this one. It's not a pretty sight. Here are some of the gems from the opinion about the value of the Proposition

65 settlement in the matter of *Consumer Defense Group v. Rental Housing Industry Members*. Prop 65 is a statute unique to California that requires businesses to label just about everything with a warning that chemicals are present that are known to the state of California to cause cancer, birth defects, and other reproductive harm. Not everyone believes it has value, as evidenced by this opinion:

> [I]nstead of $540,000, this legal work merited an award closer to a dollar ninety-eight. . . .
>
> But when litigation is as easy as shooting the side of a barn, drawing circles around the bullet holes and then claiming you hit the bull's eye…only the most minimal attorneys fees are conscionable. . . .
>
> At oral argument, Anthony G. Graham proudly proclaimed that he was a "bounty hunter. The statute was created for me." We will have more to say about exactly who Proposition 65 was created for later, but it wasn't bounty hunters. [First clue: the court believes it was created to protect the general public]. . .
>
> We are not the first to use the allusion to extortion to describe this litigation.

And that's just the light stuff. Presiding Justice David Sills has some strong opinions about what he calls the "shakedown litigation" of Proposition 65, and lets the plaintiff have it with both barrels.

To add insult to injury, he dismissed the two related cases in Footnote 23, the final footnote in the opinion. Not many cases get dismissed after an appeal, and even fewer by way of a footnote. Justice Sill's parting shot in the footnote? "We leave the parties *in pari delicto*" (that is, in equal fault).

I'm surprised he didn't also award attorneys fees to the attorney general, who objected to the settlements and filed this appeal.

The problem started when the Consumer Defense Group (CDG) sent a batch of notices of intent to sue to various apartment owners around the state, and then entered into settlements designed to provide the maximum protection from future Prop 65 litigation. The real problem came, however, when CDG and the law firm accepted some $540,000 in attorney fees to provide the "protection". The court accused CDG and Attorney Graham of falsification of time records and of not actually undertaking the required investigations that led to the lawsuits.

Ouch.

The undoing of the lawsuits, however, was the notice of intent to sue. It was so vague that in the court's opinion, it could apply to every building in the state. No wonder the attorney general was so worked up.

⁕

Of course, before you commit to an attorney, you might want to do a little research. It's always a good idea to make sure of some certain fundamental facts.

Lawyers spend a great deal of their time shoveling smoke.
—Oliver Wendell Holmes

Is Your Attorney Really an Attorney?

An "attorney" in the Bronx Public Defender's Office "practiced" for four years, handling thousands of cases.

The quotation marks are there for a reason. Turns out the "attorney," Diane Shamis, was not an actual attorney. The bar association found out when one of her clients filed a complaint against her, and she didn't show up on the statebar's list of attorneys.

That was their first clue. Apparently, the Bronx Public Defender's Office, who did not return phone calls to a news reporter asking for comments, failed to check her credentials when they hired her. When the public defender found out, she was fired on the spot.

Now, they're calling the thousands of clients to let them know about the mix-up. It is unclear whether the cases will be relitigated or overturned. At least one of the cases she handled has been overturned.

Though she faced up to a year in jail, she was only fined $500 and given a conditional discharge. Perhaps, though, it's not that much of a mix-up. Her attorney, Marvin Raskin, said she graduated from law school and passed the bar, but did not fill out the proper paperwork to get her credentials. "At this point in time, we are attempting to resolve the issues of admission to the bar as expeditiously as possible, given the circumstances of this unfortunate situation," Raskin said.

Not sure if your lawyer is really a lawyer? You can always check with your state bar association. A complete list of state bar associations can be found at *www.job-hunt.org/associations/legal associations_state_bars.shtml* or *http://tinyurl.com/2x786s*.

⌗⌗⌗

Of course, having a real-life, genuine attorney is no guarantee that there won't be any screw ups. For example, check out this next case, where marine life makes a surprise appearance in an otherwise unremarkable case.

I respect a man who knows how to spell a word more than one way. —Mark Twain

There's Something Fishy Going On: Sea Sponges Take Over Brief

Hold on to your computer mouse before you hit "Replace All" on your word processor's spell check. Here's a story that will make any spell-check conscious lawyer cringe.

A Santa Cruz solo practitioner representing a judge, now retired from the bench, sought reversal of the judge's somewhat forced resignation due to a flap over traffic ticket convictions. The lawyer submitted a brief to the Court of Appeals and dutifully ran a spell check before submitting it. The brief contained the Latin words *sua sponte*, which mean "of one's own will," and are commonly used by lawyers to refer to a court's power to do something on its own.

After submitting the brief, he got a call from his client, the former judge, asking for an explanation of the Latin phrase *sea sponge*.

A side note here, and although I haven't taken Latin classes in a while, *sea sponge* isn't Latin.

Turns out that the lawyer was using WordPerfect, which doesn't have the Latin phrase *sua sponte* in its dictionary.

The program does, however, think that *sua* was probably meant to refer to *sea*, and because you've been paying attention so far—yep, you guessed it—WordPerfect also thought *sponte* was supposed to be *sponge*.

When the lawyer clicked "Replace All" while spell-checking those two words, the word processor replaced *sua sponte* five times, and gave the brief such gems as: "An appropriate instruction limiting the judge's criminal liability in such a prosecution must be given sea sponge explaining that certain acts or omissions by themselves are not sufficient to support a conviction," as well as "It is well settled that a trial court must instruct sea sponge on any defense, including a mistake of fact defense."

⚜

Licensing requirements are one way to weed out incompetent professionals. The theory goes that if someone is licensed, then he or she must have at some point demonstrated at least a minimum level of competence.

Not all professions, however, are held to equal standards. Licensing requirements for attorneys vary wildly across the nation and other countries, which may not be the most comforting news in the world, especially if you're looking for someone to represent you.

Here in Hollywood you can actually get a marriage license printed on an Etch-A-Sketch. —Dennis Miller

Hairdressers, Yes. Lawyers, No: Investigating Professional Licenses

Certainly some large law firms have been duped by law school graduates claiming to be lawyers even though the graduates haven't passed the bar, and surely small firms have had the same experience. Most troubling, however, is the effect such circumstances have had on the general public.

New York is taking a step toward making unlicensed individuals claiming to be lawyers subject to the same criminal penalties as unlicensed individuals who claim to be doctors or other professionals, such as architects and accountants.

You might have thought that would already be the case. Impersonate a doctor in New York, and you're likely to be staring down a felony charge if this new bill passes. Impersonate a lawyer, however, and apparently it's now just a misdemeanor.

In California, an individual impersonating a lawyer can be charged with a misdemeanor and subjected to up to one year in a county jail and a $1,000 fine. Not much compared to some of the damage that can be done by those purporting to be lawyers.

In one case, a large law firm refunded almost $300,000 in fees incurred by a so-called lawyer who turned out not to be one. Even entire firms from out of state have gotten in trouble. Maybe here it will become a felony too, instead of a slap on the wrist and a minor payment.

Oh, and if you're wondering—yes, I'm licensed: in California, Washington, Iowa, and Massachusetts, and a gaggle of federal courts.

⌘

Of course, representation costs money, and good representation costs more. Sometimes the price tag for even the most basic counsel is beyond reach, and people wind up representing themselves.

As you'll read in this next case, that's not necessarily the ideal option for most people. Consider whether a pro se defendant filed a rather unique appeal really had the best lawyer.

We filed the federal suit because we are completely discriminated against and they refuse to follow the law for pro se women. We have taken our case all the way to the Illinois Supreme Court and been denied our due process rights and equal protection under the law. —Erin McRaith

Maybe It Would Have Been Wiser to Hire a Lawyer

Judges recognize that, at most, they can make only half of the parties in a case happy. Someone has to lose, after all, and even then their rulings frequently make both sides unhappy.

Lawyers are used to it; we regularly appear in front of judges, and after a while, we, too, recognize you can't win 'em all, either.

Without that experience, however, it becomes difficult to stomach a losing ruling, as in pro per or pro se (both terms are

Latin for "for one's self" and "for self, respectively") litigant George C. Swinger, Jr., aptly points out in his handwritten appeal:

> I hereby am informing you that I am appealing the asshole [judge] Ronald B. Leighton's decision in this matter.
>
> You have been hereby served notice. You're not getting away with this shit that easy.
>
> Signed this 10th day of July 2006
> George C. Swinger, Jr.
> Plaintiff/Pro Se

And shock of all shocks, U.S. District Court Judge Leighton's opinion in the Western District of Washington was upheld.

⁓⊗⁓

As you can imagine, would-be attorneys like the one in the previous case don't generally do too well. Still, some people have no option but to defend themselves—or trust to the services of a novice attorney. One court, however, is trying to help make the best of a bad situation. You might find it to be a rather provocative read.

Experience is the name everyone gives to their mistakes.
—Oscar Wilde

A Helping Hand for New Lawyers

Access to lawyers is expensive. So it's no wonder that people end up representing themselves. In legal parlance, we call it pro se litigation, as we discussed briefly in the previous case with Mr. Swinger.

It turns out to be the bane of courts, because nonlawyers rarely understand the procedure involved with litigation. Admittedly, it's frequently complicated for lawyers.

So it's not surprising that courts are trying to do something about it. Nationally, *pro se* litigants make up nearly half of all appeals filed. Likely there's a large percentage of those who are "jailhouse lawyers", (prisoners who are not really lawyers but have access to the prison law library) but still, half is a big number.

The Ninth Circuit has an information packet for *pro se* appellants. The Circuit has also proposed some rule changes designed to make it easier on *pro se* appellants by not requiring filing of certain documents.

Of course, as a pro (not a *pro se*), I have to say, I'd like to get that same break!

Former Chief Judge Mary Schroeder prepared a task force report that makes additional recommendations to ease the burden on the court and pro se appellants. Those recommendations include instructions to the lower courts to:

- Coordinate with law schools and consider using law school students to help represent *pro se* litigants, with students possibly earning credit for their work.
- Make it easy for law firms to accept *pro bono* cases by either pitching *pro se* cases as good training for young lawyers, issuing success-based fee awards or reimbursing attorneys' out-of-pocket expenses.

I like the idea of law students helping. I did that during law school, and ended up with a case in front of the Iowa Supreme Court, which was a very valuable experience.

What's really interesting is that while the Ninth Circuit is busy helping *pro se* litigants, it is also doing the same for inexperienced attorneys.

What does that tell you about the court's thoughts on the quality of practice in front of it?

❧

Now we move from those who can't afford representation to arguing who collects the money when there's a settlement on the table. This next situation is an imported case from across the pond, but we might as well look at the concepts now. They'll travel across the Atlantic soon enough.

To escape jury duty in England, wear a bowler hat and carry a copy of the DailyTelegraph. —John Mortimer

Keep a Stiff Upper Lip, Old Chap, and Pay My Fee

I don't know which is worse: contingency lawyers who want more money or insurance companies that won't pay. Across the big pond, solicitors and insurers got into a *wrangle* (that's British for fight, I guess) over no-win, no-fee cases.

First introduced in England and Wales in 1995, the no-win, no-fee program was designed to replace legal-aid funding for low-end tort cases, such as traffic accidents and the like. The idea was to encourage solicitors (a British term for lawyer) to take the case to earn a contingency fee.

The argument between the lawyers and insurers centered on—what else—money. In this case, it was how much the insurers had to pay the lawyers upon a win.

Reporter, not actress, Maureen O'Hara, of the *Guardian,* informs us that lawyers have now agreed to take 12.5 percent of a settlement as a fee, and the insurers have agreed to pay that rate. Insurers had been holding up payments to solicitors for the past two years because they believed the success fees taken before the agreement were too high.

Too high? On this side of the pond, contingency lawyers get anywhere between 20 to 50 percent of the deal, and no-win, no-fee has been part of the deal all along.

Of course, we don't have the English version of legal aid funding for tort cases. Not yet.

Heaven help us. Now someone over here will probably get that bright idea.

In England, however, the rule is that the loser pays the winner's fees. Some in the United States argue for application of the so-called English Rule. Some have even argued that because American lawyers have such an upside, they ought to also have the downside of paying the winner when they lose.

Talk about tort reform. With those rules in place, none would be needed.

No matter how you pay your attorney—via retainer, on an hourly basis, or on contingency, as just discussed—you want to know you're getting value for your money. There's a certain expectation that your lawyer will go to bat for you and do his or her best to defend you in court.

If those expectations aren't met, then what recourse do you have? I don't know about you, but if this next attorney was representing me, then I think I might be asking for my money back!

You go through a lot of these steps in any trial, criminal or civil, to build your record in case you get an adverse result.
—Gary Brown

What? You Want Me in the Courtroom?

In my practice, I occasionally handle white-collar criminal cases, mostly for companies and executives charged with environmental crimes. It's kind of a niche practice, so chances are you won't need me. But if you do, then I'm going to be there throughout the entire case, including the trial, if it ever comes to that point. That's what you pay for, and that's what I do.

Apparently not all lawyers agree with that philosophy, including New York attorney Bruce Cutler, who's carpetbagging and represented Phil Spector in his criminal trial in Los Angeles County Superior Court. Cutler was, at one point, the lead trial attorney for Mr. Spector, who was charged with murder.

Cutler, according to an Associated Press (AP) article, was off filming a new TV show, *Jury Duty,* during the trial. It's not a violation of his ethical duties, and assuming he has his client's permission, and he's otherwise complied with the Rules of Professional Conduct.

Did I mention that the lead attorney representing the defendant, who is charged with murder, was not in the courtroom during the trial?

Even so, according to Linda Deutsch's AP article, "Cutler vowed Monday to deliver the closing argument in the Spector trial even though he will not have been in court for much of the defense case. He said he has been watching the trial on TV and reading transcripts of testimony."

Watching it on TV? Reading transcripts? What's wrong with being in the courtroom?

Oh, I forgot. Mr. Cutler is the star of a new TV show. He told the AP, "I decided to do this because it's motivational and educational, and it's fun," he said. "It's good to have fun sometimes."

It's also good to be in court representing your client during a murder trial. But that's just my opinion. We'll never know whether Cutler's closing would have acquitted Spector in his first, hung-jury trial because Spector replaced him with another lawyer.

⌘

Maybe you expect your attorney to show up in the courtroom. Chances are you also expect him or her to talk a lot and generate many, many legal documents. But you can have too much of a good thing, as this next case shows.

We plan to refile in Stanislaus County and file this time with a lengthy legal brief educating the jurors themselves, written in English, so they can understand what the issue of subject matter jurisdiction is all about. We don't expect them to understand it, they've only listened to one attorney and he's the attorney we believed was already corrupted, this proves it. —Jim Robinson

They're Called Briefs for a Reason

Only lawyers and judges get excited about procedural rules and writing niceties, so if you don't fall into one of those categories, you may want to skip to the next heading. But if you're truly a writing geek, then you will appreciate Ohio Appellate Court Justice Mark Pointer's opinion, ruling on a motion filed by one set of lawyers complaining the other lawyers' appeal brief was too long.

Pointer, an author of at least three books on legal writing, says it best (edited for conciseness):

Not wishing to let stand a brief they consider too long, counsel for appellant M&M Metals International, Inc., have moved this court to strike [the insurance companies'] joint brief.

M&M advances two arguments, contending the brief (1) put the citations in footnotes (where they belong!); and (2) uses footnotes to "get around" the page limit. And counsel even goes so far as to redraft their opponent's brief, inserting the jumble of letters and numbers into the paragraphs—even the references to the record. Thus bollixed up and unreadable, the brief comes out to 38.5 pages, instead of the regulation 35. Egad!

Our dreary day has been enlivened by the thought that lawyers care about one another's prose so much as to redraft it. And that this dispute is so close that it may turn on a few extra pages of a lawyer's argument. We can't wait to read the final version—or maybe we should wait for the movie.

As to citations, they belong in footnotes. Putting goofy letters and numbers in the middle of paragraphs destroys readability. We had to do that with typewriters, just as we had to use underlining because typewriters did not have italics. No more.

We venture a guess that this court's eventual opinion resolving this dispute will be fewer than 20 pages. To both sides we suggest that less is usually more.

And because three judges of the appellate court have nothing better to do than referee a dispute about brief formatting, we [allow the insurance companies' brief to remain filed]; and,

Now that the pleadings are complete, perhaps the case can be decided on its merits.

So ordered.

Wow. Judges trying to get to the merits of a case. You have to wonder what the lawyers wanted. Billing by the word as Abraham Lincoln did. After all, he charged a penny award.

◦❧◦

We've talked a little bit about how much attorneys charge for their services. The bills are high, there's no doubt about it. But what can be done?

You don't really have any recourse when facing that sky-high representation bill.

Or do you?

You can't fire me, I quit. —Anonymous

They Said It Couldn't Be Done: Lawyer Disbarred for Overbilling

You've heard the one about St. Peter meeting the lawyer at the pearly gates? St. Peter expresses surprise that the lawyer took so long to get there. The lawyer asks why, and St. Peter responds, "According to your billing records, you should have been here years ago."

There's some truth behind every joke, according to some, and perhaps this one presents a grain or two. Seems as though a lawyer, Bobby Glenn Adkins, Jr., billed his clients for defending himself against their complaints to the bar about his billing practices.

In this case, the bill to his clients for defending himself was for $40.00.

Yep, he was disbarred by the Georgia Supreme Court, most likely because this was the third time he found himself in front of that court defending against charges of overbilling.

To add insult to injury, he defended himself in the disbarment proceedings.

Not that he didn't get a chance to avoid disbarment. Bar authorities proposed a plea bargain agreement that required Adkins to admit to illegal conduct and accept a reprimand by the Georgia Bar's ethics review panel.

Adkins refused, he said, because he doesn't think he did anything wrong: "I wouldn't capitulate to their draconian demands."

Instead, he got disbarred. Nothing draconian about that.

∽⦿∾

Adkins's bills were too high, but a bill that's too low can be a sign of trouble, as well. If you're faced with a surprisingly cheap total, then you might want to investigate a little further. After all, there's a little bit of truth in the saying:

Compromise is the best and cheapest lawyer. —Robert Stevenson

You Get What You Pay For

When you pay someone $100 to fight an eviction or ten bucks to fight a traffic ticket, you may want to ask the person doing the work to see his or her bar license. That person probably doesn't have one, and the low fee may be your first clue.

But when George Robotis appeared in an Illinois criminal court, Judge John Kirby noticed that the "lawyer" hadn't included his bar number on the pleading he filed to represent a criminal defendant. That omission was the second clue. The judge asked him for his bar number, and according to Eric Herman of the *Chicago Sun-Times*, who had a source in the courtroom, Mr. Robotis responded, "Oh, I'm not an attorney."

The judge promptly locked up Mr. Robotis, who went to jail under $75,000 bail. He was charged with one misdemeanor count, and it's likely more will follow. He's been "representing" people for over a year, not only in Illinois, but also in Indiana.

The sheriff says Mr. Robotis has an extensive criminal record, stretching to some 30 convictions, which include 23 for larceny, robbery, narcotics, and weapons charges. One guess where he picked up his legal knowledge.

Yup. That's just the kind of "lawyer" I want to hire. A bargain at twice the price.

Seriously Now: Lessons Learned

Hiring a lawyer is a highly personal choice. It's important that you find someone you trust and who communicates well. As noted above, it's likewise important that you hire one who's licensed. Check with the bar association or Supreme Court in your state. Practically all of them have online databases you can search to see whether your lawyer is licensed or has been disciplined for any untoward conduct.

If you need one and don't know a lawyer, then ask around. Your friends, business associates, and family may be able to give you some recommendations. Otherwise, there's an online service called *www.avvo.com* that ranks lawyers in various states. At the time this book was written, the service was not yet available for all 50 states, but they're expanding quickly. If you want to see how it works for comparison purposes, then go to *www.avvo.com*, and on the search tab, click "Lawyer name" (instead of "Legal practice area"), then enter *J. Craig* in the "First name" box and *Williams* in the "Last name" box, and for the "City, state, or zip code" box enter 92660, the ZIP code for Newport Beach, California. You'll have to scroll down slightly, but that search will yield results that include me, and that profile will give you an idea how Avvo's ranking system works.

When you're looking for a lawyer, the general considerations include where the lawyer went to school; what honors, qualifications, and experience the lawyer has; and perhaps most important, whether the lawyer practices the kind of law you need. We're like doctors. We all specialize or concentrate to some degree in particular areas of the law. Sure there are generalists, and that may be just the ticket you need. But if you're getting a divorce, you don't want to hire a lawyer that handles Securities and Exchange Commission regulations for big companies.

Interview your potential lawyer, look at the law firm's Web site and read the lawyer's biography, and check with the state bar. Ask how the fees and costs are to be paid and be prepared to sign a written retainer agreement defining your relationship with your lawyer. Some lawyers are willing to take cases on contingency, where they absorb the fees up front, but share in the reward (if there is one) at the end of the case. Other lawyers accept only hourly fees, and a few may work on a flat-fee basis. Flat fees are generally only offered for a defined scope of work, such as forming a corporation, drafting a will or trust, and the like. Lawyers typically don't offer flat-fee payment arrangements to handle lawsuits.

You also may want to check out the lawyer's writing, because it's likely writing will be the great majority of the work the lawyer performs for you. Most, if not all, lawyers can give you a writing sample of something they've filed with a court or some otherwise public document. Beyond the basics of typos, grammar errors, and spelling mistakes, look to see if you understand what the lawyer is saying. Chances are if you don't, then the judge won't, either.

Here's my test when I'm considering hiring a new lawyer: We look at the writing sample of a legal brief to see whether the first paragraph clearly communicates what the lawyer wants the judge to do for the client and why the client is entitled to the relief sought. That's it, plain and simple. If it's not there, then I don't look further for it, because most judges won't, either. We won't hire a lawyer who can't clearly communicate those two points in the first paragraph, and preferably in the first sentence or two.

Step 3

Go in Front of the Judge

Chapter 12

Tell It to the Judge

Cause determined and, counsel selected, you're now ready to go. It's time to present your case to the judge. This step is where the rubber meets the road, where your (or your lawyer's) carefully constructed arguments meet the harsh light of reality.

Sometimes this step is a good thing, especially if opposing counsel's arguments succeed in making their side look bad and your side look wonderful. Some lawyers, however, fail to endear themselves to the judge—and some decisions will leave you scratching your head in confusion.

Let's also take a brief look at the lengths people will go to avoid jury duty. At this point, all you can do is hold your breath and make a wish that you've done a good job with the first two steps.

It's time to face the music!

⟪⟫

Judges really are a breed unto themselves. I've had the honor of appearing in front of some of the most colorful individuals to ever hold a gavel, but I have to admit that none of them could hold a candle to the guy in our next case.

Play it straight, come out with the simple truth: He was abducted by space aliens, taken aboard their flying saucer and subjected to various probes. —Scott Ostler

Aliens Captured Me, Took Me up to Their Spaceship, and Then...

You're simply not going to believe what happened next. "The state of New Jersey injected me in the left eye with a radium laser beam, and now I hear voices in my head."

That's Ned Searight talking, way back in 1976, and he sued the state of New Jersey, claiming it owed him—I know you'll never guess it, so I'll just come right out and say it—money.

No kidding. You don't say ... ? Is there a police officer nearby? (At least that was my first reaction.)

Judge Vincent Pasquale Biunno, God rest his soul, had to struggle with this in pro per lawsuit (that is, he didn't get any help from a jury), but after reading the following excerpt, you may wonder which of the two was beamed up. Judge Biunno refused to hear the case, passing it off in stead to the FCC. Here's the judge's own observations in the case.

> But, taking the facts as pleaded, and assuming them to be true, they show a case of presumably unlicensed radio communication, a matter which comes within the sole jurisdiction of the Federal Communications Commission, 47 U.S.C. § 151, *et seq.*
>
> And even aside from that, Searight could have blocked the broadcast to the antenna in his brain simply by grounding it. See, for example, *Ghirardi, Modern Radio Servicing,* First Edition, p. 572, ff. (Radio & Technical Publishing Co., New York, 1935). Just as delivery trucks for oil and gasoline are "grounded" against the accumulation of charges of static electricity, so on the same principle Searight might have pinned to the back of a trouser leg a short chain of paper clips so that the end would touch the ground and prevent anyone from talking to him inside his brain.

Right, your honor. Let me get out my tinfoil antenna hat.

Of course, you have to have a little sympathy for the judiciary. They didn't wake up one day stringing paperclips together to keep the alien transmissions away. It's a long, slow process to reach that state, composed largely of listening to cases like this next one.

The beauty of religious mania is that it has the power to explain everything. Once God—or Satan—is accepted as the first cause of everything which happens in the mortal world, nothing is left to chance...logic can be happily tossed out the window.
—Stephen King

Maybe He Should Have Waited until *The Devil's Advocate* Came Out

Gerald Mayo is a troubled soul. In fact, he's so troubled he tried to sue not only Satan, but also Satan's staff, in a Pennsylvania federal court, back in 1971.

Surely there's a class-action lawyer somewhere who wants to get in on his act.

Think about it. Here are our hero's allegations, right out of his complaint: "Satan has on numerous occasions caused plaintiff misery and unwarranted threats, against the will of plaintiff, and Satan has placed deliberate obstacles in plaintiff's path and caused plaintiff's downfall."

And who hasn't suffered at the hands of Satan and his staff?

The court, however, would have no truck with Mr. Mayo's claim or his attempt to help the rest of us out. But hold on, here. Think about it for a moment.

Imagine a world where the court issued an injunction against Satan and his staff to stop causing misery, making threats and placing obstacles in our path. *Imagine*, as John Lennon sang.

In seven short paragraphs—less than one page—however, the court killed off his lawsuit by not allowing him to file it on his own. Despite my prior speculation, however, apparently no lawyer signed on to take his case.

In ruling on Mr. Mayo's case, the court said,

> Even if plaintiff's complaint reveals a *prima facie* [Latin for "at first view"] recital of the infringement of the civil rights of a citizen of the United

States, the court has serious doubts that the complaint reveals a cause of action upon which relief can be granted by the court. We question whether plaintiff may obtain personal jurisdiction over the defendant in this judicial district. The complaint contains no allegation of residence in this district.

While the official reports disclose no case where this defendant has appeared as defendant, there is an unofficial account of a trial in New Hampshire where this defendant filed an action of mortgage foreclosure as plaintiff [*The Devil and Daniel Webster*]. The defendant in that action was represented by the preeminent advocate of that day, and raised the defense that the plaintiff was a foreign prince with no standing to sue in an American Court. This defense was overcome by overwhelming evidence to the contrary. Whether or not this would raise an estoppel in the present case, we are unable to determine at this time.

If such action were to be allowed, we would also face the question of whether it may be maintained as a class action. It appears to meet the requirements of Fed. R. of Civ. P. 23 that the class is so numerous that joinder of all members is impracticable, there are questions of law and fact common to the class, and the claims of the representative party is typical of the claims of the class. We cannot now determine if the representative party will fairly protect the interests of the class.

We note that the plaintiff has failed to include with his complaint the required form of instructions for the United States Marshal for directions as to service of process [an satan].

For the foregoing reasons we must exercise our discretion to refuse the prayer of plaintiff to proceed *in forma pauperis* [Latin for "in the form of a pauper"].

And I thought federal judges had unlimited power. Guess not. Maybe he should have tried to sue God, instead.

Oh, right. They already made that movie.

～●●●～

The relationship between your attorney and opposing counsel can have a big impact on the outcome of your case. After all, if the lawyers are too busy sniping at each other to pay attention to you, the judge, or anything else, then how well can things turn out?

I don't think highly of this kind of behavior, and neither does Judge Sam Sparks. He's seen better behavior from little children, and he's not afraid to say so.

You can only be young once. But you can always be immature.
—Dave Barry

Kindergarten and Sandbox Litigators

In the past, I've called it sandbox litigation. You know, the kind where the fight gets personal between opposing counsel. Here, the fight is in Texas, and like the state, it's pretty big.

In one corner, we have William Davidson, local counsel, with lead counsel Irwin Gilbert. On the other, we have Richard Milvenan and an associate at Vinson & Elkins, a nearly 100-year-old law firm based in Houston with offices around the world.

Apparently, the two sides can't get along. Texas federal district court judge, Sam Sparks, who has a reputation of his own, has blasted the lawyers. He's been a judge for a while, so this missive should not have come as a surprise to these litigators.

As could have been expected, Judge Sparks did it again, and this time with a little more flair. You know it's not good when the order starts out:

> When the undersigned accepted the appointment from the president of the United States of the position now held, he was ready to face the daily practice of law in federal courts with presumably competent lawyers. No one warned the undersigned that in many instances his responsibility would be the same as a person who supervised kindergarten.

Yee-ouch. It sounds like it's naptime for everyone involved!

⁓◈◈⁓

While we're on the topic of kindergarten, let's take a look at everybody's favorite children's author, Dr. Seuss, and the rare cases where he shows up in the courtroom.

Restrict bankruptcy rules. —Jerry Weller

Bankruptcy, Dr. Seuss-Style

Congress recently changed the bankruptcy laws, leaving many judges and practitioners scratching their collective heads over the meaning of some of the new laws. One statute in particular troubled Florida Bankruptcy Judge A. Jay Cristol. He noticed 11 U.S. Code section 521(a)(1) required automatic dismissal if the bankruptcy debtor had not filed certain paperwork by the 46th day after filing a bankruptcy petition.

As most lawyers know, virtually nothing is ever done in court without a judge's order (or sometimes by certain clerks). In other words, *automatic* really isn't in the legal lexicon. In one case pending before him, *In re: Riddle*, 344 B.R. 702 (Bankr. S.D. Fla. 2006), Judge Cristol took to a Seuss-style rhyme to convince Congress to fix the word in the statute, excerpted here:

> I do not like dismissal automatic,
> It seems to me to be traumatic.
> I do not like it in this case,
> I do not like it any place.
>
> As a judge I am most keen
> To understand, *What does it mean?*
> How can any person know
> What the docket does not show?
>
> What is the clue on the 46th day?
> Is this case still here, or gone away?
> And if the debtor did not do
> What the Code had told him to
> And no concerned party knew it,
> Still the Code says the debtor blew it.
> What that is what it seems to say;
> The debtor's case is then *"Oy vay!"*

...

What does automatic dismissal mean?
And by what means can it be seen?
Are we only left to guess?
Oh please Congress, fix this mess!
Until it's fixed what should I do?
How can I explain this mess to you?

If the Code required an old-fashioned order
That would create a legal border,
With complying debtor's cases defended
And 521 violator's cases ended
From the unknown status of dismissal automatic
To the certainty of a status charismatic
The dismissal automatic problem would be gone
And debtors, trustees, and courts could move on.

Mr. and Mrs. Riddle had, in fact, filed their required papers in time, and Judge Cristol did not dismiss their case. But he chose the right case name to pose the requested fix to Congress.

⁂

While we're on the Dr. Seuss theme, let's take a look at a legalistic reinterpretation of what may be the good doctor's most famous book, *Green Eggs and Ham.*

Green Eggs and Ham *was the story of my life. I wouldn't eat a thing when I was a kid, but Dr. Seuss inspired me to try cauliflower.* —Jim Carrey

Judicial Ham and Eggs

Charles Jay Wolff is a 61-year-old, Concord, New Hampshire, inmate currently serving ten to twenty years for felony aggravated sexual assault of a minor. Mr. Wolff claims he is entitled to receive a kosher diet while in prison. He claimed he couldn't stomach hardboiled eggs, but the prison kept serving them to him. Wolff's petition alleges the prison's director of food services, Jeff Perkins, took away his kosher diet after discovering Wolff ate nonkosher ice cream, though Wolff alleges the ice cream was, in fact kosher. Not surprisingly, he received no sympathy from the warden, so Wolff sued and filed papers in court, seeking $10 million in damages.

In support of his petition for a special diet, he attached a hard-boiled egg to his pleadings to prove his point. Not amused, the federal magistrate judge assigned to the matter struck the egg from the pleadings, and did so in style. Here's a word-for-word transcript of his order.

No fan I am
Of the egg at hand.
Just like no ham
On the kosher plan.

This egg will rot
I kid you not.
And stink it can
This egg at hand.

There will be no eggs at court
To prove a clog in your aort.
There will be no eggs accepted.
Objections all will be rejected.

From this day forth
This court will ban
Hard-boiled eggs of any brand.
And if you should not understand
The meaning of the ban at hand
Then you should contact either Dan,
The deputy clerk, or my clerk Jan.

I do not like eggs in the file.
I do not like them in any style.
I will not take them fried or boiled.
I will not take them poached or broiled.
I will not take them soft or scrambled
Despite an argument well-rambled.

No fan I am
Of the egg at hand.
Destroy that egg!

Today! Today!
Today I say! Without delay.

It is so ordered (with apologies to Dr. Seuss).

James R. Muirhead, United States Magistrate Judge

Unverified reports claim the egg was indeed green by the time it arrived in court. It was tossed out rather unceremoniously by the clerk.

༺༻

Lest you think that the honorable members of America's judiciary never made it past kindergarten or grade school–level reading, rest assured that that is not the case. In fact, some judges are quite accomplished poets, as you can see here.

I think that I shall never see/A poem lovely as a tree/ Poems are made by fools like me,/ But only God can make a tree. —Joyce Kilmer

Ode on a Tree; Ode on a Judicial Opinion

Keats aside, three judges in Michigan thought they'd pass on an appeal seeking to overturn a judgment against a tree owner and in favor of the driver of a car who hit the tree and the driver's insurance company. In the case of *Fisher v. Lowe, Moffett and State Farm Ins.*, 122 Mich. App. 418, 33 N.W.2d 67 (1983), they rhymed:

We thought that we would never see
A suit to compensate a tree.

A suit whose claim in tort is prest
Upon a mangled tree's behest;

A tree whose battered trunk was prest
Against a Chevy's crumpled crest;

A tree that faces each new day
With bark and limb in disarray;

A tree that may forever bear
A lasting need for tender care.

Flora lovers though we three,
We must uphold the court's decree.

Affirmed.

For every opinion, West Publishing typically writes a short summary of the case with all of the procedural details, including the name of the trial judge and the names of the appellate justices, and then provides links to other similar opinions. The summary is generally known as a set of "headnotes." The editors, however, apparently couldn't resist some repartee with the Court of Appeals. In turn, the editors wrote in the syllabus:

A wayward Chevy struck a tree
Whose owner sued defendants three.
He sued car's owner, driver two,
And insurer for what was due
For his oak tree that now may bear
A lasting need for tender care.
The Oakland County Circuit Court,
John N. O'Brien, J., set forth
The judgment that defendants sought
And quickly an appeal was brought.

Court of Appeals, J. H. Gillis, J.,
Gave thought and then had this to say:
1) There is no liability
    Since No-Fault grants immunity;
2) No jurisdiction can be found
    Where process service is unsound;
And thus the judgment, as it's termed,
Is due to be, and is, affirmed.

No. I'm not going to rhyme a coda. I'm a writer, not a poet…don't you know it?

You might want to send a little sympathy your attorney's way. She's not in the easiest position in the world, especially now that attorneys are expected to call federal judges on the carpet.

If I had to live my life again, I'd make the same mistakes, only sooner. —Tallulah Bankhead

Trading Lightning Bolts with Federal Judges

Have you ever tried to correct a federal court judge? You know, the ones with the lifetime appointment, and who are not subject to losing their jobs for anything other than perhaps their own mistakes or high crimes and misdemeanors?

After grabbing a lightning bolt and tossing it at you, their response is something akin to, "If you don't like it, then you know where to go," and they're usually referring to the appeals court, not down to the netherworld, though that destination is an equally possible meaning.

In other words, federal judges are accountable to virtually no one except the various circuits. And who holds them accountable?

Anyway, enough with my soapbox. Besides, not all federal judges are cantankerous. Some are actually nice, and a select few are very nice.

No, my objection is not so much the lack of supervision over the federal judiciary, but more about a pair of cases from the Third Circuit, *Caprio v. Bell Atlantic Sickness and Accident Plan* and *U.S. v. D'Angelico*. The court said, "In future cases where the district court overlooks the [proper] procedure, ...the parties should not hesitate to bring that to the court's attention."

Now, apparently, we lawyers are required to correct mistakes in the trial court. Sure, we can object, and argue the point, but I wasn't aware that Congress suddenly endowed us lawyers with the ability to actually tell a federal judge what to do.

That's like trying to herd cats, except these cats have big teeth.

I already speak up when I'm in court. Maybe now, I'll start throwing those lightning bolts back.

⁓⊰⊱⁓

If that's not enough, then you can, if you're an attorney, run the risk of alienating a judge with what seems like a simple request. In this case, we see what happens when an East Coast attorney forgot the central tenet of Southwestern law: Don't Mess with Texas!

Give me an army of West Point graduates and I'll win a battle. Give me a handful of Texas Aggies, and I'll win the war. —General George S. Patton

Judge Kent Takes the Bench, Pen in Hand—and by the Way, Don't Mess with This End of Texas

We can always count on Galveston's U.S. District Court Judge Samuel B. Kent to skewer the litigants and their attorneys with his prose, and the case of *Smith v. Colonial Penn Insurance* (1996), 943 F.Supp. 782, is no exception.

The Pennsylvania insurance company's lawyer filed a motion to change venue from Galveston to Houston because Galveston did not have a commercial airport, which required the East Coast party and its lawyer to make a 40-mile trip from Houston's Hobby Airport to the Galveston courthouse.

Judge Kent sharpened his quill for this ruling, first recognizing that folks back east have a different perspective on travel: "…but in this vast state of Texas, such a travel distance would not be viewed with any surprise or consternation," and this footnote: "The sun is 'rize, the sun is set, and we is still in Texas yet!" Judge Kent continued;

> Defendant should be assured that it is not embarking on a three-week-long trip via covered wagons when it travels to Galveston. Rather, Defendant will be pleased to discover that the highway is paved

and lighted all the way to Galveston, and thanks to the efforts of this
Court's predecessor, Judge Roy Bean, the trip should be free of rus-
tlers, hooligans, or vicious varmints of unsavory kind.

In fact, it appears Judge Kent is quite fond of the surrounding
countryside: "The Court notes that any inconvenience suffered in
having to drive to Galveston may likely be offset by the peaceful-
ness of the ride and the scenic beauty of the sunny isle."

He wrapped up his denial of the motion with this gem: "Alas,
this Court's kingdom for a commercial airport," and this footnote:
"Defendant will again be pleased to know that regular limousine service is available from Hobby Airport, even to the steps of this humble
courthouse, which has got lights, indoor plummin', 'lectric doors, and
all sorts of new stuff, almost like them big courthouses back East."

Howdy, pardner. Welcome to Texas.

⌘

Sometimes courtrooms are the scene of unintentional humor.
Consider the following.

***Well, take the word friendly out of it because it is England versus
Wales.*** —Shaun Edwards

Strangers in a Courtroom

Straight in from the appellate courts are these case names:

- *United States v. Caesar*, 368 F.Supp. 328 (1973)
- *United States v. Estate of Grace*, 395 U.S. 316 (1969)
- *In re: Love*, 61 B.R. 558 (Bankr. S.D. Fla. 1986)
- *Truelove v. Truelove*, 855 N.E.2d 311 (Ind. Ct. App. 2006)
- *Silver v. Gold*, 211 Cal.App.3d 17, 259 Cal.Rptr. 185 (1989)
- *State of Indiana v. Virtue*, 658 N.E.2d 605 (1995)
- *Plough v. Fields*, 422 F.2d 824 (9th Cir. 1970)

⌘

Judges may be hard on attorneys, but they're not necessarily
any kinder to the defendants who appear in front of them. In this

next case, a criminal thought he had a witty response to a judge's inquiry.

No, I was not born under a rhyming planet. —William Shakespeare

Judges Not Only Rhyme, but They Also Sing

The drudgery of sentencing petty crimes all day, day after day, tends to drive some judges crazy, and unless assigned to another, more interesting, court calendar, judges look for something to make the job more interesting. That's certainly true for Montana 13th District Court Judge Gregory R. Todd, sitting in Department 4, in Yellowstone County, who likely had enough one fine day.

Defendant Andrew McCormack thought he'd be cute when Judge Todd asked for his recommendation for a sentence for stealing beer, and said, "Let it be." Judge Todd didn't take kindly to McCormack's suggestion to do nothing. In *Montana v. Andrew McCormack*, Judge Todd handed down probation, community service, and a fine.

But it's how he got there in his February 26 sentencing memorandum where the drudgery disappears.

On the *Harper's Magazine* Web site, Judge Todd posted his "Memory Almost Full" ruling:

> Mr. McCormack, to the question of "Give your recommendation as to what you think the Court should do in this case," you said, "Like the Beatles say, 'Let it be.'"
>
> If I were to overlook your actions and let it be, I would have to ignore that day in the life on April 21, 2006. Evidently, you said to yourself, "I feel fine," while drinking beer. Later, whether you wanted money or were just trying to act naturally, you became the fool on the hill. As Mr. Moonlight at 1:30 A.M. you did not think for yourself, but just focused on I, me, mine. Because you didn't ask for help, wait for something else, or listen to your conscience saying, "Honey, don't," the victim later that day was fixing a hole in the glass door you broke.

After you stole the eighteen-pack of Old Milwaukee, you decided it was time to run for your life and carry that weight. But when the witness said, "Baby, it's you," the police responded, "I'll get you," and you had to admit, "You really got a hold on me." You were not able to get back home because of the chains they put on you. Although you hoped the police would say, "I don't want to spoil the party" and "We can work it out," you were in misery when they said you were a bad boy.

When the police took you to jail, they said, "Hello, goodbye," and you became a nowhere man. Later, when you thought about what you did, you may have said, "I'll cry instead." Now you're saying, "Let it be," instead of, "I'm a loser." As a result of your hard day's night, you are looking at a ticket to ride that long and winding road. Hopefully, you can say when I'm sixty-four, "I should have known better."

If you were counting, then you caught all 39 different titles of Beatles songs. Now there's a judge who can carry a tune.

⊷❧⊶

In between dodging lightning bolts and listening for musical references from the bench, I make a few calls on my cell phone every day. Actually, scratch that. In between dodging a few lightning bolts, I make a few dozen calls on my cell every day—just like most attorneys.

That just got a little trickier, now that there's a move to keep cell phones out of the courtroom.

I don't answer the phone. I get the feeling whenever I do that there will be someone on the other end. —Fred Couples

Cell Phone Police in the Courtroom

In federal court the other day, the Marshall asked me whether my cell phone took pictures. Actually, it's a PDA, and it does. After waiting in line for 20 minutes, I got to return to my car to deposit my cell phone.

Arrrgh. Cell phone police. Now i've traded it in for a camera-less phone.

Court stories about cell phones abound. Like the judge who orders ringing cell phones to be dropped out of his courtroom's fifth story window—without the offending owner, thankfully.

My personal favorite: the bailiff who took a ringing cell phone and couldn't figure out how to turn it off, so he answered it.

"It was a man on the other end," the bailiff said. "It wasn't clear to me whether he was trying to complete a drug or a prostitution deal. I said, 'Can I tell her who's calling?' and he hung up."

Yeah, I know the story would have been better if the guy had given the bailiff his name and phone number, but you can't have everything, can you?

Of course, then there's the stun gun that masquerades as a cell phone, and another cell phone that fires a .22-caliber long-rifle bullet.

I don't advise trying to take those through security.

◦⊰⊱◦

Cell phones are one of life's little annoyances, but they're not the only petty problem judges encounter. In this next case, the court was called upon to decide luncheon arrangements.

There is no conversation more boring than the one where everybody agrees. —Michel de Montaigne

Would You Like Some Cheese with That Whine?

When lawyers can't get along, they turn to the judge. The judge, who frequently can't imagine how it got to that point, then embarrasses the lawyers into compliance.

This ruling, by Maricopa County, Arizona, Superior Court Judge Pendleton Gaines, gets right to the point.

Plaintiff's Motion to Compel Acceptance of Lunch Invitation

The Court has rarely seen a motion with more merit. The motion will be granted.

The Court has searched in vain in the Arizona Rules of Civil Procedure and cases, as well as the leading treatises on federal and Arizona procedure, to find specific support for Plaintiff's motion. Finding none, the Court concludes that motions of this type are so clearly within the inherent powers of the Court and have been so routinely granted that they are non-controversial and require no precedential support.

The writers support the concept.

Conversation has been called "the socializing instrument par excellence" (Jose Ortega y Gasset, *Invertebrate Spain*) and "one of the greatest pleasures in life" (Somerset Maugham, *The Moon and Sixpence*). John Dryden referred to "Sweet discourse, the banquet of the mind" (*The Flower and the Leaf*). Plaintiff's counsel extended a lunch invitation to Defendant's counsel "to have a discussion regarding discovery and other matters." Plaintiff's counsel offered to "pay for lunch."

Defendant's counsel failed to respond until the motion was filed.

The best part is yet to come. The judge gives us the setup for the problem that generated the motion:

Defendant's counsel distrusts Plaintiff's counsel's motives and fears that Plaintiff's counsel's purpose is to persuade Defendant's counsel of the lack of merit in the defense case.

The Court has no doubt of Defendant's counsel's ability to withstand Plaintiff's counsel's blandishments and to respond sally for sally and barb for barb. Defendant's counsel now makes what may be an illusory acceptance of Plaintiff's counsel's invitation by saying, "We would love to have lunch at Ruth's Chris with/on…[date]."

The court doesn't miss a beat, as a footnote explains: "Everyone knows that Ruth's Chris, while open for dinner, is not open for lunch. This is a matter of which the Court may take judicial notice."

Then, concluding his ruling, Judge Gaines passes along some paternal advice to help the lawyers resolve their differences in his final footnote: "The Court suggests that serious discussion occur after counsel have eaten. The temperaments of the Court's children always improved after a meal."

Surely the judge isn't implying the lawyers are acting like children, is he?

You can flip to the appendix at the end of this book for a full copy of judge Gaines's ruling.

⁓✺⁓

When you put your fate in the hands of the jury, the cynical statement goes, you're trusting everything to a dozen people who weren't smart enough to get out of jury duty. It could be worse. You could be leaving your fate to the woman in this next case.

Jury: a group of twelve men who, having lied to the judge about their hearing, health, and business engagements, have failed to fool him. —H. L. Mencken

How Not to Get out of Jury Duty

Jury duty—it strikes fear in the hearts of most Americans, and is almost always followed by the question, how do I get out of it?

Well, friends and neighbors, not like this. Our heroine in this particular story called in "stressed out," and failed to show up for the trial where she sat as an alternate juror.

The judge was not pleased. Circuit Judge Thomas Clark sent his deputy to find her and bring her to court.

He then instructed the jury (the same one she was sitting on) to sentence her. Ouch.

The choices: 1.) one day in jail; 2.) a return trip to the jury pool next week; or 3.) a sentence of sitting somewhere in the courthouse for the rest of the trial.

The jury picked Door Number 2 and Door Number 3.

But wait, we didn't hear the excuses. First, let's get this out of the way. She was a juror in a murder trial. OK, now the stage is set.

The recalcitrant juror said that she didn't want to view crime scene and autopsy photos, that she had an asthma attack the night before, and that she was worried about her mother in a nursing home. No one on the jury bought any of the excuses, probably because they were there sitting for jury duty, and she wasn't. Who better to sentence her than fellow jurors?

The moral of the story? Cross those off your list of excuses to get out of jury duty.

Or don't serve on a murder trial in Missouri if you're squeamish.

Seriously Now: Lessons Learned

Judges are human, too. They put on their robes one arm at a time, just like you and me. Oh, wait a minute. That's right; it's supposed to be "put on their pants one leg at a time." Well, you catch my drift.

Judges are different than the rest of us—for a lot of reasons, most of all because they have to make a decision at the end of the day that at least one party isn't going to like.

Further, and despite the several examples above, the words *humor* and *judge* usually aren't used in the same sentence, let alone the same courtroom. The courtroom is a serious place, where decorum and respect is the call of the day. You've seen some jailhouse lawyer examples of the way not to approach the judge. Indeed, most of those motions will earn only a DENIED stamp from the judge, if only because of their inherent disrespect.

Having sat as a pro tem (i.e., temporary) judge, I can give some perspective from behind the bench. Judges want to make the correct decision and be fair, as much as possible, to all the parties. Sometimes parties have created situations that preclude fairness, and judges have to make tough calls. As an example, contracts may require one party to do something that has become more expensive to do and won't yield the profit anticipated in the beginning of the deal due to some unforeseen event. That party may go to court seeking a way out of the contract, but the judge may be required to enforce it despite the added cost to the party. Though it may be unfair in that party's eye, it's not at all unfair in the other party's view, and in any event, that possible result was the deal the parties struck. Judges typically won't rewrite contracts to restore an element of fairness to them.

In an equity proceeding, where contracts or strictly legal issues aren't involved, judges have more flexibility. Divorce and juvenile law are two prime examples of equity proceedings. Judges try to bring fair results for all the parties involved, but most of all the children, because that's the judge's primary concern in a divorce.

All in all, judging is a tough job because one of the two parties in every case is going to lose. A judge once commented to me,

"When I've made my ruling, I've made one enemy for a lifetime and one friend for fifteen minutes." It's perhaps an obvious statement to make, but clients have a hard time understanding that one side has to lose in order for the other side to win, and on top of it both sides have to pay their lawyers. And in the American justice system, occasionally the losing party also has to pay the winner's attorneys fees and costs, too. That eventuality typically only happens in contract cases where the parties put that requirement in their written agreement. In contrast, the English justice system, always requires the loser to pay the winner's fees and costs.

Step 4

Do Your Time in Style

Chapter 13

Lock It Up

We've almost arrived at the end of our journey.

You made your choices, hired an attorney, and took your chances with the judge. Now we're looking at two options. Either you walked away from the courtroom the victor, in which case you don't need this chapter, or things didn't go so well for you.

If the latter's the case, then don't despair. As you'll see from some of these cases, incarceration can really be quite pleasant, as evidenced by Paris Hilton's brief trip to the slammer. It's the little things that make all the difference: the cold beer and the flat-screen TV.

Of course it might all be too much, and you'll want to make a break for it. I can't tell you how to make a successful escape, but if you read carefully here, then you'll be sure to find a couple of methods that really, really don't work.

⁓ॐ⁓

Women! Can't live with them...pass the beer nuts.
—Norm, from *Cheers*

One Thing Missing from Jail? Beer

After spending a lot of time in jail, what do you think you'd miss most? Give that one some thought, because four inmates have already answered it.

Beer. Plain and simple. No complicated tastes for these four guys.

Two of the inmates walked out of the Hawkins County Jail, in Rogersville, Tennessee, through a fire exit, leaving the door propped open, and made a hole in the exercise yard fence. They walked to a market, bought some beer, and returned to the jail to share it with other prisoners. When the booze ran out, the other two inmates made another beer run to a different store.

Authorities believe the inmates bought more than two cases of beer in all.

And surprisingly enough, they evidenced no desire to run away from jail. They simply went on a beer run to a local liquor store, and then went back to their cells.

Apparently, a jail door didn't lock, and no warning lights came on to tell the jailers that it was open. Open door, inmates—what did you think would happen next?

That's right, escape. But permanent departure wasn't in the minds of these inmates, because they returned to their cells. In the minds of the jailers, however—and perhaps more out of embarrassment—they're charging the inmates with escape.

The best part? The inmates used a Bible to prop open the door while they were on their beer run.

The storekeeper did not raise an alarm because the inmates were wearing street clothes borrowed from other prisoners. The crowded jail did not have enough orange jumpsuits to go around.

That jail has more than just escaping inmates for problems.

◦◦◦

A strong hankering for beer can get you out of jail, apparently. But it can also get you in, as demonstrated in this instance.

Operator! Give me the number for 911. —Homer Simpson

This Better Be a Beer Emergency

Liquor stores are trying to keep up with the times. They really are. One of the more recent ideas getting a cold reception most everywhere, however, is the drive-through liquor store.

No, I'm not kidding. There really are such things.

Now that you're over that shock, perhaps you won't be too surprised by the frustration felt by 35-year-old Brian Poulin, of Hebron, Connecticut, when he couldn't get his beer delivered.

If you think about it, liquor and beer delivery is the next logical step, so perhaps it's easy to understand Brian's frustration.

Just not his choice for dialing the phone for the delivery service.

You're going to love this one: He called 911, not just once, but several times. He asked the emergency dispatcher to have some beer sent over because he was out. Once the dispatcher got up off the floor after Brian's calls, the dispatcher sent someone over—just not the someone Brian was looking for.

Police arrived at his home, but forgot the extra order of wing tips. They arrested him instead, charged him with disorderly conduct, and reached an undisclosed plea agreement.

⁓⊛⁓

Few people go to prison for the perks. Considering this next story, however, that option might be about to change.

If it weren't for my lawyer, I'd still be in prison. It went a lot faster with two people digging. —Joe Martin

Go to Prison, Get a Flat-screen TV

Most people assume that when you go to prison, you deserve some level of punishment.

Not true in Oregon.

There, you get to watch a flat-screen TV in your cell, if you're good and you've earned it, according to prison officials. They claim relegating prisoners to their cells instead of the common TV room cuts down on violence.

But the prisoners who get the flat-screen TVs are basically "trustys" (trusted inmates). Did I miss something?

Most people, including me, do not yet have a flat-screen TV at home.

Maybe I need to go to prison to watch one. Nah.

⁓⊛⁓

Your day in court might not just result in prison time. Oh, no. If you're responsible for a considerable amount of damage, then the court might order you to pay some kind of restitution.

Which could be an itty-bitty, teeny-tiny problem, unless you're a multimillionaire.

I used to work in a fire hydrant factory. You couldn't park anywhere near the place. —Steven Wright

Can You Pay Back These Fines?

There you are, out wandering—let's be generous and say patrolling—the Arizona forest during high fire season. You're a U.S. Forest Service Forestry Technician. You got a letter from your estranged husband earlier that morning. You're upset—very upset. What do you do with the letter?

You know the answer. Of course, you burn it: in a campfire ring, in the middle of one of the hottest summers on record, during the time of highest possible fire danger. The fire gets away from you, and you report it. Not surprisingly, they ask you how it started.

You lie about it.

Next thing you know, you owe $42.2 million in fire suppression costs, $14.7 million of which was upheld by the Tenth Circuit Court of Appeals. Add to that fine twelve years in state prison, and six years in federal prison. At least you get to serve the sentences concurrently.

Plus, they took your matches away. Go figure.

∾

You would think that prison would be punishment enough. That's not necessarily the case. Some groups, tired of watching crime tear their communities apart, have renewed an old tradition—but they're not talking much about it.

Be gone, vulgar one. I am best not trifled with. Return to your petty games. —Kiasyd

Silence Speaks Louder Than Words

Wondering what to do with your rebellious teenagers? If you're a member of an Indian tribe, then you can try banishment. An age-old punishment, it's now coming back into vogue as a means to deal with drugs and gangs on the reservation.

The practice was long ago used to force violators out of tribal lands to fend for themselves in the wilderness. Because there's not as much wilderness left these days, banishment has sparked a debate that the Indians are just moving their problems into the general population.

The punishment is more personal for many Indians, though. According to a recent article, Kay Commodore, a Lummi Indian, was stripped of her tribal membership and banished from the reservation after she was convicted of drug trafficking in 1992. She served three years in prison, but said banishment is worse. She is allowed on the reservation only to visit a plot of land she owns, and is forbidden to visit family members.

"They're taking away a piece of who I am," Commodore said. "I can go out to my land, but I can't stop and see anybody—that's the thing that hurts me."

Banishment speaks to deeper human emotions, and how they can be used to trigger remorse and regret for criminal behavior.

The concept of banishment is nothing new. It was practiced by the Greeks and Romans, and likely by people who lived in caves, too.

৵৵৽

When you're inside prison, you have a lot of time on your hands. You can use the time to reflect and rehabilitate—or you can do as this next fellow did, and become that scourge of the legal system: the jailhouse lawyer.

The creative act is not pure. History evidences it. Sociology extracts it. The writer loses Eden, writes to be read and comes to realize that he is answerable. —Nadine Gordimer

When You're Serving Life in Prison, Perhaps You Can Say Anything You Want to a Federal Judge, but Don't Be Surprised If He Doesn't Want to Listen

This one goes to the Head of the Leader Board for the Most Creative Motion. Back in 1976, Matthew Washington bought a 12-gauge shotgun and later killed one policeman investigating a civil disturbance complaint against Washington for firing the gun in the open. Washington also injured two other police officers in that investigation, and, among other sentences, received life in prison. He had earlier been acquitted of another murder charge based on an insanity plea.

Since then, he's become a jailhouse lawyer (a derogatory term referencing an inmate who has studied the law but not passed the bar), filing lawsuits in Georgia federal and state courts. Jailhouse lawyers aren't, well, lawyers. They're completely untrained in the law—save for spending too much time in the jailhouse law library researching (and I use that term loosely) the law. They file motions and briefs that have little to do with the law, but more about the way they're feeling.

In one case, where our friend Mr. Washington filed a Motion to Kiss My Ass, the judges observed,

> "Plaintiff has shown in his dealings with the courts in this district that he lacks the ability or will to govern his suits with the civility and order required by the local rules and by the Federal Rules of Civil Procedure. He has wasted the time of many an innocent party and he has flippantly used the resources of the judiciary with his abusive motions filing practice."

His novel "Kiss My Ass" motion was not his first. In the case that engendered this caustic remark, and other cases, he has filed:

- Motion to Behoove an Inquisition. This motion sounds like something from the Middle Ages, but he likely means a motion for a new trial.

- Motion for *Judex Delegatus*. It's Latin for a "delegated or specially appointed judge," and he likely means he wants a different judge. In other words, if Dad doesn't give you want you want, ask Mom.
- Motion for Restoration of Sanity. Even if you could grant such a motion, would you?
- Motion for Deinstitutionalization. This one's the Monopoly motion, or "Get out of jail free." Not going to happen here.
- Motion for Publicity. Also known as "Look at me." Just what we need, here—someone with something better to do to pay more attention to someone who has nothing else to do.
- Motion for *Cesset pro Cessus* (*sic*—it's *"processus"*). An attempt to direct a stay of execution. There's no death penalty here, since he was sentenced to life, but probably an attempt to stop him from being incarcerated.
- Motion for *Nunc pro Tunc*. A Latin phrase meaning "now for then." This phrase is usually used by a judge to make an order today retroactive to sometime in the past—something that didn't happen, which should have. Other than existentially giving the police officers another shot at Washington, I can't imagine how it applies to him.
- Motion for Psychoanalysis. I don't know—I might have granted this one if I were the judge.
- Motion for a Skin Change Operation. Euphemism for sex change operation. This motion presents such an easy setup to make an insult that I'm not going to take the bait. You can, however. Just jump right in.
- Motion for Catered Food Service. I'd deny that one as already provided. Maybe he wants outside catering.
- Motion to Renounce Citizenship. Right. I don't want to be in the United States, so let me go be free in another country. Not. Going. To. Happen.
- Motion to Vacate Jurisdiction, which Washington created in the first place, so it's hard to logically imagine how you could vacate it, but I suspect that once again he simply wants to see if another judge would be more sympathetic.

In another shocker, the courts denied all of these motions. Fed up, the court enjoined Washington from filing any further motions or lawsuits unless he both posted a $1,500 contempt bond and signed a statement under penalty of perjury that he had read the Federal Rules of Civil Procedure, Rule 11.

The second condition was a warning issued by the court. Once Washington submitted the statement, the court could simply sanction him without further notice and put an end to this frivolity.

On top of it all, the court dismissed his case. Finally.

⌘

Great escape plans are few and far between. Luckily for those of us looking for a little humor in the legal system, not-so-great escape plans are far more plentiful. Like this.

If you chase two hares, both will escape you. —Proverb

From the Dog House to the Big House

In the category of "you're never going to believe this," we have a 48-year-old dog trainer who allegedly helped a 27-year-old murderer escape from Leavenworth by using a dog crate. They were on the lam for two weeks, but now they're both in jail. The prison is continuing the program where outside dog trainers teach inmates how to handle dogs from shelters to assist in their adoption into homes in the area.

They've also instituted a new search program for the dog crates. They look inside.

⌘

If you're going to have visitors while you're inside, then you might want to brief them on the nuances of contraband: what is or isn't allowed inside the facility. Of course, you'd think some of this information would be obvious, but apparently not.

"Oh, Miss West, I've heard so much about you."
"Yeah, honey, but you can't prove a thing." —Mae West

Is That a Gun in Your Pocket, Or Are You Just Glad to See Me?

Bawdy actress Mae West is credited with that question in her 1978 movie, *Sextette*, and perhaps in her 1933 film *She Done Him Wrong*, but in an entirely different context than a prison visit, if you know what I mean. Mae was inviting someone upstairs to come and see her sometime, but our heroine in this story surely understood the context of Mae's question as she went to visit her husband in prison. At least I think she understood it.

In the category of things not to bring with you on a prison visit, a gun seems like an obvious no-no. On the other hand, some prisons allow conjugal visits, and perhaps you might want to bring along a condom or two if you plan on…well, conjugal activities.

Robin Adkins, 43, went to visit her husband in Tomoka Correctional Institution, a medium-security state prison in Daytona Beach, Florida. She was, in fact, smart enough not to bring a gun with her.

She brought two condoms with her, however, despite the prison's ban on conjugal visits. But I don't think intercourse was on her mind. During her visit, she visited the ladies' room and came back with her arms held tightly against her waist.

Officers spotted her, walking oddly without her arms swinging back and forth. Naturally, the correctional officers detained her and asked whether she had brought contraband with her.

Robin promptly handed over the two condoms, and once in the officers' possession, they allegedly discovered marijuana inside both condoms. She was charged with possession and is pending trial at the time of this writing.

And yes, the headline gave it away. She hid the condoms in her pants.

⌘

Of course, you have to consider what happens when you get out of jail. Presumably rehabilitated, it's time to reenter society and begin a productive life. However, some former felons find it hard to find employment. For some reason, no one wants to hire them—can't imagine why!

One fellow had an innovative approach, as you'll see below.

Martha in jail would be fairly disastrous for the company. She cannot remain on the board of directors as a convicted felon.
—Henry Mazurek

Wanted: Honest Felon

No, it's not an oxymoron. It's true. Here's the setup. You went down the wrong path, got caught, and then decided the follow the straight-and-narrow.

But after you get out of jail, you can't find a job. No one will hire you because of your criminal record. After all, you're a felon.

And who'd want to hire a felon?

Consider this classified ad, published in the *Toronto Financial Post*, on February 23, 2001.

Former Marijuana Smuggler

Having successfully completed a ten-year sentence, incident-free, for importing 75 tons of marijuana into the United States, I am now seeking a legal and legitimate means to support myself and my family.

Business experience—Owned and operated a successful fishing business: multivessel, one airplane, one island, and processing facility. Simultaneously owned and operated a fleet of tractor-trailer trucks conducting business in the western United States. During this time I also co-owned and participated in the executive level management of 120 people worldwide in a successful pot-smuggling venture with revenues in excess of U.S. $100 million annually. I took responsibility for my actions, and received a ten-year sentence in the United States while others walked free for their cooperation.

Attributes—I am an expert in all levels of security. I have extensive computer skills, am personable, outgoing, well-educated, reliable, clean, and sober. I am well-traveled and speak English, French, and Spanish. References available from friends, family, the U.S. District Attorney, etc.

Only one problem, as I see it. He may be good, but he got caught. No word whether anyone hired him.

Seriously Now: Lessons Learned

Jail is not a fun place. I know, I've been there. No, it's not what you're thinking—I've been there to visit with clients. I first learned the lesson as a young boy of six or seven, back in West Pittston, Pennsylvania. My grandfather, a charter member of the hose house (that's Pennsylvanian for fire department) took me to meet the policemen because the police department was attached to the hose house. I met the man in blue and learned that he was a friend and I could trust him if I had any type of problem.

To teach me the next lesson, my grandfather asked the policeman (a friend of his) if he could take me back to see the jail cells. The small station had two tiny cells, all painted in drab gray, complete with bars, a small metal bench bolted into the floor, and an open toilet. I went in and as I had my back to my grandfather, he slammed the door shut and walked out of my sight before I could turn around. I spent ten or so harrowing minutes wondering whether I would ever get out.

I'll never forget that "clank" sound of metal hitting metal, or the feeling of abandonment. I've heard that same sound many times in my professional career, and I still don't like it. I've never forgotten the lesson my grandfather taught me, and I'm grateful for it now, despite the trauma at the time.

No amount of food, water, shelter, beer, flat-screen TVs, work-out rooms, or libraries could make me want to spend time in jail. Watching it on the movies or on television is as close an experience as I want to have to jail, apart from my professional career.

If you have any doubts, then I suggest you try an overnight stay. That's all it will take to convince you.

Conclusion

Before we part ways, let's take a look together at what you can expect once you step into the courtroom. Generally speaking, you can become involved with the legal system in two ways: as a party in a civil lawsuit or as a defendant in a criminal action. There are also administrative proceedings involving the civil side of the government, and we'll look briefly at those, too.

On the civil side, you can be involved, among others, in a divorce, will contest, probate, contract dispute, or tort (civil wrong). On the criminal side, it's either as an adult or a juvenile. The procedure varies from state to state, but it generally involves some version of the steps outlined below.

Though I provide some estimates on the fees and costs, please recognize that these numbers vary wildly, given all the considerations that go into them. I may be way off for your particular matter, but the dollar figures I estimate are based on a highly unscientific study from talking to lawyers across the country and listening to their tall tales.

Special rules that apply in juvenile proceedings are designed to keep the parties' names confidential, and they're mostly designed to get the child back on track as a responsible citizen. When the child falls short of that goal, the last resort tends to be juvenile hall, which typically starts a downward spiral. The number-one cure for juvenile delinquents is two concerned parents who participate in the process. With a loving and concerned family, most kids can be put back on the right track.

As an adult, the criminal side starts with an arrest and jail, and moves next to an arraignment, during which you enter your plea of either guilty, not guilty, nolo contendre (i.e., no contest), or some version of either insanity or diminished capacity. At that point, you can be released "OR" (on your own recognizance) or post a bond to gain your freedom. Assuming you've pleaded not guilty, then the court will next hold a pretrial hearing to determine whether you'll be *bound over* for trial. The prosecutor merely has to demonstrate probable cause that a crime was committed and that the defendant committed the crime, which is the same standard that the police employed to arrest you in the first place. It's not a very high standard, and consequently most defendants are bound over for trial. At any point in this process, you can strike a plea bargain with the district attorney. If you don't *plea out,* then you're going to have a trial before twelve of your peers or directly in front of the judge. There are two possible results: guilty and not guilty, with several exceptions. If you're guilty, then you may want to reread the last chapter.

Criminal actions aren't cheap, either. Though the court will appoint an attorney for you if you can't afford one, conventional wisdom places the current cost of one driving-under-the-influence charge (without considering any property damage or injury) at around $15,000, when all is said and done, including the increases to insurance premiums. Although you have a constitutional right to a speedy trial, most defendants give up that right and have their cases resolved in something less than a year.

On the civil side, the process is entirely different. One side files a complaint against the other and the pleading is then challenged for sufficiency or answered, denying the claims made. The parties then move to the discovery phase, in which they ferret out each other's facts, witnesses, and documents. Settlement of the case is possible at any time, even after trial or while on appeal.

Next, the motion phase results in briefs filed before the judge in an attempt to eliminate some or all of the other party's claims or defenses. Once the judge issues rulings establishing the legal issues in dispute, the parties go to trial, which, other's like the criminal side, other's can either be before a judge or before a jury. On the civil side, you may have between six and twelve jurors, depending on local procedure. At the end of the trial, the judge or jury awards a verdict for one side or the other. It's impossible to predict the cost of civil litigation, but it can range from $5,000 to $5 million, and even more, depending on the scope of the legal issues involved. Civil litigation typically lasts a year to a year and a half, and can be as long as five years or as short as just a few months.

In both criminal and civil actions, there's generally only one appeal "of right," which means that the lowest appellate court must hear your appeal. You can expect your appeal to last from one to two years. Appeals generally start at $25,000 and go up from there. All the higher courts have discretion on whether or not to hear an appeal from the lower appellate court. Of all the cases filed, for example, the U.S. Supreme Court chooses to hear less than one percent. It's a small docket at the top, and a big one at the bottom.

If you can avoid it, then, it's much less expensive to stay out of the litigation system, in terms of money out of your pocket, time gone from your life, and the worry over an unknown outcome.

So there you go: a start-to-finish tour of the legal system, presented for your enjoyment. Now you're prepared to start your own journey. You know the best ways to invite litigation into your life, as well as the value of securing competent counsel. No one can say for certain what will happen when you step in front of a judge, or a jury, but I hope this book gives you examples and some idea of what to expect—or more accurately, what you want to avoid.

Thanks for taking this trip with me. It's been fun, and I hope you've enjoyed it as much as I have.

Cheers!

Disclaimers

The author, J. Craig Williams, is admitted to practice law in California, Iowa, Massachusetts, and Washington, but actively practices only in California. Readers should not rely on this book for legal advice. If you have questions of a legal nature, then you should consult an attorney licensed to practice in the appropriate jurisdiction.

Just to be sure we've covered everything, here's the rest of our disclaimer: Used without permission. If you do not understand, or cannot read, all directions, cautions, and warnings, then do not use this book. This product is meant for educational purposes only. Any resemblance to real persons, living or dead, is purely coincidental. Void where prohibited. Some assembly required. List each check separately by bank number. E-mail transmission cannot be guaranteed to be secure or error-free since information could be intercepted, corrupted, lost, destroyed, arrive late or incompletely, or contain viruses. The sender therefore does not accept liability for any errors or omissions in the contents of this message that arise as a result of e-mail transmission. One prize per customer. Contains wheat. Batteries not included. Contents may settle during shipment. Use only as directed. No other warranty expressed or implied. Do not use while operating a motor vehicle or heavy equipment. Postage will be paid by addressee. Subject to CARB [California Air Resources Board] approval. This is not an offer to sell securities. Apply only to affected area. May be too intense for some viewers. Do not stamp. Use other side for additional information. For recreational use only. Do not disturb. All models over eighteen years of age. If condition persists, then consult your physician. No user-serviceable parts inside. Freshest if eaten before date on carton. Contains paper, glue and ink. Subject to change without notice. Times approximate. Simulated picture. No postage necessary if mailed in the United States. Breaking seal constitutes acceptance of agreement. For off-road use only. As seen on TV. This private communication may be confidential or privileged. If you are not the intended recipient, then any disclosure, distribution, or use of information herein or attached is prohibited. Many suitcases look alike. Contains a substantial amount of nontobacco ingredients. Colors may, in time, fade. We have sent the forms that seem to be right for you. Slippery when wet. For office use only. Not affiliated with the American Red Cross. Drop in any mailbox. Edited for television. May be formatted to fit your screen. Keep cool, process promptly. Post office will not deliver without postage. List was current at time of printing. Return to sender, no forwarding order on file, unable to forward. Not responsible for either direct, indirect, incidental, or consequential damages resulting from any defect, error, or failure to perform. Available at participating locations only. Not the Beatles. Penalty for private use. See label for sequence. Substantial penalty for early withdrawal. Falling rock. Slippery slope. Seamless web. Lost ticket pays maximum rate. Your cancelled check is your receipt. Add toner. Place stamp here. Avoid contact with skin. Sanitized for your protection provided by management. Be sure each item is properly endorsed. Sign here without admitting guilt. Slightly higher west of the Mississippi. Check contents for damage before accepting package. Employees and their families are not eligible. Beware of owls. Contestants have been briefed on some questions before the show. Limited time offer, call now to ensure prompt delivery. You must be present to win. You need not be present to win. No passes accepted for this engagement. No purchase necessary. Processed at location stamped in code at top of carton. Shading within a garment may occur. Use in small area first. Use only in well-ventilated area. Replace with same type. Not approved for veterans. Booths for two or more.

Check here if tax deductible. Some equipment shown is optional. Price does not include taxes. No Canadian coins. Not recommended for children. Not endorsed. Prerecorded for this time zone. Not tax advice. Reproduction strictly prohibited. No solicitors. No alcohol, dogs, or horses. No anchovies, unless otherwise specified. Restaurant package, not for resale. List at least two alternate dates. First pull up, then pull down. Caution, this book may have been exposed to peanuts. Call toll-free before digging. Driver does not carry cash. Some of the trademarks mentioned in this book appear for identification purposes only. Record additional transactions on back of previous stub. Ticket limits our liability. Not all materials may be applicable in your jurisdiction. Not intended to be a substitute for professional advice. No implied endorsement of, or affiliation with, any linked sites. Path to individual pages may change, Please link to home page only. Serving suggestion. This disclaimer is meant for humorous purposes mainly. Send no money now. Ask your doctor or pharmacist. To prevent electric shock, do not open back door. You may or may not have additional rights, which may vary from country to country and state to state, and may be even either county to county or city to city and quite possibly town to town and perhaps even boroughs and townships. Not recommended for children under twelve years of age, adults, senior citizens, animals, insects, plants, or dead people. Limit one per customer. or two per pack. Does not come with any other figures. Keep away from fire, open flame, or spark. All rights reserved. Use only as directed; intentional misuse by deliberately concentrating and inhaling contents can be harmful or fatal. Parental discretion advised. Subject to copyright laws. No other warranty expressed or implied. Unauthorized copying of this disclaimer strictly prohibited. Do not read while operating a motor vehicle or heavy equipment. Postage will not be paid by addressee. Don't paint yourself into a corner. In case of eye contact, flush with water. Subject to approval. This is not an offer to sell securities. Apply only to affected area. May be too intense for some viewers. Do not fold, spindle, or mutilate. For recreational use only. Shipping and handling extra. No animals were harmed in the production of this disclaimer. Do not disturb. If condition persists, then consult your physician. Prices subject to change without notice. If swallowed, do not induce vomiting. Do not leave funds without collecting a receipt. Count your change. Contains a substantial number of nonactive ingredients. This product is only warranted to the original retail purchaser or gift recipient. Net weight before cooking. Surfaces should be clean of paint, grease, dirt, etc before applying. Read the prospectus. $2.98/min AE/V/MC. No Discover card. For certified investors only. Penalty for private use. Do not expose to direct sunlight. No warranties or representations that this book is fit for a particular purpose. Do not puncture or incinerate empty container. Do not write below this line. Time lock safe—clerk cannot open. At participating locations only. Serial numbers must be visible. Align parts carefully, then bond. Read all instructions first. Keep out of reach of children. Check paper path. Nonpotable water. May be PEBKAC error (problem exists between keyboard and computer). Plug computer into electrical outlet before use. Be sure each item is properly endorsed. Prices slightly higher east of Alaska. Storage temperature: -30° C (-22° F) to 40° C (104° F). Beware of dog. No purchase necessary. Plastic gloves available inside. Extinguish all pilot lights. Processed at location stamped in code at top of carton.Backstage pass only. No shirt, no shoes, no service. Some equipment shown is optional. Price does not include taxes. Hard hat area. This is off the record. Reproduction by mechanical or electronic means, including photocopying, is strictly prohibited. Adults 18 and over only. Do not drink. Detach and keep for your reference. Demo package, not for resale. This supersedes all previous notices. Tag not to be removed under penalty of law. Take a number. Not rated by the Motion Picture Association of America. Call for nutritional information. FBI warning: Do not copy. Mind the gap. Printed on recycled paper. Prizes are not redeemable for cash equivalent. To be used as a supplementary restraint system only. Always fasten your safety belt. Subject to change without notice. Do not staple or paper clip. Do not X-ray. Magnetic media, nonreturnable if seal is broken. Prolonged exposure to vapors has caused cancer in laboratory animals. Phenylketonurics: contains phenylalanine. Road construction ahead. These examples are highly exaggerated for the purpose of getting a point across. Keep your finger in the dike. Open other end. Dealer participation may affect final price. Wash your hands. Lavese los manos. May not be present in all tap water. Park at your own risk. Employees and their families and friends are not eligible. Book ink may contain lead, copper, and other chemicals. See Uniform Code of Military Justice. Indicates a low-fat item. Tax, tag, and title not included in advertised price. Avoid spraying into eyes. An 18 percent gratuity will be added for parties of eight or more. Contains fluoride. Parking for Harleys only. For qualified buyers. Contents under pressure. Unix is a registered trademark of AT&T. No transfers issued until the bus comes to a complete stop. No one may stand in front of the yellow line. All passengers must be behind the white line while bus is in motion. Package sold by weight, not volume. Carpool is two or more riders. Strollers only. No MSG. Proposition 65 warning: This book contains chemicals known to the state of California to cause cancer, birth defects, or other reproductive harm. Your mileage may vary. No smoking, food, or drink. This book does not reflect the thoughts or opinions of either myself, my company, my family, my roommate, my friends, or my cat or, for that matter the publisher. Don't quote me on that. Don't quote me on anything. You may not distribute this book freely and you may not make a profit from it. Management not responsible for loss or theft. Maximum speeding fine: $371. Terms are subject to change without notice. Illustrations are slightly enlarged to show detail. Warning: The Surgeon General has determined that smoking is hazardous to your health. We have kosher and nonkosher foods. Hand wash only, tumble dry on low heat. No substitutions allowed. This article is void where prohibited, taxed, or otherwise restricted. *Caveat emptor*. All taxes become liability of the winner. Handicapped parking—tow zone. User assumes full responsibility. An equal opportunity employer. Dry clean only. We do not discriminate an the basis of race, color or creed. We accept food stamps. Quantities are limited while supplies last. If any defects are discovered, do not attempt to fix them yourself, but return to an authorized service center. Use at your own risk. Parental advisory—explicit lyrics. Text may contain explicit materials some readers may find objectionable, parental guidance is advised. You must be taller than Mickey's ears to ride this ride. Disconnect spark plug wire before servicing. Keep away from pets and small children. Limit one per family, please. Do not swallow. No money down. Do not try this at home. Closed course professional drivers. Instructions are included. Action figures sold separately. No preservatives added. May cause blindness. Product does not really fly. Coated with food-grade vegetable, beeswax, and/or shellac-based wax or resin to maintain freshness. This product contains Olestra. Safety goggles required during use. Sealed with printed foil for your protection, do not use if safety seal is broken. Not liable for damages arising from use or misuse. Warning: May cause cirrhosis of the liver, inflammation of the brain, heart damage, pancreatic damage, kidney damage, spleen implosion or explosion, thyroid combustion, severe nasal hair growth, eruptia, pregnancy, infertility, fecal incontinence, impotence, loss of genitalia and/or hermaphroditism, hair loss, skin blemishes, bone deformity, throat cancer, ulcers, hangnails, bladder leakage, sores, scabs, elephantiasis, hepatitis, conjunctivitis, gingivitis, appendicitis, bronchitis, and/or athlete's foot. Your e-mail session may be monitored at the university's discretion. The best safeguard, second only to abstinence, is the use of a condom. No salt, artificial color, or flavoring added. Use type GR927 battery. Warning: Pregnant women, the elderly, and children should avoid this book. Discontinue use of book if any of the following occurs: itching, vertigo, dizziness, tingling in extremities, loss of balance or coordination, slurred speech, temporary blindness, profuse sweating, or heart palpitations. May stick to certain types of skin. Contains no fruit juice. Push down, then twist. Labor disputes may cause delays. UL listed. Articles are ribbed for your pleasure. Offer valid only at participating sites. Allow four to six weeks for delivery. Must be 18 to use. Warranty does not cover misuse, accident, extraterrestrial impact, lightning, floods, tornadoes, solar flares, tsunami, volcanic eruptions, earthquakes, supernovas, hurricanes, other Acts of God, neglect, damage from improper or unauthorized use, incorrect line voltage and/or frequency, broken antenna or marred cabinet, missing or altered serial numbers, chemical reactions, electromagnetic radiation from nuclear blasts, sonic boom shock waves, customer adjustments that are not covered in this list, and incidents owing to an airplane crash, Divine Intervention, extraterrestrial intervention, ship sinking or taking on water, motor vehicle crashing, explosive decompression, hard vacuum, dropping the item, falling rocks, falling anything, falling on rocks, falling on anything, caustic chemicals, napalm, leaky roofs, post-traumatic stress syndrome or disorder, broken glass, magnetic fields, laser or other energy weapons, subatomic particle bombardment, emissions of X-rays, microwave, ultraviolet, cosmic, and/or gamma rays, mud slides, forest fires, or projectiles (which may include, but are not limited to, arrows, bombs, artillery shells, mortars, missiles, bullets, snowballs, hand grenades, buckshot, BBs, flares, shrapnel, liquid-filled balloons, torpedoes, knives, stones, nuclear or atom bombs, spears, swords, maces, pikes, clubs, morning stars). These words are listed as a convenience to our readers. If you use these words, we take no responsibility and give no guarantees, warranties, or representations, implied or otherwise, for the content or accuracy of any of them. Caution: The contents of this book should not be fed to fish. Do not use while sleeping. Do not use in shower. Exclamation points used for emphasis only. Warning: This product can burn eyes. No drugs or nuclear weapons allowed inside. Caution: Hot beverages are hot! For external use only! Warning: May contain small parts. Do not use orally. Please keep out of reach of children. Do not recharge, put in backwards, or use. Warning: Do not use on eyes. Do not look into laser with remaining eye. Do not shine on flying objects. Do not use for drying pets. Do not use as ear plugs. Please store in the cold section of the refrigerator. Warning: Knives are sharp. Sharp curves. Keep out of microwave. Not for weight control. Twist top off with hands. Throw top away. Do not put top in mouth. Theft of this container is a crime. Do not use intimately. High voltage. Warning: has been found to cause cancer in laboratory mice. Fragile. Do not drop. Cannot be made nonpoisonous. Caution: Remove infant before folding for storage. Excessive dust may be irritating to skin and eyes. Look before driving. Do not iron clothes on body. High winds ahead. Do not drive car or operate machinery. For indoor or outdoor use only. Reading this book does not enable you to fly. Stay off the sidewalk. Concrete not dry. Paint is wet. BHT added to preserve freshness. Do not inhale. This door is alarmed from 7:00 P.M. to 7:00 A.M. Beware! To touch these wires is instant death. No hunting. Anyone found doing so will be prosecuted. Warning: Do not use if you have prostate problems. Product will be hot after heating. Danger: thin ice. Do not turn upside down. Do not light in face. Do not expose to flame. Choking hazard: This toy is a small ball. Not for human consumption. May be harmful if swallowed. Using Ingenio cookware to destroy your old pots may void your warranty. Do not attempt to stop the blade with your hand. Do not dangle the mouse by its cable or throw the mouse at coworkers. Warning: May contain nuts. Sharks may be present in ocean. Access hole only—not intended for use in lifting box. Warning: May cause drowsiness. Warning: Misuse may cause injury or death. Do not use orally after using rectally. Turn off motor before using this product. Not to be used as a personal flotation device. Bend with your knees. Please remove before driving. Trespassers will be shot. Remove plastic before eating. Not dishwasher safe. For lifting purposes only. Do not put lit candles on book. Warning: This is not underwear! Do not attempt to put in pants. Do not use house paint on face. Do not drive cars in ocean. Always drive on roads—not on people. No stopping or standing. Do not sit under coconut trees. Keep off the grass. Do not point a loaded weapon at another person. These rows reserved for parents with children. Scuba diving is a dangerous activity with inherent risks of death and serious injury. All cups leaving this store, whether full or empty, must be paid for. No refills. Malfunction: Insufficient water. Contains polyester. Prescriptions cannot be filled by phone. Not a pedestrian walkway. Caution: Bridge freezes before roadway. Keep zippers shut at all times. You could be a winner! Ski trails contain unmarked hazards. Slopes are steep. Always stay in control and be able to stop or avoid other people or objects. People ahead of you have the right of way. It is your responsibility to avoid them. Do not stop where you obstruct a trail or are not visible from above. Whenever starting downhill or merging onto a trail, look uphill and yield to others. Always use devices to help prevent runaway equipment. Observe all posted signs and warnings. Caution: low ceiling. Keep off closed trails and out of closed areas. Before using any lift, you must have the knowledge and ability to load, ride, and unload safely. Watch the movie first. Details are inside. Park at your own risk.

Fits one head. Payment is due by the due date. Take care: New nonslip surface. In case of flood, proceed uphill. In case of a flash flood, proceed uphill quickly. Hundred percent pure yarn. Remove the plastic wrapper. Open packet. Do not ride motorcycle without a helmet. Eat the contents. Remove wrapper, open mouth, insert muffin, eat. Use like regular soap. Federal law prohibits the smoking of tampons in the lavatory. Instructions: usage known. Serving suggestion: Defrost. Boil water before drinking, Simply pour the biscuits into a bowl and allow the cat to eat when it wants. In order to get out of car, open door, get out, lock doors, and then close doors. Please include the proper portion of your bill. Optional modem required. Actual product may not match expectations.

Finally, you agree, by using this book, that your use of this book is at your sole risk, that you assume full responsibility for all losses, damages, fees, and costs associated with either some or all the words that you read or use in connection with this book, and that neither its author, editors, or publishers shall be responsible or liable for any damages of any kind whatsoever arising out of, caused by, or related to your use of this book. Material in this book may contain inaccuracies or typographical errors and quite possibly grammar mistakes. We are not liable or responsible for any loss or damage caused by or arising from any reader's reliance on information obtained from or through this book. It is your responsibility to evaluate the information and other content available through this book. This book and the information and materials contained in this book are subject to change at any time, and from time to time, without prior or subsequent notice, which may be published in later editions. You agree also to defend us, indemnify us, and hold us harmless, together with our affiliates and their officers, directors, agents, and employees, from and against any and all claims, damages, losses, costs, and expenses, including, but not limited to, reasonable and actual attorneys' fees and court costs, including those incurred on appeal arising from or related to your use of this book.

Finally go away, and thank you for reading. We appreciate the opportunity to be of service. Push one to leave a message. Your call is important to us. Some calls may be recorded or monitored for quality assurance. Stay within the lines.

Appendix

CV 2003-020242   07/19/2006

                                              CLERK OF THE COURT
JUDGE PENDLETON GAINES   A. Beery
                                                     Deputy
                                    FILED: 07/21/2006

PHYSICIANS CHOICE OF   DAVID A SELDEN
ARIZONA, INC.

v.

MICKEY MILLER, *et al.*   DOW GLENN OSTLUND
                            DAVID ROSENBAUM

                            ROSENBAUM & ASSOCIATES
                            650 DUNDEE RD
                            STE 380
                            NORTHBROOK IL 60062

RULINGS ON PENDING MOTIONS

SUPERIOR COURT OF ARIZONA
MARICOPA COUNTY

CV 2003-020242   07/19/2006

The Court has reviewed the pending motions. Two will be granted. The others will be deferred.

Plaintiff's Motion to Compel Acceptance of Lunch Invitation

The Court has rarely seen a motion with more merit. The motion will be granted.

The Court has searched in vain in the Arizona Rules of Civil Procedure and cases, as well as the leading treatises on federal and Arizona procedure, to find specific support for Plaintiff's motion. Finding none, the Court concludes that motions of this type are so clearly within the inherent powers of the Court and have been so routinely granted that they are non-controversial and require no precedential support.

The writers support the concept. Conversation has been called "the socializing instrument par excellence" (Jose Ortega y Gasset, *Invertebrate Spain*) and "one of the greatest pleasures in life" (Somerset Maugham, *The Moon and Sixpence*). John Dryden referred to "Sweet discourse, the banquet of the mind" (*The Flower and the Leaf*).

Plaintiff's counsel extended a lunch invitation to Defendant's counsel "to have a discussion regarding discovery and other matters." Plaintiff's counsel offered to "pay for lunch." Defendant's counsel failed to respond until the motion was filed.

Defendant's counsel distrusts Plaintiff's counsel's motives and fears that Plaintiff's counsel's purpose is to persuade Defendant's counsel of the lack of merit in the defense case. The Court has no doubt of Defendant's counsel's ability to withstand Plaintiff's counsel's blandishments and to respond sally for sally and barb for barb. Defendant's counsel now makes what may be an illusory acceptance of Plaintiff's counsel's invitation by saying, "We would love to have lunch at Ruth's Chris with/on..." Plaintiff's counsel.[1]

SUPERIOR COURT OF ARIZONA
MARICOPA COUNTY

CV 2003-020242   07/19/2006

Plaintiff's counsel replies somewhat petulantly, criticizing Defendant's counsels' acceptance of the lunch invitation on the grounds that Defendant's counsel is "now attempting to choose the location" and saying that he "will oblige," but Defendant's counsel "will pay for its own meal."

There are a number of fine restaurants within easy driving distance of both counsels' offices, e.g., Christopher's, Vincent's, Morton's, Donovan's, Bistro 24 at the Ritz-Carlton, The Arizona Biltmore Grill, Sam's Café (Biltmore location), Alexi's, Sophie's and, if either counsel has a membership, the Phoenix Country Club and the University Club. Counsel may select their own venue or, if unable to agree, shall select from this list in order. The time will be noon during a normal business day. The lunch must be conducted and concluded not later than August 18, 2006.[2]

Each side may be represented by no more than two (2) lawyers of its own choosing, but the principal counsel on the pending motions must personally appear.

The cost of the lunch will be paid as follows: Total cost will be calculated by the amount of the bill including appetizers, salads, entrees and one non-alcoholic beverage per participant.[3] A twenty percent (20%) tip will be added to the bill (which will include tax). Each side will pay its *pro rata* share according to number of partici-pants. The Court may reapportion the cost on application for good cause or may treat it as a taxable cost under ARS § 12-331(5).

---

[1] Everyone knows that Ruth's Chris, while open for dinner, is not open for lunch. This is a matter of which the Court may take judicial notice.

[2] The Court is aware of the penchant of Plaintiff's counsel to take extended cruises during the summer months.

SUPERIOR COURT OF ARIZONA
MARICOPA COUNTY

CV 2003-020242   07/19/2006

During lunch, counsel will confer regarding the disputes identified in Plaintiff's motion to strike Defendant's discovery motion and Defendant's motions to quash, for protective order and for commission authorizing out-of-state depositions.[4] At the initiative of Plaintiff's counsel, a brief joint report detailing the parties' agreements and disagreements regarding these motions will be filed with the Court not later than one week following the lunch and, in any event, not later than noon, Wednesday, August 23, 2006.

Defendant's Motion to Strike Proposed Amended Complaint

To demonstrate to counsel that the Court has more on its mind than lunch, the Court has considered Defendant's motion to strike Plaintiff's proposed amended complaint. The motion will be granted.

Plaintiff's proposed amended complaint is 56 pages long and has 554 separately numbered paragraphs. It contains 19 counts. It is prolix and discursive in the extreme. It violates the Court's order of July 22, 2005, permitting the Plaintiff to file "an agreed-upon form of Amended Complaint to clean up housekeeping matters." It is not the "short and plain statement" required by Rule 8(a)(2). It is a pleading of a type specifically condemned in *Anserv Insurance Services, Inc., v. Albrecht*, 192 Ariz. 48, 49-50 (1998) (trial court should have stricken 269-page, 1322-paragraph complaint). Most importantly, it violates the observation of French philosopher Blaise Pascal, who concluded a long letter with an apology, saying

---

[3] Alcoholic beverages may be consumed, but at the personal expense of the consumer.

[4] The Court suggests that serious discussion occur after counsel have eaten. The temperaments of the Court's children always improved after a meal.

SUPERIOR COURT OF ARIZONA
MARICOPA COUNTY

CV 2003-020242   07/19/2006

he "had not the leisure to make it shorter." Since this is a 2003 case with no end in sight, Plaintiff's counsel has the leisure to make his complaint shorter.

H IS SO ORDERED.

/s/

Judge Pendleton Gaines

Index

A

Aaron, Hank, 121
Abbey, Edward, 88
Additional living expenses,
    173-74
Adkins, Bobby Glenn Jr., 189
Adkins, Robin, 225
Advertising, 145-46
Airplane travel, 127-28, 132
Albrecht, Tina, 9
Alcohol consumption
    driving and, 134-35
    inmate beer run, 218
    public intoxication, 136-37
    public intoxication with ax,
    137-39
Ale, H. Fred, 55
Ali, Muhammad, 87
Alien abduction claim, 196
Allen, Woody, 45, 79
*Alliance for Environmental
    Renewal, Inc., v. Pyramic
    Crossgates Co.,* 86
Allstate, 172
American Beverage Association,
    143
American Safety Institute, 99
Americans with Disabilities Act,
    161
Antismoking campaigns, 140
Apparent authority, 70-71
Appeals, 231
Ardeaga, Carlos, 53
Arillotta, Albert, 70-71
Armed robbery, 53

Arraignment, 230
Arson, 220
Assault, 51-52, 55
Assumption of the risk, 55, 112,
    120, 132, 159
Atlanta Freethought Society, 97
Atlantic Casualty Insurance
    Company, 168-69
Attorneys. *See* Legal
    representation
Avvo ranking system, 191
Ayas, Albert, 160

B

Backyards, 166-67
Baker, Ross, 124-25
Balboa Island Village Inn
    (Newport Beach, CA), 33-34
Banishment, 221
Bankhead, Tallulah, 205
Bank robbery, 45-46, 47-48, 65
Bankruptcy, 200-201
Barry, Dave, 35, 146, 199
Barth, Aston, 48
Barz, Anton, 22
Batelle, Phyllis, 135
Bayan, Rick, 171
Beard, James, 142
Bedsworth, William, 137
Beethoven Orchestra, 26
Bell, Lauire, 163
Bierce, Ambrose, 167
Biunno, Vincent Pasquale, 196
Black letter law, 70
Blake, William, 60

Blue Butterfly, 87-88
Bolen, Bobby Lee, 51-52
Bombeck, Erma, 95
Bowen, Louie, 42-43
Bowers, Timothy J., 65
Braugher, Andre, 64
Breaking and entering, 58
Breathalyzers, 134
Brown, Gary, 186
Bryant, Gordon A., 46
BSE (bovine spongiform
    encephalopathy), 75
Buckwalter, Ronald, 169
Buddha, 85
Burglary, 46-47, 62-63
Business ownership, 25-44
    Beethoven Orchestra (Bonn),
    26
    "boobie" pillow sales, 32-33
    comb-over patent, 35-36
    costumes as signs, 42-43
    free speech and defamatory
    statements, 33-34
    furniture store square footage
    conflict, 31
    handwritten documents, 38-39
    Harrah's Casino makeup
    requirement, 28-30
    Krispy Kreme, 37-38
    legal assistance in, 44
    Rent-a-Husband, 39-40
    Sloppy Joe's name conflict,
    36-37
    stripper's copyright, 27
    wine shipments, 41

Butterfly protection, 87-90
Byrne, Robert, 165

C
California Civil Code section
    3343 (strict liability dog bite
    statute), 158
Campbell, Joseph, 22
Cape Wind Associates, 171
*Caprio v. Bell Atlantic Sickness
    and Accident Plan,* 205
Carey, Drew, 41
Carnival Corporation, 67-68
Carrey, Jim, 201
Carter, Jimmy, 112
Cefora, Christopher, 131-32
Cell phone, in courtroom, 209-10
Cell phone towers, 169-70
Censorship, 141-42
Center for Biological Diversity, 87
Center for Science in the Public
    Interest, 143
Chanel, Coco, 161
Channing, William Ellery, 78
Chase, Chevy, 37
"Cheeseburger Bill," 147
Chengdu Chop, 11-12
Chevrolet, 146
Childhood obesity, 143
Children, 103-17
    conceived after death of parent,
    108
    egg and sperm donations, 110
    juvenile proceedings, 229-30
    naming issues, 112-15
    ownership of contraband
    by, 111
    parents representing legal
    rights of, 105
    paternity issues, 103-4
    school rules on self-expression
    of, 115-16
    sex education and, 107
    sports injuries and, 112
    support of, 106
China, censorship and, 141-42
Cho, Margaret, 81
Civil proceedings, 230
Clark, Thomas, 212
Clarke, Hope, 50-51
Clarke, W.A., 7
Clear Play, 141
Clinton, Bill, 66
Coca-Cola, 143
Comb-over patent, 35-36
"Coming to the nuisance," 100
Commodore, Kay, 221

Consumer Defense Group, 178-79
*Consumer Defense Group v.
    Rental Housing Industry
    Members,* 178
Continental Airlines, 127-28
Contract disputes, 72
    handwritten documents, 38-39
    written and oral, 43-44
Cook, Ewa, 34
Cook, G. Lee, 21
Copyright issues, 130, 132
Costumes as signs, 42-43
Couples, Fred, 209
Court TV viral campaign, 9-10
Craigslist.com, 49
Creekstone Farms Premium Beef,
    LLC, 75-76
A Criminal Waste of Space blog,
    137
Criminal activity, 45-66
    accepting responsibility for, 66
    assault, 51-52, 55
    bank robbery, 45-46, 47-48, 53,
    61-62, 65
    breaking and entering, 57-58
    burglary, 46-47
    destruction of property, 56
    driving under the influence, 61,
    134-35, 230
    escape from custody, 63, 224
    illegal possession of a weapon,
    62
    impersonating a police officer,
    53-54
    leprechaun defense, 57-58
    lewdness, 60
    pickle assault, 51-52
    police officers and, 64
    s'mores violation, 50-51
    theft, 48-50, 56, 58-60, 62
    trespassing, 124-25
Criminal proceedings described,
    230
Criminal stupidity, 53
Cristol, A. Jay, 200
Critical habitat designations,
    87-88
Crystal, Billy, 151
CSI contract disputes, 72
CSX Transportation, Inc., 70-71
Cutler, Bruce, 186-87

D
Dana, Charles Anderson, 158
D'Angelico, U.S. v, 205
Davenport, Lindsey, 62
Davidson, William, 199

Defamatory statements, 34
Del Campo, Antonio, 63
de Montaigne, Michel, 210
Destin, Florida beachfront
    restoration, 92-93
Destruction of property, 56
Deutsch, Linda, 186
de Visser, Mark, 46
Deweese, Connie, 15
Dieckmann, Barbel, 26
Dietary supplements, 153
Dietrich, Marlene, 78
Dinky the Chihuahua, 162
Directors Guild of America, 141
Disclaimers, 129, 233-41
Discovery phase, 230
Discrimination, sexual, 29-30
Disorderly conduct, 218-19
Divorce
    Austrian divorce fair, 22
    no fault, 6
    paternity issues, 103-4
Dog bites, 158-59
Doherty, Chad, 113-14
Donnelly, Annie, 145
Dozeman, Douglas, 162
Drinking water, 95-96
Driver safety, 80
    driving while watching DVDs,
    126
    drunk drivers, 61, 134-35, 230
    speeding, 131-32
Drunk driving (DUI), 61,
    134-35, 230
Drunken horsedrawn carriage
    driving, 150-51
Drunkenness, 61
Drunk horseback riding, 149
DUI, 61, 134-35, 230
DVD Copy Control v. Bunner
    (2003), 130
DVDs
    driving while watching, 126
    filtering objectionable content
    from, 141

E
Eads, George, 72
Eakin, J. Michael, 149
Edwards, Herman, 47
Edwards, Shaun, 207
Eilert, Regina, 38
Einstein, Albert, 82, 90
Eisenhower, Dwight D., 93
E-mail
    apparent authority and, 71
    theft, 17-18

Employees, insubordination and, 73-74
Employment (public and private sector employment compared), 74. *See also* Workplace conflict
Endangered Species Act, 88
Engagement rings, 7-8
English Rule, 185
Environmental issues, 85-101
  consumer warnings, 98-99
  critical habitat designation, 87-88
  drinking water purity, 95-96
  Monarch butterfly protection, 89-90
  ocean-use and overfishing, 94-95
  offensive smells, 99-100
  salt as pollutant, 86
  scenic views, 91-92
  sea turtle protection, 92-93
  sewer sludge as fertilizer, 98
  tree removal, 90-93
  waste disposal, 94
Environmental Protection Agency (EPA), 95, 98
Epicurus, 48
Epstein, Marlene, 168-69
Equity proceedings, 213
Escape from custody, 63, 224
Espinosa, Richard, 160-62
Estrada, Vincent Jr., 59
Exercise program copyright, 27

F
Family Movie Act, 141
Farmers Insurance, 172
Fax.com, 82
Federal Communications Commission (FCC), 82
Feng shui, 91
Finances
  joint accounts, 10-11, 23
  marriage and, 6-11
Firefighter's rule, 158
Fisher, Raymond C., 140
Fisher v. Lowe, Moffett and State Farm Ins. (1983), 203
Fish & Wildlife Service, 87-88
FlexYourRights.org, 111
Floyd, Ray, 121
Foranyic, Robert Francis, 137-39
Ford, Betty, 40
Forster, E.M., 109
Fox, Jorja, 72
Franken, Rose, 13

Franklin, Benjamin, 134
Free speech and defamatory statements, 33-34
freethegnomes.com, 167
Furniture store square footage conflict, 31

G
Gabor, Zsa Zsa, 5
Gaines, Pendleton, 210
Gambling, 144-45
Garden gnomes, 166-68
Geist, George, 80
Gelbman, Shalom, 54
Georgia drought, 97
Gilbert, Irwin, 199
Global positioning system disclaimers, 129
Gluttony, 142-44
Gnomes, 166-68
Goldenberg, Rene, 104
Golden Rule, 17
Golf accidents, 121-22
Gordimer, Nadine, 221
Gottlieb, Sherman, 67-68
GPS disclaimers, 129
Grace, Janet, 7-8
Graham, Anthony G., 178
Graham, Heather, 126
Gratuities, 122-24
Great South Bay Surgical Associates, 145
"Greed provision," 72
Griggs, Steve, 47
Gulley, Robert, 61

H
Hambright, Tom, 37
Handwritten documents, 38-39
Handy, Jack, 61
Handyman business, 39-40
Haque, Abdul, 58
Harassment, 23, 83
Harbison, Matthew, 150
Harrah's Casino, 28-30
Haskell, Molly, 26
Hecht, Ben, 54
Heimel, Cynthia, 8
Heller, Matthew, 7-8
Hell's Angels, 155-56
Hemingway, Ernest, 36
Herman, Eric, 190
Heubach, Randolph E., 110
Hilton, Richard, 87
Hobbs, Michael W., 46-47
Hoffman, Abbie, 33
Hoffman, Douglas, 91-92

Holmes, Oliver Wendell, 179
Home ownership, 165-74
  cell phone towers and, 169-70
  deodorizers as contaminants, 165-66
  garden gnomes, 166-68
  insurance coverage, 173-74
  insurance denial of cleanup costs, 168-69
  insurance premiums for destroyed houses, 172
  windmills, 171
Hopper, Hedda, 35
Horace, 91
Hormel Corporation, 68-69
Hubbard, Elbert, 19, 97
Hughie & Louie's (costume shop), 42-43
Hurricane Katrina, 92

I
Impersonating a police officer, 53-54
Incarceration, 217-27
  contraband, 225
  inmates on beer run, 218
  personal televisions and, 219
In-dash DVD players, 126
Infidelity, 10-12
Injury
  resulting in loss-of-consortium, 12-13
  sports injuries, 119-22
In re: Riddle, 200
Insubordination, 73
Insurance
  additional living expenses, 173-74
  contingency fees and, 185
  home ownership, 173
  liability, 173
  personal property, 174
  pet insurance, 163
  renters and, 174
  replacement cost *vs.* actual cash value, 173
Internet surfing, in workplace, 73
Interstate Demolition & Environmental Corporation, 70
Irving, Washington, 16
It Takes a Thief, 47

J
Jackson, Billy, 125
Jailhouse lawyers, 221-24
Jefferson, Thomas, 140
Jerry Springer Show, 54-55
Jespersen v. Harrah's Casino, 29-30

Jesperson, Darlene, 28-30
Jim Henson Productions, 69
Job conflict. *See* Workplace conflict
Job wanted ad, 226
Jones, Carl, 104
Jones, Greg, 151
Judges, 195-214
  accountability of, 205-6
  cell phones in courtrooms and,
    209-10
  equity proceedings, 213
Junk mail faxes, 67-68, 82-83
Jury duty, 212
Jury Duty (television), 186
Juvenile proceedings, 229-30

K
Kaczynski, Theodore, 65
Kahn, Oliva, 112
Kelley, Sheila, 27
Kelly, Kevin, 125
Kempf, Jerry, 46
Kennard, Joyce L., 112
Kennedy, Robert Burns, 160
Kent, Samuel B., 206-7
Kentucky bluegrass, 93-94
Kern County, California, 32
Kiasyd, 220
*Kids & the Law: An A-to-Z Guide
  for Parents,* 116
Kilmer, Joyce, 203
King, Stephen, 197
Koch, Dietmar, 9
Kozinski, Alex, 29-30
Krispy Kreme, 37-38

L
Land-banking, 95
*La Porte v. Associated
  Independents Inc.,* 160
Larkin, Robert, 81
Lawn statuary, 166
Lawrence v. Texas, 21
Lawyers. *See* Legal representation
Learned intermediary rule, 81
Lebedeff, Diane, 128
Leblanc, Kim, 57
Lebowitz, Fran, 133
Leckie, John, 168
Lee, Angel, 17-18
Lee, Jody, 51-52
Lefler, Ofer, 153
Legal representation, 177-92
  appeals, 182-83
  briefs, 187-88
  contingency payments, 185-86
  cost of, 189, 191

finding, 190-91
  inadequate, 186-87
  interviewing potential, 191
  jailhouse lawyers, 222-24
  licensing requirements,
    179-82, 190
  Proposition 65 and, 177-79
  pro se litigation, 183-84
  state bar associations, 180
  writing skills and, 191-92
Legal system, involvement in, 229
Lemen, Anne, 33-34
Leno, Jay, 145
Leprechaun defense, 57-58
Lesbian rights, 110
Lewdness, 60
Lewis, David, 98
Liability insurance, 173
Libel, 34
Lindh v. Surmand (1999), 7-8
Litigation, cost of, 230
Liu, Lucy, 76
Long, Jim, 129
Lo Pu-yi, 91
Loss-of-consortium, 12-13
Lunch invitation motion, 210-11,
  243-47
Lyons, Seamus, 54

M
MacArthur, Douglas, 128
McCormack, Andrew, 208
McDonald, Kyle, 18
McDonald's, 144
McGinn, Dan, 141
McGraw, Phillip C., 31
McRaith, Erin, 182
Mad cow disease testing, 75-76
MADD, 134
Maggie's Law, 80
Mailer, Norman, 17
Makeup requirement for female
  employees, 28-30
Marquis, Don, 56
Marriage
  counseling, 23
  finances and, 6-11, 23
  knowledge of partner, 4, 23
  loss-of-consortium, 12-13
  multiple, 18-20, 21
  occupation of partner, 5-6
  polygamy, 19-20, 21
  pre- and postnuptial
    agreements, 23
  same-sex, 19
  wedding vows, 8-9
Marshall, Jason, 58

Martin, Aaron, 48-49
Martin, Joe, 219
Martinez, Luis, 53
Marx, Groucho, 109
Maryland v. Pringle, 110
Mass, Brian, 50
Matsch, Richard P., 18
Matthews, Marcieau, 15
Maugham, W. Somerset, 39
May It Please the Court blog, 140
Mayo, Gerald, 197
Mazurek, Henry, 226
Mele, Mario, 7
*MetroPCS Inc. v. City and County
  of San Francisco,* 170
Michaux, Fred, 60
Miller, Dennis, 181
Milvenan, Richard, 199
Mire, Charles, 124
Monarch butterfly protection,
  89-90
Money, marriage and, 6-11
Montagu, Mary Wortley, 99
Montana v. Andrew McCormack,
  208
Moore, Dudley, 145
Mortimer, John, 184
Mothers Against Drunk Driving
  (MADD), 134
Motion phase, 230-31
Muirhead, James R., 203
Muppet Treasure Island, 69

N
New Zealand obesity legislation,
  147-48
NIMBY, 95
Nixon, Richard, 66
No fault divorce, 6
Nunn, Gregory, 63

O
Obesity, 143-44, 146-47, 147-48
Obscene display, 126
Occupation, of spouse, 5-6
Off-road vehicles and endangered
  species, 87-88
O'Hara, Maureen, 185
Ostler, Scott, 195
O'Sullivan, John J., 51
Ottawa County, Michigan, 100
Overfishing, 94-95
Overlawyered blog, 156

P
Palmdale School District, 107
Palm frond theft, 56

Parker, Richard and Margaret, 104
Passenger Bill of Rights, 128, 132
Paternity issues, 103-4
Patterson, Daniel R., 87-88
Patton, George S., 206
Perdue, Sonny, 97
Perez, Arturo, 34
Perkins, Jeff, 201
Persing, Carl Warren, 152
Personal property insurance, 174
Personal responsibility, 148-49
Personal Responsibility in Food
  Consumption Act, 147
Pets, 155-63
  custody battles over, 161-62
  dog bites, 158-59
  emotional damage suits and,
  160
  Hell's Angels guard dogs, 155-56
  pet industry, 155
  reckless endangerment an, 157
  Taco Bell mascot dispute, 162-63
Petterson, Erwin J. Jr., 126
Pfizer, 81
Phelps, William Lyon, 96
Phillips, Bob, 144
Phillips, Emo, 49
Physicians Choice of Arizona, Inc.
  v. Mickey Miller, et al (2006),
  243-47
Pickle assault, 51-52
Pilaar, Thomas, 49
Planty, Donna, 145
Plea bargain, 230
Pointer, Mark, 187
Polyamory, 19
Polygamy, 19-20
Pornography, 126, 141
Pregnancy, wrongful, due to
  botched sterilization, 109
Prenuptial agreements, for pets,
  162
Prescription drug side effects, 81
Privacy issues, 17-18
Private Citizen, 82
Product liability, 132
Professional standards, violations
  of, 79
Property, destruction of, 56
Proposition 65, 99, 177-78
Pro se litigation, 183-84
Prostitution, 77

Q-R
Quayle, Dan, 98, 107
Quist, Gordon J., 163
Ramsay, Duongladde, 17

Raskin, Marvin, 179-80
Ravenhead, Kirk, 151
Reckless endangerment, 157
Recovery Express, Inc. (REI), 70
Rehnquist, Warren, 111
Relationships (romantic)
  see also Marriage
  counseling, 23
  points to consider, 4, 22-23
  rights of unmarried partners,
  16
Rent-a-Husband, 39-40
Renters insurance, 174
Resource Conservation and
  Recovery Act, 94
Restaurant dining, and gratuities,
  122-24
Restrictive deeds, 91
Reynolds v. United States, 21
Rice, Donald, 18
Riddle, In re:, 201
Ritchie, Guy, 146
Rivers, Joan, 147
Robbery. See Burglary; Theft
Roberts, Tommy, 135
Robinson, Jim, 187
Robotis, George, 190
Rocchi, Gerald A., 62
Rogozensky, Ben, 63
Romanski, J.W. III, 52
Roosevelt, Teddy, 70
Royles, William, 150
Russell, Mark, 127

S
Safeco, 172
Salinas, CA sobriety checkpoints,
  134
Same-sex marriage, 19
Sand Mountain Blue Butterfly,
  87-88
Santa Claus, 144
Santa Monica Collection, 38-39
Satan lawsuit, 197-98
Scalia, Antonin, 21
Scenic views, 91-92
Schofield, Scott, 52
Schroeder, Mary, 29, 184
Schwarzenegger, Arnold, 75
Searight, Ned, 196
Sea turtle protection, 92-93
Self-expression, 115-16
Separation of church and state, 97
Sewell, Dawn Elizabeth, 152
Sewer sludge as fertilizer, 98
Sex-as-therapy, 77-78
Sex-change operations, 4-5

Sex education, 107
Sexual activity
  dietary supplements and,
  153-54
  on airplane, 151-52
Sexual discrimination, 29-30
Sexual harassment, 83
Shaffer, Josh, 43
Shakespeare, William, 208
Shakur, Tupac, 58
Shamis, Diane, 179-80
Sheppard, Derrick, 130
Signage, 42-43
Sills, David, 6, 178
Skiing and snowboarding, 119-21
Slander, 34
Smith, Donald J., 35
Smith, Frank J., 35
Smith v. Colonial Penn Insurance
  (1996), 206
S'mores, 50-51
Smothers, Tommy, 141
Sodomy, 21
Solid Waste Disposal Act, 94
Sonner, Scott, 87
Soprano's Restaurant and Italian
  Grill (Great Neck, NY), 123
Spamalot, 69
SPAM (meat product), 68-69
Sparks, Sam, 199
Spector, Phil, 186
Speeding, 131-32
Sports injuries
  children and, 112
  golf accidents, 121-22
  skiing and snowboarding
  accidents, 119-21
Spur Industries v. Del Webb
  (1972), 100
St. Johns, Adela Rogers, 4
Stanton, Frank, 20
Stein, Marcia, 80
Stein, Sidney, 157
Sterling, Donald, 38-39
Stevenson, Adlai E., 10
Stevenson, Robert, 189
Stone, Thatcher A., 127-28
Strickland, Larry, 43
Strict liability dog bit statute, 158
Stripper's copyright, 27
Supreme Court, 231
Swinger, George C. Jr., 183

T
Taco Bell Chihuahua mascot,
  162-63
Tancredo, Tom, 130

Taveras, Humberto A., 123
Taylor, Lawrence, 38
Telecommunications Act of
    1996, 170
Telephone Consumer Protection
    Act, 68
"That Girl Emily" blog, 9-10
Theft. *See also* Bank robbery
    auto, 58
    of ice cream store, with stapler
        as weapon, 62-63
    from a jail, 48-49
    library, 49-50
    of palm fronds, 56
    of services, 123
    of tracking device, 59-60
Thompson, Debra, 125
Thongs, exposure of, 130-31
Thurber, James, 160, 169
Tipping, 122-24
Tobacco, taxation of, 139-40
Todd, Gregory R., 208-9
Toiv, Barry, 103
Toll, Aric, 34
Toll, Theresa, 34
Tom, Andrew, 122
Toxic chemicals, consumer
    warnings and, 99
Toxic waste, 98
Trade secrets, 130
Tree removal, 90-93
Trespassing, 124-25
Trezise, Richie, 148
Twain, Mark, 59, 139, 155, 162,
    180

U
Underwear, exposure of, 13-31
Uniform Parentage Act, 106

United States Department of
    Agriculture (USDA), 75-76
Unmarried partners, rights of, 16
U.S. Supreme Court, 231
U.S. v. Syufy Enterprises (1990),
    29

V
Valencio, Alejandro, 15
Vandalism, 16-17
Vazzana, Andrea, 144
Veterinary variant, 158-59
Vices
    alcohol, 134-39, 149-50
    gambling, 144-45
    gluttony, 142-44, 146-47
    obscenity, 140-42
    sex, 151-52
    tobacco, 139-40
Violinists' lawsuit, 26
Volcano Winery, 41
Voltaire, 105

W
Walton, Sam, 25
Warren, David, 16-17
Washington, Matthew, 222-24
Waste disposal, 94
Water purity, 95-96
Weiland, Scott, 68
Weinstick, Louis, 159
Welfare Group for Disability and
    Sexuality, 78
Weller, Jerry, 200
West, Kanye, 18
West, Mae, 28, 224, 225
Whannell, Leigh, 136
Wilde, Oscar, 72, 106, 183
Wilkins, Otis Cecil, 13-14

Wilkinson, Randall, 6
Williams, J. Craig, 233
Williams, Montel, 119
Wilson, Larry, 34
Wind farms, 171
Winenergy, LLC, 171
Wine shipments, 41
Wizner, Christy, 113-14
Wolff, Charles Jay, 201-2
Woods, Brian, 105
Woods, Daniel, 105
Workplace conflict, 67-84
    contract disputes, 72
    driver safety, 80
    Fax.com, 82
    Hormel Corp. and *Spamalot*,
        69
    Internet surfing for personal
        reasons, 73-74
    junk faxes, 67-68
    sex-as-therapy, 77-78
    sexual harassment, 83
    sufficiency of warnings, 81
    USDA and Creekstone Farms,
        75-76
    violations of professional
        standards, 79
    wage and hours, 84
Wright, Stephen, 92, 131
Wright, Steven, 67, 220
Wrongful death, 6

Y-Z
Yanbin, Dong, 142
Yards (backyards), 166-68
Yates, Antoine, 157
Yoneda, Ryan, 122
Young, William G., 71
Zemp, Ahia, 78